Roger Maris*

A Title to Fame

ISBN 0-911007-12-1

First printing 1991

Prairie House Inc.
Box 9199
Fargo ND 58106

Library of Congress Cataloguing-in-Publication data:

Rosenfeld, Harvey.
    Roger Maris : a title to fame / Harvey Rosenfeld.
        p.   cm.
    Includes bibliographical references.
    ISBN 0-911007-12-1 : $19.95
    1. Maris, Roger, 1934–1985. 2. Baseball players—United States—
Biography. 3. New York Yankees (Baseball team). I. Title.
GV865.M34R67 1991
796.357'092—dc20
[B]   89-37318
                                                            CIP

Roger Maris*
A Title to Fame

Harvey Rosenfeld

PRAIRIE HOUSE

... but a court as of angels, a public not to be bribed, not to be entreated, and not to be overawed, decides upon every man's title to fame.

Ralph Waldo Emerson
Spiritual Laws

Table of Contents

Preface *ix*

I. *A Prairie Spirit Forged on the Iron Range* 11
II. *Growing Up in North Dakota* 19
III. *Baseball Begins at Home* 27
IV. *Short Stops in Cleveland and Kansas City* 37
V. *Suited for Pinstripes and New York* 47
VI. *A Season of Triumph and Despair* 55
VII. *A Star, Not an Asterisk** 61
VIII. *The Babe versus Roger: 1927 versus 1961* 71
IX. *Roger and the Mick* 79
X. *Days of Torment* 83
XI. *The Roger Maris Watch* 94
XII. *Countdown to 154* 109
XIII. *Three for Number 61: Maris, Stallard, Durante* 121
XIV. *'Pull Down the Curtains ...*
 Shut Out the Crazy World' 137
XV. *1962: 'Sour from the Start'* 149
XVI. *Summers That Were Bummers* 161
XVII. *A Spirit Rekindled in St. Louis* 179
XVIII. *Post-Baseball: As Before, Family Comes First* 193
XIX. *The Road Back to Yankee Stadium* 203
XX. *Come Lovely and Soothing Death* 215
XXI. *In Appreciation of Roger — After Death* 223
XXII. *Preserving a Legacy* 235
XXIII. *Of Heroes and Cooperstown* 245
XXIV. *A Title to Fame* 255

Appendices:
Chronology of the Year 1961 275
Babe Ruth's Home Run Record 279
Roger Maris' Home Run Record 282
Further Reading 285

Preface

In January 1988 we left New York on a trip that was to eventually take us to Hibbing, Minnesota, the birthplace of Roger Maris. At the time our father was at a Brooklyn hospital, but in no serious danger. We stopped for a few days vacation in Miami, where we began the chapter on Roger's fatal illness.

On the eve of our visit to Hibbing, we received the tragic news that our father had died suddenly. We never made it to Hibbing and we never said goodbye to our father. We also lost our mother before the completion of the book. The lesson of mortality needs no elaboration.

We were fortunate in visiting Fargo twice in the writing of this book, where we experienced the warmth and cooperation of its people in telling us of the Roger Maris they knew. The publication of the story of his life is most appropriate by Prairie House, located in Fargo. For their graciousness and friendship, we dedicate this book to the people of Fargo, as we do to the encouragement of our family, Pearl, Marcel and Robbie.

The list of people who helped us in this project would be quite long, but we must single out Sister Bertha Hill; Robert Johnson, Fargo Parks Superintendent: Dr. George Surprise, and Julius Isaacson. We are especially grateful to Mrs. Pat Maris for her understanding, consideration and time. Charles R. Allen, Jr., had helpful suggestions, and the Baseball Hall of Fame in Cooperstown made available its resources. Once again, Barbara Bergstrom has proven her talents as an editor. Nancy Edmonds Hanson and Carl Wichman of Prairie House were very patient and professional in this undertaking.

All-time home-run champion Roger Maris.
(New York Yankees Promotion Pictures).

Chapter I
A Prairie Spirit
Forged on the Iron Range

Roger Maris had many days of triumph. But despite his achievements – despite his victories – the finest of them all eludes him even after death: The all-time home-run record-setter still has not been welcomed into the Baseball Hall of Fame.

He set a baseball record of sixty-one home runs in a season on October 1, 1961, topping Babe Ruth's sixty-home-run mark. During the course of his illustrious career, he also won the Most Valuable Player Award in two consecutive seasons and made the crucial plays that brought seven pennants to the Yankees and the Cardinals.

On July 21, 1984, at the New York Yankees' annual Old Timers' Day celebration, Roger finally received his due from his team. The Yankees honored the slugger by retiring his Number 9 jersey and by placing a bronze plaque in the memorial park behind the fence in left center field. The plaque's engraved tribute read: "In belated recognition of one of baseball's greatest achievements ever. ... " With permanent enshrinement in Yankee Stadium, Maris took his place alongside other baseball greats: Joe DiMaggio, Mickey Mantle, Casey Stengel.

Roger received a tribute of a different sort on December 19, 1985, as a saddened baseball world prepared to say farewell to one of its legends. While mourners paid their final respects in the subzero winter weather of an ice-covered North Dakota, a headline in that day's *New York Daily News* pronounced: "Maris Doesn't Merit Hall."

In his life the insensitivity, coarseness, and crudeness of his critics had blunted Roger's moments of happiness and triumph. Even death did not keep Roger safe from the brickbats of others.

Those who knew him well felt that Roger was misunderstood and unappreciated. The slugger who audaciously surpassed Babe Ruth's home-run record had roots and values nurtured on the prairie. Any attempt to understand Roger must also consider the Maris family and the rigorous lifestyles of the Iron Range and the Red River Valley of the North.

Although Roger lived in Raytown and Independence, Missouri, for most of his life and spent his final years in the warmer clime of Gainesville, Florida, in death he came back to Fargo and the prairie. "He was buried *here*," wrote Jerome D. Lamb, editor of *The Small Voice*, a Fargo bimonthly newsletter. "After all this time, all those days in the sun and nights under the lights, this frozen piece of earth perched on the near side of nowhere was still and always home."

Roger grew up in the quietude and privacy of the North Dakota prairie, where one's abilities are displayed without show. As Lamb observes, North Dakotans must "make do with the quiet talents — the mechanic who knows at first hearing that what's in order is a minor adjustment, not a major overhaul; the piemaker at such and such a cafe; the trapper who could track a weasel across the asphalt of a shopping mall parking lot if he had to."

In his professional career Roger faced the challenge of preserving his North Dakotan openness, honesty, and anonymity in situations more suited to evasiveness, deceit, and grandstanding for the media.

Roger Maris called Fargo, North Dakota, home. He even listed the North Dakotan city as his place of birth for the Major Leagues, causing errors in some of the fact books. In fact, Roger was born in Hibbing, Minnesota. When someone once asked him about his birthplace, Roger responded, "What do I know about Hibbing? I didn't live there long enough." Despite his brief stay in the northeastern Minnesota city, the Iron Range spirit had an important influence on him.

The Mesabi Iron Range lies approximately 200 miles north of the Twin Cities. In *Three Iron Mining Towns*, Landin describes the Iron Range as "a wilderness of burned-over stumps, second-growth evergreens, tamarack, and underbrush scattered over rocky hills intervened by swampy valleys or crystal lakes." Hibbing, like other towns on the range, became world-famous for the rich iron ore beneath its harsh terrain.

The Iron Range had a large immigrant population, including the South Slavs, Bulgarians, Montenegrins, Serbs, Slovenes, and Croatians. Minnesota's largest concentration of South Slavs occurred in St. Louis County, Hibbing's location. The Croatians constituted about 60 percent of the South Slav newcomers. They were the forefathers of the Maris family.

Most of these South Slavs left Croatia to seek their fortunes in America. Many of these "ambitious" and "self-uprooted" South Slavs hoped to reap the economic benefits of life in the United States and then return home; however, many immigrants remained on the Mesabi.

The Mesabi forests and swamps of the 1890s had already given way by 1910 to thirteen communities totaling 50,000 residents, including almost 3,500 Croats. The Mesabi's iron ore mines — the largest in the world — gave Hibbing the title, "Iron Ore Capital of the World." Hibbing's blend of many nationalities led one early-1900s commentator to observe, "The babel of more than thirty different alien tongues mingle with the roar of the mine blasts and the clash and clank of machinery."

The Maras family began its immigration to the United States in 1906, when Paul Maras, Roger Maris' great-uncle, arrived on the range. The Hibbing Marases still retain the traditional spelling of their name, while Rudy Maras changed the family name to Maris at the beginning of his son Roger's professional baseball career.

Soon after his emigration, Paul Maras welcomed to Hibbing his four brothers, Mike, Peter, Joso, and Steve, Roger's grandfather. According to Mrs. Tilly Sandborn, Paul Maras's daughter and Roger's aunt, many South Slavs had difficulty learning English, so Paul Maras became an interpreter at the Oliver Iron Mining Company, the biggest operating company on the range. Mrs. Sandborn told us that Paul Maras also operated a Hibbing saloon, for which he was better known, and his brother Steve Maras worked for him there.

Life on the Iron Range was difficult and austere. The Marases, like others on the range, had to sustain themselves with an inner toughness. Roger inherited that legacy of the Iron Range and it served him well throughout his life and throughout his battle with cancer.

The Maras family lived on the Leetonia mining location, which was a settlement close to a mine site. Between 1892 and the 1920s, more than 175 locations appeared on the Mesabi. While the companies thought these locations were adequate, social workers and community leaders viewed these sites as breeding grounds for unique social and communal problems.

The settlement at Carson Lake differed little from that at Leetonia or other Hibbing-area locations. Alanen describes Carson Lake in *Minnesota History*:

> The Carson Lake enclave was approached by picking one's way amid the muddy alleys to houses set helter

skelter without rhyme or reason, through ... mazes of stick fences and pig sties. Her colleague, who questioned Carson Lake as 'a fearful place,' also questioned how the residents could joke about the location to the extent they did. She concluded that it was the only way they made life tolerable.

Leetonia's physical environment had at least one advantage that contributed to Roger Maris' professional development. The arctic climate of the range made winters ideal for hockey. The ponds and lakes froze early and stayed solid until late in the spring, giving hockey devotees a long season. The senior Maris, now 80, played amateur hockey in the Hibbing area and later nearly tried out for the Boston Bruins in 1932. Instead, he married Anne Corrine Sturbitz from the nearby town of Calumet and put aside his skates for a while. Rudy Maris Sr. was never in top form again.

Roger himself played a lot of hockey in his early school years. Hibbing had one of the first indoor hockey rinks in that part of the country. "My father liked to see me on skates as often as possible," Roger told former Olympic speed-skating champion Irving Jaffe. Some credit the development of Roger's powerful wrists to those hockey workouts.

Aside from comments on his father's hockey abilities, Roger had almost no recollections of his life in Hibbing. Sketches and biographies of Roger note that the slugger was born in Hibbing. Then the story moves quickly to Fargo, stopping in Grand Forks, where the close ties between Roger and Fargo began.

The people of Hibbing never took kindly to that. As Maury Allen writes in his book, *Roger Maris: A Man for All Seasons*, according to the senior Maris: "Roger just felt like Fargo was his hometown because he grew up there. I think people in Hibbing resented that. Some of the newspapers wrote about it when he died. I have a sister who lives there in Hibbing, and she said some people made a big fuss about that."

Al Zdon, editor of the *Hibbing Tribune*, told us, "After Roger Maris died, the paper got lots of mail, for about three weeks, to locate his birthplace, which is on the west side of Hibbing.

Why, then, was homage never paid to Roger in Hibbing? "You know the adage," said Zdon, "'No man is a prophet in his own country.' This is especially true in Hibbing, where we don't dwell on fame. ... If Roger

Maris had spent his formative years in the area, things might have been different."

However, on December 17, 1985, the *Hibbing Tribune* featured an editorial "Roger Maris, 1934-1985," parts of which could have been written in Fargo as well: "Only now that Maris has died is he getting the recognition he deserved in his lifetime. He was a good man, close to his family, generous to others, and a gifted athlete. He only lived in Hibbing for a few years of his childhood, but the city is proud to claim the distinction as his birthplace."

From Hibbing, Minnesota, the family moved to Grand Forks, North Dakota. If Hibbing could take pride in claiming Roger as a native son, how much more so could North Dakota, where Roger Maris spent his youth, began his professional career, and so often returned in later years.

Celebrating its one-hundredth year of statehood in 1989, North Dakota has a colorful and distinctive history. Like Roger Maris, North Dakotans take fierce pride in their personal and civic accomplishments. They defiantly preserve their independent lifestyles and values from attacks by those who wish to change them. Roger Maris lived his life as a true North Dakotan.

In his travels through America reported in *Inside U.S.A.*, John Gunther noticed the "peculiarities" of North Dakota:

> There are more idiosyncrasies per square inch in North Dakota than in any state I know. Quite possibly this cross-grained inflammatory state is the most complex in the nation. Contrasts are sharp in almost every field: for instance, the state capital is a handsome skyscraper; ... the governor's mansion near by is a small white frame house that would be modest even for a farmer of very modest means. No state except possibly Oklahoma has a history so bursting with wackiness and furor.

According to Gunther, North Dakota could boast of progressive, advanced government, "the reform state par excellence." Gunther enumerated such reforms as the state-owned Bank of North Dakota, compulsory state insurance for public buildings, a state-run program of hail insurance for farmers, workmen's compensation, and a highly developed system of cooperatives. The Nonpartisan League, founded in 1915, proposed reforms similar to much New Deal legislation.

The late Dr. Elwyn B. Robinson, professor of history and chairman of the department at the University of North Dakota, provides valuable insight into understanding North Dakotans in "The Character of a People," the final chapter in his *History of North Dakota.*

Dr. Robinson claims that North Dakota was destined from the beginning to be different because its frontier differed from earlier ones to the east or later ones to the west. In addition, it had a different mix of settlers foreign and native than that of other states.

North Dakota had an unusual combination of physical factors: a flat and featureless terrain; temperature fluctuations that range from oppressive summer heat to subzero winter cold. North Dakota was more markedly rural than any other state: by the 1920s more than eighty-five percent of the population lived in the country or in small towns. In addition to the rural isolation, sixty-seven percent of the North Dakotan population was of foreign stock, primarily Norwegian and German native-born persons of immigrant and mixed parentage. Thus the geography and citizenry of North Dakota made the northern plains unlike the Midwest, South, East, or any other American region.

"Most North Dakotans were undergoing the process of casting off old, traditional ways of living and adopting new ones," writes Robinson. Over the years, this unhappiness often resulted in mass departures. Father William C. Sherman, pastor of St. Mary's Church in Grand Forks and associate professor of sociology at North Dakota State University, speaks of "North Dakota Days" held especially in California, Arizona, and Washington. During these periods, thousands of former North Dakotans reunite and celebrate the North Dakota way of life.

According to Robinson, North Dakotans felt "as if they were looked down upon as inferior by the rest of American people. ... Part of a rural state, they felt like country cousins toward the city folk of the nation." Radio-TV commentator Eric Sevareid of Velva, North Dakota, recalls his youthful experience of staring in wonderment at the map showing "the meaningless rectangle of Dakota."

However, throughout its history, North Dakotans transformed the unique qualities of their state — the physical environment, the isolation, the foreign stock — into their strong and admirable personality traits. As Sevareid observes with pride, "It was a trial of the human spirit just to live there, and a triumph of faith and fortitude

       Roger Maris* — A Title to Fame

for those who stayed on through the terrible blasting of the summer winds, the merciless suns, through the frozen darkness of the winters when the deathly mourn of the coyote seemed at times the only signal of life." To survive and grow in North Dakota, as the Marises and other families discovered, required courage, energy, optimism, self-reliance, fraternity, and a democratic spirit.

Washington Grade School basketball champs,
1945–1946. Players include (front row, left to right)
Eugene Goodwin, Roger Maras – co-captain,
Galen Telander; (middle row) Colin MacDonald,
James Hadland, Lyle Thorson, Wallace MacDonald
– co-captain, Ron Ahlness; (third row) Jackie Lowe,
Jimmie Lowe, Duane Walsh and Dewey Walsh.
(Grand Forks Herald photo)

Chapter II
Growing Up in North Dakota

Roger Maris said little about his days in Grand Forks, North Dakota, where the family stayed until he was ten. However, his uncle Jerry March, who now lives in Los Gatos, California, does remember his nephew's childhood.

My thoughts of Roger revert to the early days before the time of fame and fortune. He never seemed to have changed. There was always that youthful, innocent-like quality so present in him during the times we played in the sand piles with our trucks or sneaked a cigarette made from Indian tobacco.

I still have in mind the picture of Roger when the Empire Builder train came through Grand Forks during the dinner hour. He had newspapers and magazines under his arms ready for sale. But he was so small then that he didn't know how to make change. When people gave him money for the paper or magazine, he would just pull out a handful of coins and hold it out to the buyer. He looked so confused, but the people usually let him keep the change.

John Velaski remembers the Maris family when they lived in an eight-unit building in Grand Forks. "You could tell that Roger had exceptional skills even in his Grand Forks days," Velaski said. "There was a vacant lot near the parochial school. It was close to 200 yards to the railroad track. Only Roger and his brother, Buddy, could just about reach the tracks in stickball."

Gailen Telander of Grand Forks also remembers his grade-school friend Roger. They were both guards and co-captains of the Washington Elementary School city-league basketball team that took the championship in the 1945-46 season.

"Roger was a popular kid," Telander recounted, "and very strong-headed. He was the team leader." Telander also spoke of Roger's natural abilities in baseball and the track relays they ran together. "Roger was faster than me," Telander conceded, "but I could beat him in the high jump though."

Gailen recalled their childhood relationship. "Roger and I were very close friends. We did things together, as good buddies do. We were at each other's houses frequently and often slept over. After school we played soccer together."

Once Roger used Telander's backside as a target for BB-gun practice and scored a bull's eye. "I was very mad at first," Gailen said, "but what could I do about it? It wasn't long before we laughed the whole thing off."

The friends parted — never to meet again — when Telander moved to Michigan, North Dakota, for the seventh-grade term. Shortly thereafter, Roger and his family left for Fargo, where he spent his formative years. As Fargo turned into his real home, the tradition and heritage of North Dakota became deeply ingrained in his being.

Fargo today has changed little since the 1940s and the 1950s, the decades of Roger's youth. The city along the Red River of the North has lost nothing of its pre-statehood Dakota character. Although its 1876 population of 600 has swelled to more than 60,000 citizens, making it the state's largest city, Fargo has retained the North Dakota spirit of self-reliance, courage, cooperation.

Fargo Mayor Jon Lindgren extolled the city's many virtues and proudly noted that people rarely lock their cars because of the "basic honesty of our people." Parks Superintendent Robert Johnson said, "We're thinking of taking the word 'crime' out of the dictionary because it hardly exists here." The mayor cited the low crime statistics: From January through August, 1986, the police logged no homicides for the year, monthly figures for forcible rapes ranged from zero to four, and assaults, from five to 16. Fargo's quiet, anxiety-free atmosphere has resulted in its rating as the least stressful city in the United States, according to a recent survey by the Washington-based Zero Population Growth Inc.

The people of Fargo speak openly and directly. Strikingly missing from their conversations are the earthy words and obscenities that so frequently pepper dialogues in the East and West. Neighbors watch out for each other and show concern for the safety and well-being of those around them.

Such neighborly interest and concern resulted in the fond memories of Roger Maris' youth that linger with his former teachers, friends, and classmates. Fargo will never forget Roger Maris. In the words of editor Lamb, Roger remains "a distinct presence, part extraordinary natural phenomenon, part myth, and part something uniquely the region's own."

Roger and his older brother, Rudy Jr. (Buddy), first entered Fargo Central High School, where both felt their athletic abilities went unappreciated. Roger was on the "B" football team while Rudy did not play regularly.

Father John E. Moore of St. Mary's Church, himself an athlete and coach and a long-time friend of the Maris family, claimed to have encouraged Roger to enroll at Shanley High School, a parochial school, where football excellence is a tradition. However, Rudy Maris Sr. disputed Moore's claim and maintained that Roger chose Shanley on his own.

When Roger was a sophomore and Rudy a junior, they transferred to Shanley in time for the spring term. Because of this change, they lost their eligibility to compete in sports until the following fall. Some Fargoans blamed the boys for leaving Fargo Central bereft of athletic talent. Roger felt that some local media people stayed angry with him for a long time. He blamed Rudy and his transfer on the new Fargo High coach who, according to Roger, "didn't like the Maris brothers." "If Fargo had no use for us," Roger said, "then it was time to find a school that would use us."

Dr. Pat Colliton, a Shanley High teammate, remembers the incident from a different perspective. "It is true that people were upset at first, and there were charges of pirating and recruiting on the part of Shanley," he said. "However, there was little lingering animosity toward Bud and Roger. People in town have always respected Roger, not only because of his accomplishments but because he was honest and open in what he did. What Fargo Central High lost, Shanley gained, and so obviously did North Dakota."

Shanley High took its name from Bishop John Shanley. Run by the Presentation Order of Sisters, Shanley had one of the nation's top football mentors, Sid Cichy, who won a place in the High School Coaches Hall of Fame. More than just a coach, Cichy was very close to his players and always accompanied them to mass before a game.

The coach welcomed both Roger and Rudy Maris Jr. — halfback and star in his own right — for the 1950-51 season. Cichy recalls that Roger's great offensive playing abilities matched his defensive skills:

How can I forget the kid in the red jersey with the blond crew cut? He had such a smooth movement about him that he could be deceiving. And he did things with such a flair.

Roger ran out of the single wing and nobody stopped him. On the defense, he would come up from the secondary to nail the runner for no gain on one play and intercept a pass twenty-five yards down field on the next. As a blocking back, we'd run him in motion and then bring him back to crack back on the line backer. In those days, it was legal.

Cichy's memories of Roger's outstanding individual performances include two involving games against Devils Lake. In one contest he led Shanley to victory by scoring five touchdowns, a state record only recently eclipsed. In another battle against Devils Lake, Roger caught four kickoffs and took them all in for touchdowns. "The Devil's Lake coach shook his head in disbelief as Shanley rolled up the score," Cichy reminisced. "He told me that he hoped his team would not score because he was getting tired of seeing Roger run the kickoffs back for touchdowns. That record still stands for national high school competition.

Shanley could always depend on Roger, remembered Pat Colliton, who played both quarterback and fullback. "Whenever we needed those four yards," he said, "we gave the ball to Roger, and he always got the yardage on a quick pitchout."

Roger's formidable gridiron skills had their counterpart in his unselfishness as a player. Cichy remembers the touchdown that Roger didn't score. In a game against Park River, Roger had already scored three touchdowns and was ten yards away from a fourth as he raced toward the goal line. "Suddenly he turned around," Cichy said, "and looked back and saw his brother Rudy trailing the play. He tossed him the ball and let him score. That was typical Roger: generosity and devotion to family."

Cichy also commented on Roger's forthrightness. "One day we were running a ridiculous drill in practice," Cichy remembered. "I was a young coach at the time. And then Roger told me how ridiculous the drill was. You don't want to hear that when you are a young, self-important coach. But Roger was right, and I called the drill off."

Shanley won the eastern division title during 1950-51, and Roger made the Associated Press East-West High School Football Team. Roger scored two touchdowns on passes from Rudy in a game with

Fargo High, and the Maris boys tasted sweet revenge when Shanley defeated their former school. A Dakota blizzard forced the cancellation of the championship game against Minot.

Roger had a reputation for physical endurance. During his two years with the Shanley Deacons, he missed only one football practice. In his first season he played three-and-a-half quarters in every game, and all sixty minutes in most of them. "The 1951-52 season was a particularly tough one," Cichy said, "and we were without Rudy, who graduated. Yet, Roger went all the way in every contest."

In addition to football, Roger played basketball and ran track for Shanley under Cichy's tutelage. As a hoopster, Roger was a good shooting guard and ball hawk, and was excellent on the fast break and defense, his coach said. In track he ran the dashes, earning second place in the one-hundred-yard dash in state competition. He was lead-off on two relay teams, gained third place statewide in the shot put, and was the school's best long jumper. Roger could even pole vault.

Cichy doubled as a history teacher at Shanley and recollected Roger's academic performance. "Sitting in the classroom wasn't always his thing, although he was a good student. You see, Roger was one of these guys who was very antsy and liked to be on the move. He was always in a hurry. As things turned out, you can say that he had a lot of living to do with not too much time to do it in."

Another member of the Shanley faculty, Sister Bernice echoed these thoughts. "Roger's priorities were not in the classroom," she said. "However, he was a conscientious student who wanted to maintain his eligibility in sports. For that reason he sought help in geometry and came in before class to brush up on the subject."

Sister Bertha — Roger's favorite teacher — spoke about Roger with a gleam in her eye.

Roger really enjoyed my typing class. The hands were always busy, and there were not many tests and assignments. I would walk around the classroom encouraging Roger and the other students. I do remember that Roger had great respect and love for the sisters.

Roger was a quiet person, always affable, no matter what. He was very gracious not only to his teachers but to his classmates as well. I was always grateful for his cheery, "Good morning, Sister," and his friendly smile at the start of class.

Over the years Sister Bertha maintained very close ties with Roger and with another of her students, Patricia Ann Carvell, who later became Pat Maris.

Roger and Pat did not meet in one of Sister Bertha's classes, but in the gymnasium of St. Anthony of Padua Church, where another football player, Gene Johnson, introduced them. "I still can go to St. Anthony's and point out the precise spot," Johnson said. "Roger noticed two girls on the other side of the gymnasium. 'Do you know those two?' he asked. 'Yes,' I told Roger. 'One is Pat Carvell; the other is Jeanie Williams.'"

Sid Cichy followed the courtship closely. "There was only one girl for Roger. He was very dedicated to Patsy from day one."

Pat received her first corsage ever from Roger at the senior prom. "Roger came dressed in a suit because hardly anyone in Fargo could afford to rent a tuxedo. He borrowed his dad's beat-up 1932 Chevrolet and came up the steps with that nervous half-smile of his, self-conscious. In his right hand there was a box with a corsage," recalled Pat Maris.

"Roger was always very considerate," she added. "That's one of the first things I noticed about him."

Bob Wood, a high school friend who manages Ralph's Tavern in neighboring Moorhead, Minnesota, recalls an incident.

> Roger gave Pat a gold football ring that he received when Shanley won the championship. Roger and Pat had some sort of squabble, and she gave him his ring back. On our way home that night, Roger took the ring and flung it in the grass. "Who needs it now?" he shouted. A few moments later, he turned around: "Let's go back and find it. Patsy is going to want it." There we were on our hands and knees, in the dark, looking for a ring in thick grass. We did find it — finally.

The misguided journalism of the 60s pictured Roger the teenager as surly, sulky, a sourball, but he was a fun-loving teenager and adult — even a prankster. "Roger had a great sense of humor," said boyhood friend Don Gooselaw, now proprietor of Mr. Don's State College of Beauty in Fargo.

> We were very close and we often double-dated. Roger's sense of humor was refreshing, but on one occasion it

really backfired. It was the Annual Pancake Dinner bringing together parents, students, and teachers.

As Roger and I and two others left, we noticed sacks of pancake flour in the corridor. I can't say that it was Roger's idea, but he certainly enjoyed the prank of taking the flour and pouring it in the nuns' overshoes. All the flour turned to messy black stuff. It was great fun until the school called a meeting and the superintendent pledged, in obvious anger: "If necessary, I will call in the FBI to find the culprits." All four of us stood up. As punishment, we had to clean up the gymnasium with scrub brushes.

At Shanley, Tom Conmy III, now an attorney, became a target for Roger's horseplay. He said:

I was a freshman while Roger was an upperclassman. He was one of those who initiated us. It wasn't very rough, just harassment and some fun. It involved, for example, bowing down to the upperclassmen, washing their cars, and doing other chores. One day Roger sent me to the local grocery store, with a long list of inconsequential items. But all I had to spend was fifteen cents. Roger had a good laugh, but it was a little irritating to me.

Roger and Bob Wood found time for other mischief. They posted themselves in Lover's Lane on Fargo's north side and put on kerchiefs. As the would-be lovers made their appearance, Roger and Bob would initiate "harmless" combat.

Bob Wood, Don Gooselaw, and Dick Savageau were intimate friends of Roger. Now president of Butler Machinery in Fargo, Savageau as a Shanley end, once brought in the plays from coach Cichy. "Roger received much enjoyment from playing practical jokes," Savageau recalled. "I won't forget that Sunday afternoon in 1952 when we planned to clean his dad's restored Chevrolet, but, instead, Roger took a hose and squirted me down."

Savageau saw significance in Roger's tripartite friendship. "Woodsie (Wood) was ebullient; Goose (Gooselaw) was amiable and obliging; and I was thought of as intense and thoughtful. Roger liked to think of himself as an individual who not only could give to his friends but could also learn from them. It would be reasonable to say that Roger's personality was somewhat of a composite of the three friends."

When not in school, involved in sports competitions, or socializing with friends, Roger held some odd jobs. One summer he worked at the Great Northern Railroad, where his dad was an engineer. Retiree George Tchouban of Moorhead also worked at the railroad that summer. "The young Maris was a clerk who handled mail and freight. He was a very good worker and was well liked by other workers. Young Maris was a very private person who minded his own business," said Tchouban.

Cichy believes that summer job had an important connection to Roger's future success in baseball. "Roger was a great hitter because of his powerful wrists," the coach reasoned. "The work on the railroad was very physical and went beyond just being a clerk. In tapping ties for the railroads, he developed wrist strength."

Roger's summer job at Fargo Floral may not have enhanced his athletic potential, but Jerry (Dede) Cossette remembers the 16-year-old who worked around the store and delivered flowers. "He was a very active youngster," Cossette said, "and got enjoyment from playing pranks." Cossette recalled such an occasion.

> The front and back offices were separated by a short partition. As the girls worked in the back, Roger was in front with some funeral sprays, mounted with doves of peace. From his position on top of the refrigerator, Roger floated a dove down on top of one of the girls. The girls shouted in fright, as Roger had his little joke.

Cossette said that when the shop no longer needed Roger's services, "we told him to go to the local pool hall across the street until there was a change in the situation. He never returned."

Roger had enough to do without working in a flower shop: with summer came baseball, and only a short time after that, a professional career awaited.

Chapter III
Baseball Begins at Home

Like many other baseball stars, Roger Maris began his career in American Legion baseball. He played the outfield and also pitched for the Fargo American Legion junior baseball team. His teammates named him the Most Valuable Player on the North Dakota championship team when he hit .367 for the 1950 squad. Coach Chuck Bentsen noted that those home runs "were not cheap shots. They were driven out in legitimate parks, including the home park, Barnett Field."

Leo Osman coached Roger's team in 1951, Maris' last year as an amateur. The coach remembered him well. "He had a perfect eye and perfect timing. Roger was so sincere at wanting to get a hit instead of a walk that he'd swing away on the first pitch. He felt it was a disgrace to take a walk.

"He was close to a ten-second man in track. I can't figure out why they didn't let him run. I'm sure he could have stolen with the ability of Mickey Mantle if given the practice."

Pat Colliton recalled how good Roger and Bud Maris were during their Legion ball days: "I was playing for the Moorhead team, and our coach 'Oats' LeGrand warned our pitcher about the brothers: 'Don't you dare throw them anything above the waist.'"

Roger had an excellent season that year but did not play well enough to salvage his team. In the double-elimination championship tourney, Fargo suffered 3-2 and 12-2 defeats. In the first game, the left-handed slugger gave up all three runs in one inning of pitching, but no one could fault his hitting. At midseason Roger was batting .480, and scored more hits, runs batted in, doubles, triples, and home runs than any member of this club. Although he finished the season with an average over .350 and led Fargo in almost all offensive departments, Roger did not win the Most Valuable Player award. Instead, the award went instead to Don Gronland, an outfielder and pitcher whose stats were comparable to Roger's. In the 3-2 finals loss, he knocked in one of the runs and struck out twelve after relieving Roger.

Even though Roger had been voted MVP the year before, he felt keenly disappointed at Gronland's selection. "Throughout his life, Roger had to contend with many adversities, and he accepted things well," Sister Bertha said, "but not receiving that award really disheartened him."

After graduation, Roger faced an important decision: should he go out for football or baseball? At nearly six feet and one-hundred ninety pounds, Roger had almost the same physique as he did when he joined the major leagues. Coach Cichy observed, "Roger could have gone far in football, too, but he had to want it and give it the same effort he gave baseball. He was an all-state halfback twice, so he had the credentials."

Roger visited the University of Oklahoma where famed football wizard Bud Wilkinson showed him the Norman campus. "Bud Wilkinson seemed like a nice guy," Roger said. "When I went in to take the exams, Wilkinson told me just to take my time and answer everything I could thoroughly. It was one of those multiple-choice tests, you know? Well, I sat there and tried to concentrate on the first page, but after that I just filled in numbers at random as fast as I could and got out. I realized then that sitting in a classroom wasn't for me, and that I was just too impatient for any sort of college life, football or no." Roger expressed a wish for the future: "When I get into some business after baseball, I hope it won't tie me down to an office."

Even though athletics seemed to take priority over academics in high school, Roger remained a good, conscientious student. He wanted to succeed in life. If he chose baseball and had a few good years, what would happen afterward? A college degree would allay any fears of being unable to make a living.

Even after he attained stardom with the New York Yankees, Roger wondered whether he had made the right decision. "Don't misunderstand me," he said. "I have no regrets. I'm happy in baseball and happy to be with the Yankees. But you can't help wondering to yourself what would have happened if you had gone on to college. I'd have graduated from Oklahoma in 1957. ... Would I be in some business today, or maybe playing pro football? I guess it's all for the best."

Roger turned down not only Oklahoma State, but also all the other colleges that had made offers. He chose baseball. "I liked the outdoors," he said, "and I liked being alone. I couldn't keep my mind on books. We grew up in the outdoors, on skates, playing a lot of hockey because that was the game my father loved."

Rudy Maris, Sr., also loved baseball. He had played some town and semi-pro ball in his youth. However, it was Rudy Jr., Roger's one-year-older brother, who motivated — even bullied — Roger to perfect his baseball skills.

"It was my brother who forced me to play baseball," Roger admitted, "and I mean *forced* me. If he went to play, he dragged me along. If he found me sitting around the house, he grabbed me by the ear and pulled me out. If I had been bigger I might have put up an argument. But I didn't catch up to him until we were in high school, and by that time nobody had to force me to play."

Roger always spoke with pride about his older brother, an outstanding athlete in his own right. "Do you want to know who was Roger Maris' best friend?" asked Dr. George Surprise, a friend of Roger and Pat's from Independence, Missouri. "There was never any doubt that it was his brother, Rudy."

Having decided on a career in baseball, Roger waited to be "discovered." "Our area wasn't blessed with too many scouts," Roger's American Legion coach Bentsen said. In those days big-league teams had part-time assistants helping the full-time scouts in the search. The Cleveland Indians had Frank Fahey as their part-timer or "bird dog" in the Dakotas.

During the 1961 season, Fahey, then a Dodger scout, looked through his old files. He found his first scouting report on Roger, dated August 12, 1950, and compiled at Dickinson, North Dakota, where Roger played in the American Legion tournament. "Roger weighed one-hundred fifty pounds and stood about five-eight," said Fahey. "My opinion at the time was that Maris would be a major leaguer if he filled out. ... He could run and throw and had lots of power. By the time Roger was seventeen, he had put on twenty pounds. I was convinced he was a sure-fire prospect."

Fahey recommended that the Tribe look him over. The Cleveland Indians invited Roger to a tryout camp at League Park, the Tribe home stadium before Municipal Stadium. The short right field with its high screen proved an ideal target for Roger's home-run swings. Hank Greenberg, then general manager and part-owner of Cleveland, liked what he saw when Roger creamed Red Ruffing's offerings into the seats. "As soon as you get home, have your father call me," Greenberg said in parting.

Greenberg soon made the next move by sending Cyril (Cy) Slapnicka to Fargo to sign Roger on as an Indian. Slapnicka's pitch focused less on money than on the practicality and respectability of a baseball career. News of Roger's talent spread throughout the league, and soon the Chicago Cubs joined the hunt. At Wrigley Field Chicago's brain trust looked Roger over carefully and made a negative evaluation. "Go home and forget baseball," they said. "You're too small. You'll never make it." Roger's measurements then differed little from his vital statistics as a major leaguer, but perhaps his compact, symmetrical build made him look ordinary to the Cubbies.

Slapnicka kept courting, despite the Maris family's second thoughts. How many high school boys made it to the majors? Roger himself wondered whether he should reconsider the university offers, but Hank Greenberg's agents came well prepared. Slapnicka emphasized the viability and acceptability of baseball as a profession. Scout Jack O'Connor traveled to Fargo to prove to the Marises that professional baseball had exciting financial potential.

O'Connor, general manager of the Fargo-Moorhead Twins in the Class C Northern League, negotiated a deal satisfactory to both the Marises and the Cleveland organization. The total package of $15,000 included a bonus of $5,000 and an additional $10,000 if Roger could make the majors.

Despite his parents' inducements, urgings, reservations, and thoughts, Roger decided for himself. He said, "I felt injustice to my family. I couldn't pass up a sum of money like that."

The signed contract did not settle the issue of where Roger would play. When Roger, then eighteen, reported for the 1953 Cleveland spring training in Daytona Beach, Florida, farm director Mike McNally wanted to put him in a Class D league. McNally felt Roger should stay in Daytona, where the Tribe affiliate was. Roger thought himself too good to start at the bottom. He told McNally he had his mind set on Fargo, Class C, Northern League.

Once McNally realized that Roger had made up his mind about going to Class C, he pleaded with Roger for a week to forget about Fargo. The farm director argued, "We never let a boy play in his home town. It subjects him to needless pressure in trying to make good."

Roger told McNally he planned to be in Fargo one way or another. The suggested pressure "won't bother me," Roger asserted. "I've played before those people before. I'm going to Fargo — to play, or I go to Fargo to live. Now, it's up to you to decide whether I go there on my own or to play ball for the Cleveland organization."

His words may have sounded stubborn, but Roger was just speaking frankly and saying what was on his mind — a quality he developed long before he turned professional ballplayer. As Roger told Leonard Koppett in a *Saturday Evening Post* interview, "I was in a midget league, I don't remember the exact age. I knew I was good enough to play with the age group one year up, and I insisted that they let me. They refused, and I kept insisting. Finally, they let me."

Roger persisted until Cleveland sent him to Fargo as a player. "I only had to walk across town to play ball," Roger said. He began to show impressive numbers. His colorful and spirited manager, former major-league veteran Zeke Bonura, did not push the rookie to swing for the fences, to go all out. Roger's amazing stats — batting average of .325, with nine home runs and thirteen triples — pointed to his speed.

He easily won the George Treadwell-Duluth Dukes Memorial Award as the Northern League's 1953 Rookie of the Year. He collected twelve of twenty-two first-place votes and seventy points on a 5-3-1 basis. In league history only Hank Aaron, the all-time home-run leader, garnered more votes than Roger.

Maris worked hard that year to perfect his skills. Max Olson of Grand Barber and Beauty, who gave Roger his distinctive crew cuts, noticed Roger's "diligent and dedicated" practicing. "He was a heck of a guy who never boasted how great he was or what he planned to do. He just went out and did it."

Roger became the talk of Fargo. Loren Oliver, president of the Fargo-Moorhead team, said, "We were delighted when Cleveland farm officials left Maris with us. Roger fulfilled our faith when he was chosen the Northern League Rookie of the Year."

Eugene Fitzgerald wrote in the *Fargo Forum*: "Playing in his home town, Maris had some prejudices to beat. He did it convincingly. Baseball men know the most difficult place for a player to make good is in his home town."

Fitzgerald argued that North Dakota "hasn't produced too many major league products. This has resulted in the supposition that we play an inferior brand of baseball in the state. The wide margin by which Maris won the award was a credit to junior and amateur baseball in the state, as Maris played both varieties before signing with the Cleveland farm system."

Playing baseball in Fargo was not a full-time job. While not on the diamond, Roger pumped gas at the Moorhead service station he operated. He also found time to befriend some orphaned children. "During vacation in the summer," Sister Bertha recalled, "Roger came over occasionally to chat when I was on yard duty with the children at St. John's Orphanage in Fargo. When he tossed the football around with them, they felt great. He was a regular guy and a friend to the children. Roger's coming to the orphanage was only one instance of his thoughtfulness of others."

Roger's performance pleased Fargo and delighted the Cleveland front office. They slated him to play the 1954 season in Fargo, but Roger felt it was time to move on. At training in Daytona, Roger checked out the farm-club rosters and noticed that he was still on the Fargo squad. "I got so mad," Roger said, "I just took off to the beach and lazed around a couple of days, missing some squad games. Then they got mad. Then I went down to where the officials lived and got into a shouting match. There was one man in particular who told me I was making a bad impression. I said, 'If I can't get to the big leagues on my own ability without your words, I don't want it.'"

Roger's "Move me up to Class B or I quit!" ultimatum worked and Roger headed for the Class B Three-Eye League in Keokuk, Iowa. At this turning point in Roger's professional career, he met Jo-Jo White, former Detroit outfielder. White told his new outfielder, "You're too strong to be a spray hitter. You're too big not to use your power to pull the ball and for distance. Try it."

Following White's advice, Roger hit .315 with thirty-two home runs and one-hundred eleven RBIs. Some years later, Roger spoke of White: "He was one of the great influences I had in baseball. I can't imagine a young fellow breaking into baseball being in better hands." White's steadying influence as a father figure helped the twenty-year-old Roger cope with his tensions and inexperience. Roger's own success spread to the Keokuk team, which played to a second-place finish.

Roger gave his all for White and Keokuk. According to White, Roger stole "almost a base a night." In one game he went to make a catch and ran right through a fence. He caught the ball and held on to it without injuring himself. Roger believed that injuries were as much a part of the game as hitting, fielding, and throwing. "Just because I get hurt is no reason for me to stop hustling. I'd rather stop playing than hustling. Anybody who feels otherwise doesn't belong in baseball."

The parent club promoted Roger to Tulsa, Class AA of the Texas League. Soon Roger came into conflict there with Dutch Meyer, a manager determined to have his squad stay in contention. Meyer felt that Roger's inexperience would jeopardize his team's chances. The manager kept Roger on the bench, to the slugger's dismay. "I can't help you on the bench," Roger told Meyer bluntly, "and you can't help me. I'd like to go some place where I can play regularly, and I don't particularly care where as long as I'm in the lineup every day."

After an errant throw by Roger cost Tulsa a game, Meyer told Roger to field grounders and throw to third. Roger, being open and honest, refused. He asked for a transfer to Reading.

Meyer did not object to Roger's transfer. The Cleveland organization's evaluation indicated that perhaps the youngster was being hurried. Cleveland reassigned Roger to Reading in the Eastern League, where his trusted mentor Jo-Jo White had been assigned to manage. Meyer was fired.

The change in mood and scenery made a difference. At Tulsa, Roger struggled with a .239 average. At Reading, Roger batted .289 in one-hundred thirteen games, nineteen home runs, seventy-eight RBIs, and twenty-four stolen bases, and beat out eighteen of nineteen drag bunts.

During a trying season, White steadied Roger even more than he had before. As Roger told Red Barber during a 1960 interview, "White was understanding, which every kid needs when he's inexperienced, and he was a fine teacher, both ways, hitting and fielding."

White responded to Roger's sentiments:

> Seeing a boy like Roger become a major-league star is one of the things which makes minor-league managing so worthwhile. ... When you get to send a boy to the big leagues and you see him make good, especially when he makes it as big as Maris has, it makes up for everything.
>
> When you're through yourself as a player, the only thrill you have left is seeing somebody pull off the plays you

taught him. And you can't say anything too good about Maris. He ran right through a wooden fence for me at Keokuk. I thought he was out for the year, but he held the ball, came to, and got up and won the game for me with a homer in the ninth. How much hustle can a guy give you?

White observed that Roger is "the strongest boy I ever saw. Carroll Hardy [the pro footballer] played for me, too, and I think Maris could flip Hardy over his back."

Still, the skipper recalled: "I never saw Roger look for a fight. If somebody got smart with him, he'd say, 'That's enough. If you keep it up, I won't be responsible for what happens to you.' I never saw anybody accept the challenge. And if somebody started anything with one of our players, Roger would be the first to rush right up, ready to help his teammates out."

To avoid conflicts resulting from mispronunciation or misspelling of his name, Roger *Maras* officially became Roger *Maris* in a legal change of name filed in 1955.

The Cleveland Indians considered Maris a hot prospect at the 1956 training camp in Tucson. The Tribe had won the pennant in 1954. Maris' statistics indicated that the Maris bat might win them another flag.

The New York Yankees also monitored Roger's progress. The Yankees' general manager began paying close attention to Roger in 1955. In a 1961 interview with the *New York Journal-American*, George Weiss, then head of the New York Mets, recalled the pursuit:

We were looking for a left-handed pull hitter. In the past we had fellows like Tommy Henrich, Charley Keller, and Red Rolfe. But they were gone, and we couldn't find the proper replacement. It was hurting us in that we weren't winning at home. On the road we were fine. But in the stadium there was trouble because of the lack of left-handed power. A ball club, you know, should be tailor-made to its home park.

Weiss' interest sharpened as reports came in from Reading. The Yankees wanted to know more about Roger's skills and about his personal habits. "We watched him closely," Weiss said. "We received reports on his personal habits and even assigned scouts to his hometown of Fargo, North Dakota, to find out all about him. Everything we were told convinced us that he was the player we wanted."

However, in 1955 Cleveland manager Al Lopez had a full opportunity to see Maris for himself and make a decision about his immediate future. Lopez said:

> I liked him. He could hit, he could run, he had a good arm — why wouldn't you like him? I didn't have much to do with him — the only conversation I remember having was suggesting he might stand closer to the plate if he was going to be a pull hitter. But he said he could pull an outside pitch as well as an inside pitch the way he was. And he was right. He's pulled plenty of them against me since [when Lopez managed the White Sox].

Indianapolis skipper Kerby Farrell had wanted Roger "ever since he had that good year at Keokuk" and greeted Roger warmly. When Roger did not start off well, Farrell assigned his pinch hitter and former big-league veteran Ron Northey as an advisor and friend to Roger. Northey sat next to the youngster on the bench to give Roger batting pointers and also to keep up his spirits. "Northey is funny," Roger said. "He reminds me of Lou Costello. He was like a tonic."

Despite Northey's ministrations, Roger had an inauspicious start and Farrell benched him. Again, Roger spoke his mind, but his confrontation with Farrell lacked the bitterness of his exchange with Meyer. Roger liked playing for Farrell, so he told the manager that he could only maintain his timing and achieve peak performance by being in the lineup every day. Farrell listened sympathetically. If Hank Greenberg gave his approval, Farrell told Roger, "You're in my lineup for every inning for every game for ten days, no matter what. Let's see what you can do."

Roger made a believer out of Farrell. After a bloop single the first game, the slugger fought back and finished with a very respectable .293 mark, with seventeen homers and seventy-five runs batted in. In the final month of the season, Roger batted well over .300 and was instrumental to the club's winning the Little World Series against Rochester. He saved one game with a line-drive throw to the plate and won a second game with two homers and seven runs batted in.

George Spencer, the relief ace of the '51 miracle New York Giants, remembers the professional maturation of Roger. They were roommates on that Indianapolis team. "Roger improved more in that one year," he said, "than I can personally recall any athlete improving in such a period. And I should add that he was a wonderful person. All personal attacks on him were totally uncalled for."

Greenberg was overjoyed. The $15,000 signing of the sharp-featured, blue-eyed twenty-two-year-old began to look like a steal. The fans idolized Roger Maris and named him "Cleveland's future Mickey Mantle."

Before the 1957 season began, Roger Maris married Pat Carvell in a small, double-ring ceremony at St. Anthony of Padua Church on October 13, 1956. Roger was twenty-two and Pat, twenty-one. Sister Bertha feels that although Roger and Pat had known each other for a long time, Pat's mother Mrs. Grace Carvell "was not too anxious for the marriage at that time, although she did like Roger. Perhaps she saw hard times ahead."

Chapter IV
Short Stops in Cleveland
and Kansas City

Pat remained in Fargo while Roger enthusiastically left for the Indians' 1957 training camp in Arizona. Roger happily greeted the Indians' new manager, Kerby Farrell, unworried by his competition for the right-field position, the power-hitting, strong-fielding Rocco Colavito. Maris knew that Farrell had confidence in his abilities and would play him regularly. As the Tribe broke camp, many experts chose Roger as top candidate for rookie of the year.

On opening day, April 16, Roger played left field against the White Sox ace, lefty Billy Pierce, a twenty-game winner in 1956. Cleveland countered with their star southpaw Herb Score. Roger had a fine start: three singles in the eleven-inning 3-2 loss.

The Tribe traveled to Detroit's Briggs Stadium. Roger came through with the first of his 275 home runs, a grand slammer, the first bases-loaded smash in the major leagues that season. The drive came off Jack Crimian, as the Tribe beat the Tigers 8-3 in eleven innings.

After five games, Roger was hitting .305, with seven hits in twenty-three times at bat. He sparkled in the field: in Detroit he cut down the winning run with a throw to the plate; against the White Sox he made a rolling catch of Sherman Lollar's sinking line drive.

People back home in Fargo were expressing their unabashed pride. In his sports column Fitzgerald wrote: "If North Dakota isn't getting some benefit from the feats performed by Maris, a lot of people are learning where Fargo is. Maris is beginning to excite a lot of interest in North Dakota cities outside Fargo as well as in the surrounding Minnesota area."

Many self-made experts had expected Roger to do well, but his early .300 hitting took them by surprise. Fitzgerald noted, "No one expects Maris to continue his batting average in the high .300 class. He could drop quite a little and still do it because of his fine defensive play, including a strong throwing arm."

After sixteen games, Roger had twenty hits for thirty-three total bases, with three home runs, thirteen runs batted in, and a batting average of .308. Hal Lebovitz, the veteran writer of the *Cleveland News,* did a very favorable full-page story on Roger, which appeared along with an accompanying cartoon by Lou Darvas in the May 1 *Sporting News.*

The article highlighted Roger's competitiveness, his honesty, and his maturation as a person.

> This is the same Maris ... who was classified as a "brooder" by Tribe brass when he worked out in Tucson during spring training last year.
>
> If this Maris seems a tough customer, it is only because he is such an intense competitor. He rebelled inwardly last spring because he wasn't playing in any of the exhibition games. ...
>
> There has been no trace of moodiness or surliness in Maris this spring. Now 22, he appears to have matured. In truth, we have come to know him as a friendly young man who tells what is in his heart. He puts it, "If I've got something in my bonnet, it's got to be said."
>
> The forthright rookie bluntly states: "I've been a marked man ever since I got into baseball. I've been called a brooder, a sore-head, a bad actor. I don't see it.
>
> Maybe it's because I show it on my face when I'm disgusted. I may look down, but inside me it's not that way. I never got down on myself. I have full confidence.
>
> I don't care where I am, in Class D or in the majors, if I don't play I'm not happy. You better believe it [this is his favorite expression]. But as long as I'm playing I never worry about what I did the last time at bat. I'm thinking about the next time and, if I look like I'm brooding, it's only my natural expression. Honestly, I'm not.

Lebovitz assessed Roger's talents:

> Base runners already have learned not to challenge his arm. He fearlessly charges ground balls and gets rid of them quickly and accurately. In our book, for what it's worth, Maris has the mark of greatness. This is an exciting young player who could approach the stature of a Mantle.

He has all the physical attributes plus the necessary determination.

Farrell noted that Roger played on a pennant-winning team in each of his four years in professional ball. The Tribe manager hoped to channel Roger's competitive spirit, and he would not allow his rookie to brood.

Fargo's Eugene Fitzgerald visited Comiskey Park and commented on Roger's "changed" attitude. "Maris is apparently no longer brooding," he said. "He has had supreme confidence in himself and believed he was capable of playing in the majors. Now he's there, and all he has to do is prove he can stay there."

The Marises rented a home in Parma, Ohio, fifteen miles from downtown Cleveland. Pat gave birth to their first child, Susan, while Roger was on the road in Baltimore. Roger was hitting .310, and the Associated Press's Joe Reichler had tabbed Roger as an early-season favorite to win rookie-of-the-year honors. Everything seemed to be going his way.

On May 10 Cleveland played at home against Kansas City, In the third inning Roger slid into second base and the knee of second baseman Milt Graff struck Roger in the side. Despite his pain Roger continued to play for two innings before his difficulty in swinging the bat forced him to leave. He had suffered two broken ribs that kept him out of the lineup for nearly a month.

The outpouring of good wishes from his fans made the healing process easier. Pat recalled, "He received 'Get Well' cards from fans of all ages, little children to grandmothers. It really made us feel good that so many people were interested in him."

Roger had little chance to work out and prepare himself for his return to the lineup, but Farrell wanted him out on the field if Roger could swing a bat. Farrell seemed to have made the right decision. In the first week of his return, in the lead-off spot, Roger hit three homers, two coming in a four run-batted-in contest against Detroit. Three weeks after his return, Roger again made the disabled list after his right foot got in the way of two foul tips.

He never regained his early form. "When I came back, I couldn't do a thing," he complained. "My timing was way off and my average melted. Most of the time I was helpless at the plate." Although he hit fourteen homers for the season, his average went down to .235, with only fifty-one runs batted in. Cleveland also had a poor year, finishing in sixth place with a below-.500 percentage.

Roger later told Joe McGuff of the *Kansas City Star:*

> I never did feel like I was wanted with the Cleveland organization. I got started on my way out with them after I was hurt in 1957. I was out for about a month, and as soon as I was able to swing a bat, Kerby Farrell put me back in the lineup. I hadn't been able to work out at all before and I wasn't ready. In a way, though, I don't blame Kerby because there was a lot of pressure on him.
>
> When I went back in the lineup he called me aside and explained that he knew I wasn't ready. He told me not to worry and said that I had a job regardless of how I went. Well, I went lousy and a few weeks later he called me in and said, "Kid, if you don't start hitting, we're going to have to take you out of the lineup."

An organizational shake-up in Cleveland intensified Roger's discontent and finally led to his departure. Hank Greenberg, who had had so much confidence in Roger, left. Greenberg's replacement, the pompous Frank "Trader" Lane from the Cardinals, had won his nickname by negotiating over five hundred deals on the baseball market during his career.

The Yankees were operating quietly when Lane appeared on the Cleveland scene. The New Yorkers wanted to know if Roger's 1957 injury would jeopardize his career. According to the *Forum's* Fitzgerald, the Yankees dispatched Fargo-Moorhead general manager Kenny Blackman to evaluate Roger's physical condition right after Fargo-Moorhead had completed its first season under Yankee affiliation. Since the Yankees feared that contracting Roger might be considered tampering, Blackman asked Fitzgerald to call on Roger, who had returned to Fargo for the winter.

"Of course, all were pledged to secrecy," Fitzgerald wrote. "But that's why there has been so much certainty by this department that the Yankees were interested in obtaining Maris. Not even Maris knows why the inquiry about the state of his health was made."

For the off-season, Roger joined the staff of KVOX, a Moorhead radio station. As an account executive he sold advertising and serviced existing accounts. He also did a sports show.

Trader Lane had other off-season plans for his slugger. He felt Roger had a very promising future, but he wanted him to play center field. To speed the development process and help Roger forget the memories of last season, Lane commanded Roger, "I want you to play winter ball."

A battle began between the two iron-willed personalities. Lane felt he was being very generous in offering Roger a raise for 1958, a chance to make a few extra dollars then, and an opportunity to increase his value in the long run. Lane presented his self-righteous stance in *Baseball Quarterly*:

> When I inherited Maris he was coming off a season in which he had hit .235. But I felt he had excellent potential and I particularly wanted him to play center field for us. However, despite the somewhat disappointing season he had the previous year, I sent him a contract for a raise of $1,500. That would really raise the eyebrows of our millionaires today, wouldn't it? Anyway, Maris sent the contract back to me in two pieces with no comment. So I called him at his home in North Dakota and said, "Roger, I know you accidentally tore this, but the one I'm going to send you will be the only one you'll get."
>
> In the meantime, I asked Roger if he would go to Licey in the Dominican Republic winter league. He told me he wasn't all that interested because they only paid $800 a month there. So I asked him what it would take to go and he said, "$1,500 a month." "You got it," I said, "but let me work out the details and get back to you." Well, I pulled a few strings with the local operators of the Licey Club and they agreed to help me out with getting Maris what he wanted. But when I called Roger back, he said he had changed his mind and didn't want to go under any circumstances.

Roger had no plans to leave Fargo to play winter ball. His marriage and family meant more to him than a few extra dollars. "I've been away from my wife and family too long," Roger said, ending Lane's demands.

Lane did not enjoy being challenged by a rookie who dared to put family before career. Nor could he accept Roger's disregard of his directive. "That did it," Lane said in *Baseball Quarterly*. "I made up my mind that this guy was going to be too difficult to handle to make it worth my while."

Roger determined to return to his early 1957 form and silence critics who were writing him off as a "streak hitter," a morning glory whose potential had faded. When Roger reported for spring training in 1958 he not only met an incensed Lane, but he also had to adjust to new manager Bobby Bragan, another roadblock in Roger's attempt to regain his early 1957 form. Bragan planned to alternate Roger and Colavito. Without bitterness, Roger admitted openly and honestly, "I couldn't play for Bragan. I didn't like him, and he had no use for me. He hailed me on the carpet one day and shouted, 'I am fed up with your loafing.'" Even when Roger ran into a fence retrieving a ball, Bragan still criticized.

Roger could not perform for Bragan (nor could other Indians). By June Roger had not gotten his average much above .225 and had only managed nine homers. At the beginning of June, Lane fired Bragan.

As the June trading deadline approached, it seemed inevitable that Roger would also be leaving. Roger, along with pitcher Dick Tomanek and infielder Preston Ward, was swapped to Kansas City for Vic Power and Woody Held. Lane delighted in unloading Roger for half an infield, Power at first and Held at third. Lane affirmed that he would make the deal again, given the opportunity. Lane said:

> Looking back, even if I had known Maris would hit sixty-one home runs someday, I'd still do it because I got half an infield for him [Power at first, Held at third], and his lack of ambition to improve himself by playing center field convinced me to get rid of him.
>
> I was lucky in the Maris deal because when I traded him, he was still a comparative unknown, and we got two quality ball players for him.

Greenberg, who still had faith in Maris, shook his head when learning of the deal. Roger would never have gone to Kansas City "if I ever had anything to say about it."

Fargo friends and family insist that the although Roger never spoke ill of anyone, Frank Lane would have to be an exception. Roger evaluated the Trader during the 1961 season: "I can't stand Lane's guts. I never liked Lane. Not because of what he ever did to me, but what he's done to others. He talks big. Thinks he's a big deal. Who's he kidding? ... He's no good. I don't like what he stands for. His type is no good for baseball."

Roger maintained that his assessment went beyond the 1958 trade. "I got no grievance against him for that trade. He did me a great favor. It was a good trade for both of us."

Roger's unhappiness with Lane was only part of a negative Cleveland experience. The two baseball greats, Greenberg and Tris Speaker, provided only confusing and contradictory instruction. Speaker would exhort Roger to hit the ball to left field; then Greenberg would implore the lefty to get out in front and pull the ball more. "By the time they finished with me," Roger said, "I didn't know what I was doing."

According to Roger, his attitude distressed Cleveland. The Tribe had not brought home a flag since 1954 and had become adjusted to losing. However, Roger's consuming determination to win had begun at Grand Forks, extended to Shanley and through the minor leagues, and eventually spread to the Yankees and the Cardinals. Cleveland didn't like him, Roger reasoned, "because I'd get mad in the clubhouse after losing a game. I guess they wanted gentlemen ballplayers. I don't like to lose, and I'm not going to be happy any time a club I'm with has been beaten. It doesn't make any difference how good a day I've had either. ... I don't like ballplayers who laugh and cut up in the clubhouse when they've had a good day, but the team has lost."

Roger responded to his new 1958 surroundings. Although the Athletics had been mired in the second division, Roger got a chance to play regularly. His nineteen homers and fifty-two runs batted in with Kansas City gave him a respectable season of twenty-eight homers and eighty RBIs, despite his .240 average.

Roger felt at home in Kansas City. He looked forward to his best season when he reported for spring training in 1959. He began brilliantly. By mid-May his lusty batting average of .328, with a total of ten homers and twenty-six runs batted in, made him one of the leading candidates for the All Star team.

Manager Harry Craft and Roger felt a mutual admiration. "If I mess up a play, what good does it do for the manager to come around and cuss me out?" Roger said. "I know what I've done, and I don't like it any better than he does. That's one thing I like about playing for Harry Craft. If you do something wrong, he'll call you aside later on and explain how the play should have been made. You don't learn anything from a manager that just chews you out."

Sometimes Craft criticized Roger's performance, attributing it to inexperience. "He's a very confused young ball player when he's not hitting," the manager said. Roger accepted the criticism with a touch of self-effacement: "I don't know how confused I was, but I do know that when I'm not hitting, my wife could pitch and get me out." In general, however, Craft felt that "Roger was a hard-hitting Dutchman, opinionated, yet also quiet. All he wanted to do was win — and, my, how he did that!"

At the end of May an emergency appendectomy sidelined Roger. He suffered no visible ill effects, but he went into a prolonged slump. "I never really got my full strength back, or my timing when I came back," he said. Roger might have been trying too hard to carry the Athletics: the team had finished seventh with only fifty-six wins, one .300 hit by a regular, and twenty home runs hit by the leading slugger Bob Cerv, a future roommate of Roger's. As a result, management fired Harry Craft at season's end.

Roger had still had a respectable year. He hit .273, sixteen home runs, and seventy-two RBIs and won a spot on the American League team for the second All Star game in Los Angeles. In the previous year, Roger had knocked in eight more runs, but in twenty-eight more games. In answer to those who faulted his second-half-of-the-season decline, Roger pointed to his injuries and the loss of playing time that accompanied them.

Roger felt that his 1959 slump stemmed from his timing. When he was on a tear he would use a thirty-five-inch, thin-handled bat; when he had to get around on the ball more quickly, his bat varied from thirty-one to thirty-four ounces. According to Roger,

> Any slump is a matter of timing. That's why it's so hard for a player to maintain the rhythmic swing you've got to have for good hitting if he isn't in the line-up every day. Any time I've been out, I've found it takes quite a while to adjust my timing after I get back in. It's how fast you can get back your timing that determines whether you're back on the beam or in a slump. The longer it takes you to get it back, the more likely you are to press, and once you start pressing, you're in trouble. I was pressing in the last part of 1959. Everybody was telling me I was. I couldn't see it then. But I realize it now.

The Athletics' front office had special concern over Roger's slump. He had shown power, speed, and defensive skill when the Athletics had taken him on, but what if the slump carried over to a poor performance in 1960? As Tom Meany writes in *Sport*: "Was his fade-out in the last half of 1959 an indication of permanent weakness or was it something transient? It could be, in a player of Maris' limited major-league experience, that the pitchers suddenly had discovered a weak spot where he could be pitched to."

The Yankees were well aware of Roger's slump and his statistics in the second half of the season, yet they were willing to take the risk. They had finished third in the 1959 season, after at one point sinking to last place below the Washington Senators. Yankee general manager George Weiss had tried to sign Roger for years, but Cleveland general manager Lane would not deal with the Yankees. However, Weiss circumvented Lane by promising Kansas City owner Arnold Johnson "a real deal for Maris" if the slugger ever came to Kansas City. "If Maris hadn't slumped in '59," Yankee General Manager George Weiss said afterward, "I doubt whether Johnson would have traded him."

Early in the season Roger made it known that he did not want to play under the Yankee regime. "I honestly don't want to leave Kansas City," he said of the place his family now called home. "I've been told that I could make a lot of extra money on endorsements and other things if I were with the Yankees," Roger commented to Joe McGuff. "The fence at Yankee Stadium would be better for me, but I'll still get my share of home runs in our park."

The prospect of Yankee control made him uncomfortable. "I wouldn't want to join the Yankees," Roger said, "because I don't believe I'd be happy playing there. They get on their ball players a lot and try to make them do things just the way they want it. I don't go for that sort of thing. When someone starts getting all over me, I just get mad."

At the December 1959 winter meetings in Florida, Pittsburgh entered the bidding and Roger nearly went to the National League. Realizing that Pittsburgh could be a strong contender for the 1960 flag, general manager Joe L. Brown approached the Athletics' general manager Parke Carroll about Maris and Kansas City's third baseman-catcher Hal Smith. Carroll asked about Bill Virdon and Don Hoak, but Brown was only willing to counter with shortstop Dick

Groat. The ball was literally in Brown's court, but the GM wanted to think it over. Brown thought it over and called Carroll the next day to tell him there was no deal.

Weiss had not lost interest in Maris, but the Athletics originally asked for Norm Siebern in trade. Casey Stengel refused to part with the outfielder. When Pittsburgh dropped out of the bargaining for Roger, Weiss jumped in again. Weiss desperately needed a lefty pull hitter and Cincinnati General Manager Gabe Paul wanted too much in return for Gus Bell.

The Yankees and the Athletics had cut many deals over the years; insiders joked that KC was the best Yank farm team. When the Athletics demanded substitute first baseman-outfielder Marv Thronberry, Stengel at first said no. The special relationship between Johnson and Dan Topping of the Yankees' front office kept open the channels of communication between the teams. The Athletics overcame the Thronberry problem by tossing in their own utility man, Kent Hadley.

This was no ordinary deal. The Yankees gave up Thronberry, World Series perfect-game hero Don Larsen, and veteran Hank Bauer for Roger Maris, Hadley, and infielder Joe DeMaestri.

Roger Maris — *A Title to Fame*

Chapter V
Suited for Pinstripes and New York

Roger Maris was not thrilled on December 11, 1959, when news of the swap reached him via the media. Reporters eager for Roger's comments about his trade greeted him on his way home. Other sources report that Roger learned of the trade while doing promotional work in the Consentino supermarket.

He told the press, "Kansas City is my home now." He added, after some thought, "And I'll expect more money." The news of the trade left Pat Maris "very upset." The Maris family had liked Kansas City so much that they had just bought a home.

Roger stressed that he had nothing personal against the Yankees, but that he felt very kindly about the Kansas City fans. When the fans honored him with Maris Day, he received many gifts and then showed his appreciation by striking out in the ninth with the bases loaded and two out. The fans still cheered him. "That's what I call loyalty," said Roger.

While the Yanks could not conquer Roger's reluctance to leave the Midwest, they did have a chance to increase his salary. Roger held out for more money, but "they didn't offer me any more of a raise than the Athletics did," he said. Finally, Weiss's assistant in charge of signing players, Roy Hamey, sat down with Roger and raised his salary, but not much above his earnings with the Athletics.

Once settled in New York in the summer of 1960, Roger discussed his reactions to the Yankee trade with Tom Meaney: "In Kansas City I had established myself and my family — my wife, my daughter Susan and our little boy Roger Jr. Because my wife is expecting, I couldn't bring the family to New York with 'em, so it's been something of a lonesome summer. That was one reason, maybe, why I didn't react as enthusiastically to the trade as some people thought I should when it was announced."

The greatest displeasure with Maris' trade to the Yankees came from the Chisox and Indians. Both had tried unsuccessfully to land Roger. White Sox owner Bill Veeck criticized the "apparent closed combine" of the Yankees and Athletics that had completed its fifteenth deal since 1955. Trader Lane called the deal "legal, but it should cause some eyebrow lifting."

Many Yankees, however, were excited about the trade. According to catcher John Blanchard, "The arrival of Roger Maris meant we had a good shot at the pennant and post-season money."

Yankee hill-ace Whitey Ford had followed Roger's career in Cleveland and Kansas City. As Ford states in his book, *Slick,* "I thought Maris was the one guy we needed. He always played hard. And he would plow into second base with total abandon to break up a double play. He was a complete player and he could field and throw and run."

Clubhouse attendant Pete Sheehy also welcomed Roger. Sheehy told the *New York Post,* "When Roger was with Cleveland ... I kept saying now there's a kid I hope the Yankees land. He was so quiet, peaceful, bothered nobody."

Weiss still worried about Roger's reluctance to leave Kansas City and decided to explore Roger's feelings further at spring training. "I greeted him in St. Petersburg," Weiss said, "and he seemed fine. He sat in a box next to mine during an early exhibition game and we had a very pleasant chat. After that all my fears had vanished. I felt confident we had the right guy."

The press appeared in St. Petersburg in full force. Jim Ogle, a reporter for the *Newark Star Ledger,* recalls the interview that would establish Roger's personality for the press. When asked, "How many home runs do you expect to hit?" Roger responded, "Oh, twenty to twenty-five." Pencils dropped — so few homers from a left-handed power hitter coming to Yankee Stadium? Roger explained with typical Maris candor: "If I said, 'thirty-five to forty,' and didn't do it, it would be a lousy year. With a lower figure, no one can say I had a bad year."

The Yankees had acquired Roger as a protective measure. Stengel told reporters. "We needed balance at home." The Yank's right-handed batters — Moose Skowron, Clete Boyer, Hector Lopez — could hit with power. But if Berra didn't play every day and Mantle was hitting right-handed against lefties, who would take advantage of the short right-field stadium porch?

The Old Professor used spring training to experiment with Roger, trying to turn him into a left fielder. Although unhappy with the attempted switch, Roger said nothing and went along with Stengel. Roger's hitting was impressive in the spring, but when the 1960 season opened in Boston, Stengel had him back in right field.

In 1960 a writer for *New Yorker* described Roger, the new Yankee, "as garrulous as Calvin Coolidge." Roger told the correspondent of his desire to return to Fargo after his career because "I don't much like big cities."

The Fargo native who preferred the plains or midwestern life in Kansas City didn't have to address his big-city phobia while in spring training. However, the differences in lifestyles between New York and the Midwest became immediately apparent upon Roger's arrival in the Big Apple. "Big Julie" Isaacson met Roger at the airport. Big Julie was the president of the Novelty Workers Union, has managed boxers, and lists seven years of minor league baseball experience with the Dodgers.

In his unmistakable Brooklyn accent, Big Julie recalls: "I knew Bob Cerv pretty well." Cerv had played outfield for the Athletics while Roger was in Kansas City and later in 1960 came to New York through the Athletics-Yankee conduit. Isaacson continues, "Cerv asked me to look after a kid named Roger Maris who was coming to New York.

"I know a lot of people in New York, and I like helping people. So I decided to go out to the airport to meet this Maris kid and help get him settled in the city."

Big Julie had an idea of what Roger looked like and knew he couldn't miss the blond crew cut. He searched the debarking passengers for a man in a suit and tie, someone who looked like a Yankee. Then, says Big Julie, "Suddenly, I see this kid who looks lost. It had to be Maris because of the crew cut. But what an outfit: sweater, corduroy jeans, and white buckskin shoes."

After the introductions, Big Julie immediately told Roger: "You can't dress like that; you're gonna be playing for the Yankees." Roger responded with his typical openness, "The hell with them. If they don't like the way I look or dress, I won't play for them. I can go back to Kansas City."

Later that day, Roger went in search of a Thom McAn. "I'm going to buy myself two more of these white shoes," he said.

"You must be kidding," Big Julie said, still taken aback by the new Yankee. "Nobody here wears them kind of shoes."

The battle of the wardrobe ended when Roger bought two more pairs of white bucks. Big Julie describes the result: "When I came to get Roger for his first game, he had the same shirt, pants, and funny shoes, and he added some kind of Sears Roebuck seersucker jacket. A Yankee? He looked more like some yokel."

The relationship between Roger Maris and Julius Isaacson blossomed into an unshakable friendship. "You couldn't get two more opposite people," according to Big Julie. "He was a country kid from North Dakota, and I grew up in Brooklyn. He was basically quiet, and I was very loud. He was a German, a Catholic, and I was a Jew." Despite their surface differences, Roger and Big Julie found common ground in their sincerity, openness, and straightforwardness. They both said what was on their mind without camouflage or public relations hype. As Big Julie said, "We both didn't have any time for crap."

Roger's most pressing need upon arrival in New York was finding a place to live. He tried a couple of hotels — even lived briefly above the Stage Deli — but he did not like Manhattan. Big Julie rented an apartment for Roger off the Van Wyck Expressway in Queens, a short distance from JFK airport. Former teammate Bob Cerv, a native of rural Weston, Nebraska, became Roger's first roommate. As permanent residents of Kansas City, they became all-year companions, sharing mutual friends in the off season and a fondness for hunting together. Both men had large families — another bond between the two.

The eight-year-older Cerv treated Roger like a younger brother and was an ideal influence upon him. Cerv had played in the majors since 1951 and had developed a spartan stoicism about the game. He neither brooded nor got down on himself after a bad game or during a slump. Focusing his keen eye on the baseball diamond, Cerv and Roger could always analyze a game together afterward.

Once settled in New York, Roger got off to a great start in 1960. With Mantle not at full physical efficiency, Roger gave the Yanks the lift they needed to forget a poor 1959 season. Maris' early hitting-and-power tear put him ahead of Babe Ruth's pace in 1927, his sixty-homer year. However, although the Yankees acquired Roger for his batting ability, he opened their eyes with his fielding. Veteran watchers claimed he had the best arm among Yankee outfielders since Cliff Mapes. Experts agreed that he threw better than his predecessor Hank Bauer did at his best. Runners thought better of trying to take an extra base; those who streaked for the plate found themselves thrown out.

Following the All-Star break, the Yanks came to the stadium in first place. They had lost ten of their last fifteen games, and nine of their last ten games played against second-division teams. Then the Chisox came in. They won the first three games against the Yankees and moved into first place by one game. When Chicago won the first game of a Sunday twin bill, the Sox were up by two.

In the nightcap, a struggling pitcher Eli Grba found himself one run down. In the second inning, with one man on base and one out, Gene Freese slammed the ball so quickly to right center field that Mantle had no chance to catch it. The ball traveled toward the auxiliary scoreboard when Roger, racing over, made a spectacular glove-hand catch that stopped a triple. Roger's quick action not only saved a run, but also gave Grba a breather and the boost he needed. Grba went on to pitch a complete game victory. The Yanks crawled back to one game out and put together a 9-2 mark that took them back into the lead.

Most of the press covering the Yanks felt that Roger's catch had done more for the Yanks' pennant drive than any other hit, home run, or play that season. Whitey Ford had no doubt: "I've been with the club for ten years, and nearly always we've been right up there fighting for the lead. ... There is always a game you can look back on, maybe even one play and say to yourself, 'This is the one.'... We *could* have been out of it if Roger hadn't caught the ball Freese hit."

As happened so often in his career, injuries stopped Roger's streak. In August, he ripped a muscle in his side crashing into Washington's Billy Gardner at second base. While nursing his injury, Roger received good news from home: his son Kevin had been born.

Roger's nearly .325 batting mark made him a valuable player, and Stengel was anxious to bring the slugger back into play as soon as possible. Roger came off the disabled list and returned to the lineup before Labor Day. He finished the season with a .283 batting average, 39 homers, 112 runs batted in — in 136 games.

The Yankees lost a heartbreaking World Series to Pittsburgh when they dropped the seventh game after thirteen innings . Although Roger knocked in only two runs with his two homers, the series did not diminish his great season.

Writers remembered his sensational play during the first half of the season. In the second closest victory in the Most Valuable Player competition, Maris beat Mantle 225-222. A surprised but pleased Roger heard about the award in his home in Raytown, a Kansas City suburb: "I thought it was possible, but I didn't really think I'd win it. I feel happy about it. Every player in the League hopes that he can win this honor at least once before he retires. It's just about the greatest award you can get in the American League."

Roger also received a Gold Glove for his outfield play, and because of the .581 slugging average that went along with his home-run and runs-batted-in stats, he was crowned Sultan of Swat for 1960.

The Old Professor, Casey Stengel, gave Roger top evaluation:

> I give the man a point for speed. I do this because Maris can run fast. Then I can give him a point because he can slide fast. I give him another point because he can bunt. I also give him a point because he can field. He is very good around the fences — sometimes on top of the fences. Next, I give him a point because he can throw. A right fielder has to be a thrower or he's not a right fielder. So I add up my points, and I've got five for him before I even come to his hitting. I would say this is a good man.

In 1960 Roger had begun proving that he was suited for the Yankee pinstripes. Unfortunately, few of the talents that served the Yankees so well on the baseball diamond helped Roger in his relationships with the New York-based media.

He was neither verbose nor flippant, and evasiveness had never been part of his nature. Roger quickly became disillusioned at the press's misinterpretation of his statements. For example, when reporters asked why he objected to playing in the stadium's left field, Roger candidly replied, "I'd sooner play right field because I think I play better there." His interviewers neglected to add Roger's concluding sentence: "If they want me to play there, I'll have to."

The Fargo favorite was ill prepared for the cameras that focused on his every move, the reporters that shouted intrusive questions, and the microphones that were thrust in his face everywhere in New York. Cleveland or Kansas City had nothing like this. The horde of New York newspapermen and other media personnel often asked repetitious questions, and the interviewers seemed to come in an endless stream.

In a 1960 preview of the torturous 1961 spotlight, the media began to barrage Roger with Babe Ruth questions as Maris forged ahead of the Bambino's homer record. The standard question — "Did Maris have a chance to break the record?" — had many, many variants. Roger prepared a standard response that expressed the truth as well as he could say it: "I'm not interested in breaking Babe Ruth's record. I'm only interested in having a good year for myself and seeing the Yankees win the pennant."

As more and more interviewers recklessly and carelessly asked more personal and probing questions, Roger began to withdraw. Soon some of the press began to describe Roger as a brooder; a sulky complainer; a surly, suspicious red-neck. Other journalists, however, found Roger Maris refreshing. As Jack Ryan wrote in *Family Weekly*. "Here was an 'old-time ball player,' not a walking corporation as exemplified by some modern Yankee like Mantle," but one whose old-time spirit was "as modern and as calculating as an electronic scoreboard."

Roger's success on the baseball field began paying dividends away from the diamond, and the slugger's brother, Rudy, guided these new endeavors. The ingenious Rudy had worked for Allis Chalmers in Milwaukee. According to Fargo's Bob Johnson, "Rudy would methodically learn how to get endorsements for Roger, examine the contracts, and take care of any necessary detail." As *New Yorker* proclaimed, Roger "reached a new plateau in his career; he made his first television commercial for Camel cigarettes. This is perhaps the most tangible evidence that he is a success in his chosen occupation." Endorsements for shaving creams and razor blades soon followed. An amazed Roger said, "They pay a lot of money, and it takes no time at all."

Roger Maris signs a baseball
for President John F. Kennedy in 1961.
(Courtesy of New York Yankees)

Chapter VI
A Season of Triumph and Despair

A Yankee-produced videotape, "Pinstripe Power," relates how 1961 became the year the most awesome team in baseball history won 109 games and defeated Cincinnati in the World Series. In narrating the glory of the 1961 Yankees, the "Pinstripe" video recounts the advent of a new era for the team.

The same year also marked the zenith of Roger Maris' baseball career, but he paid a price for achieving those sixty-one home runs in 1961. His time of triumph became a time of despair and disheartenment when he reflected on those summer days.

Roger's glorious but turbulent passage to his "61 in '61" achievement occurred during what the *New York Times* called "a year of dreadful events" on the national and international scenes. *[See Appendix for a chronology of 1961 events.]*

The CIA-backed invasion of the Bay of Pigs in Cuba brought the United States and the Soviet Union closer to the brink of nuclear confrontation than they had ever been before or since. The Berlin Wall, constructed to keep East Germans securely within the Iron Curtain, made freedom-loving peoples all over the world reexamine their commitment to democracy. In the American South, blacks and whites marching together to test the promise of integration, suffered beatings and other indignities at the hands of hostile crowds. These events created emotional uncertainty for millions: basic notions like justice, right, and wrong were challenged, giving rise to fear that the end might be near. In such a climate of doubt, people tend to reach back into a past that is fixed and immutable. As the *New York Times* observes, in an article entitled "Roger Maris*" written after his death, clinging to Babe Ruth and his record is "just one generation's way of trying to preserve its youth by preserving a youthful hero undiminished."

The Marises' spring began inauspiciously. As they drove from Raytown to St. Petersburg for a brief vacation before spring training, the Marises' car broke down somewhere in Alabama. "Nothing was going right," Pat Maris said. "It looked like I was going to have a miscarriage, and it was a week before the crisis was over. I'm certain that the situation was the reason Roger did not get off to a good start in the season."

Roger and the Yankees began the season very poorly. By mid-May Maris was hitting an anemic .210 with four homers. At one point, the Yankees were 16-14 and trailed Detroit by five games. Some speculated that Roger might be traded for the third time in his brief major-league career. In the *Sporting News,* Joe King wrote that manager Ralph Houk "has to be wondering about Maris. Which Maris would he be? The MVP who showed .320 with 27 homers and 69 RBIs in the first half of 1960 or the ordinary batsman who fell to .239 with 12 homers and 43 rbi's in the second half of that season?"

Dan Topping and Roy Hamey invited Roger in for a chat. Roger expected to hear that he had been dispatched to another team. Instead, Topping told him not to worry about averages; the Yankees were paying him to hit homers. To ensure that Roger was all right physically, Topping told him to have his eyes checked. The doctor diagnosed a slight strain and prescribed some eyedrops that had an unfortunate negative reaction.

Kubek and Pluto make much of this examination in *Sixty-One.* Houk claims that "Roger thought he couldn't see well and wanted his eyes checked." *Roger Maris at Bat,* coauthored with Jim Ogle, clearly indicates that Topping ordered the examination. Using a quote from teammate Clete Boyer as reinforcement, Kubek and Pluto interpret the Houk position as the beginning of strained relations between Roger and his manager and feel that "The eye exam did little for Roger's confidence." *Maris at Bat* says nothing of Houk's involvement in this matter. More importantly, Roger's book notes that the slugger greatly appreciates the front-office advice and considers the meeting to be the turning point of the season. "For the first time," Roger states, "I was beginning to look ahead rather than backward. Things were at last going my way."

Roger hit the hundredth homer of his major-league career off Eli Grba in Los Angeles's Wrigley Field on May 6. Although 1961 still held more impressive milestones for Roger, he often longingly remarked, "I would have liked the [ball from the] hundredth of my career which I hit at Los Angeles. But nobody brought it back."

When Roger began the May 17 game against Washington at the stadium, he had hit nine homers and knocked in thirty runs. He raised his batting average fifty points and closed out the month of May with twelve home runs.

Off the field, the two-bedroom Queens apartment, rented in Big Julie's name and occupied by Roger Maris and Bob Cerv, gained a third tenant, Mickey Mantle. The roommates found the apartment an ideal place to preserve their privacy and to avoid attention and autograph seekers. The neighbors had seldom bothered Roger and Cerv. Since his wife had remained in Dallas, Mantle was delighted to be part of the arrangement. Mantle comments in *Sixty-One,* "I liked it in Queens. The press couldn't find us. ... The apartment was perfect for him and it was good for me. He wanted to get away from everything, and I needed to get away from it all, too."

"Because the apartment was in my name," Big Julie said, "I spent a lot of time in Queens." Relaxing meant watching television — especially quiz shows — playing cards, or listening to music. Roger favored jazz, Mantle preferred country, while Big Julie liked his Jewish records. Isaacson remembers, "My [musical] tastes didn't suit Roger and Mickey. One day when I came to the apartment and was looking for my records, Roger said, 'Oh, we decided to toss them out on the Van Wyck.' Of course, this was not Roger's way of being mean, but simply a proof of his wonderful sense of humor."

Their cooking reflected the different tastes of each of the four. Cerv cooked for Mantle and himself. Roger did his own cooking because only his wife, his mother, and himself made eggs the way he wanted them. Big Julie often went to the market for the players. He said, "A typical list might be eggs, bacon, pork and beans, ham, juices, soda, vegetable soup, bean soup, and a *TV Guide.*

Big Julie and the Yankees often played cards — usually hearts or pinochle. When they played in Big Julie's house, Roger and Mickey competed as partners against Big Julie and New York City detective Paul Levy. "One day as we're playing pinochle," Julie recounted, "I noticed that they're looking at each other and passing baseball signals. So they hitch the belt and pass one hand over the chest. That means hearts. I tried to get even by speaking Yiddish to Paul. It didn't work. ... But we had a lot of fun."

Big Julie even tried introducing Roger to horse racing.

I knew there were no race tracks in North Dakota. I would tell Roger to go with me to the track and watch the ponies run. It's a great way to relax. Finally, Roger came with me and bet no more than two bucks a race. Roger won fourteen bucks, and I had a very big day. Roger tried the track again a few weeks later. However, this time he was six bucks behind and turned to me, "I'm not coming back here to throw my money away." He never did go with me to the track again.

Roger took every opportunity to demonstrate his friendship for Big Julie. When Roger learned that Big Julie was at a loss for an appropriate bar mitzvah gift for a friend's son, Roger made an excellent suggestion. "I got a great idea," Roger recommended. "Give him me." After the Yanks' game at the stadium, Roger showered and taxied to the Astor Hotel. He approached the celebrant and asked, "Are you the Yankees fan who became a man today?" Big Julie recalled, "Roger sang along for 'Havah Nagilah.' I couldn't even sing the words myself. Roger just worked hard to show his friends he cared."

In June Roger and the Yankees got into high gear, posting a 23-10 record. Whitey Ford won all eight of his starts. Roger had a sensational month. He slammed fifteen homers and ended June with twenty-seven round trippers, only three short of the one-month major-league record set by Rudy York.

When Roger hit his fourteenth homer off Bob Shaw in Comiskey Park, he pulled even with Mantle for the home run lead. Number fourteen marked the beginnings of the great home run race and chase. The next day Roger hit number fifteen off Russ Kemmerer and, for the first time, forged ahead of Mantle. However, the Mick tied him in the next game, against Minneapolis.

Roger got two homers against Minneapolis and added his eighteenth against Kansas City. The press corps made daily visits to the club house and, in an allusion to the popular candy, dubbed the sluggers "the M & M boys."

The seesaw battle for homers continued when the Los Angeles Angels visited the stadium on June 11. In the first game of the twin bill, Roger made no home runs. However, he short-circuited an Angels' home run by jumping as high as he could for the ball, toppling over backwards into the stands, and landing in a lady's lap. He victimized player Ken Hunt, a 1960 teammate with the Yankees and a fellow North Dakotan against whom Roger had competed in high school football.

In the nightcap, Mantle took one downtown for number eighteen and another tie in the homer derby. The statistics changed quickly as Roger scored numbers nineteen in the third and twenty in the fourth. While the press had yet to capitalize on tales of the Mantle-Maris home-run antagonism, Roger was becoming very aware of the positive influence the home-run competition had on both players. As Roger observes in *Roger Maris at Bat,* "It was becoming pretty obvious that Mickey and I were helping each other to hit home runs. ... It is hard to say just how much we helped each other, but definitely the way we were going after home runs made each of us try that much harder. It was like having someone pace you as you tried to break a record."

Roger slammed three home runs against his old team, the Athletics, on June 19, 20, and 22 in Kansas City. At the series end, he had a total of twenty-seven home runs for the season, but he hit no more during the last seven games in June. "For the first time," Roger said, "I was playing under the pressure of trying to attain something. Once you start consciously trying for home runs, you've had it."

Both Maris and Mantle finished June slightly ahead of Ruth's 1927 pace, with Roger leading Mickey 27-25. Those who knew Roger well during his first two seasons with the Yankees noticed a change in his spirit now that he was doing well and gaining the recognition he deserved.

On July 1 at the stadium, Mantle hit two rockets to tie Roger at twenty-seven apiece. In the ninth inning Roger against Dave Sisler put one into the right-field stands for number twenty-eight. The next day, Maris added numbers twenty-nine and thirty against Washington's Pete Burnside and Johnny Klippstein, respectively. Mantle slammed his twenty-eighth.

League-leading Detroit came to the stadium one game ahead of the Yankees on July 4. A crowd of 75,000 fans gathered for the twin bill. The Yanks took the first game and trailed 2-0 in the nightcap until Roger came to bat in the eighth against Tiger pitcher Frank Lary. Roger put one beyond Al Kaline, making number thirty-one and a tie game. Nevertheless, the Yanks lost in extra innings and failed to move into first place.

At about this time in the season, the press began sharpening their pencils with questions about Roger's chances of eclipsing the Babe's record. One reporter baited him: "I bet you lie awake at night, thinking how you're going to break Ruth's record." Roger gave the interrogator a steely gaze: "Listen, I don't' give Babe Ruth a thought. Not now or ever. I don't think about the record, and I'm surprised I've got as many homers as I do."

Frank Funk, the Tribe's workhorse from the bullpen, allowed Roger his thirty-second homer in game number seventy-eight. In game eighty, the Yanks passed the Tigers and took a one-half game lead. On July 9 Roger walloped one — his thirty-third — off Bill Monbouquette in Fenway Park. Going into the All-Star break, Roger had thirty-three home runs to Mantle's twenty-nine. As an All-Star selection, Roger had an average over .280 and felt he had excellent chances to win both the home-run and runs-batted-in titles. When the second half of the season opened, Roger hoped that for the first time he could have two good halves in a season.

Chapter VII
A Star, Not an Asterisk*

The media scrutinized Roger's home-run total at the All-Star break. For the first time the baseball schedule had 162 games, an extra eight added to accommodate the league's expansion to ten teams.

Dan Daniel explored the ramifications of this enlarged schedule in the *Sporting News:*

> Commissioner Ford Frick will soon call a conference with the Records Committee of the Baseball Writers of America. ... The commissioner is quite aroused over the chance that the new 162-game schedule, eight games more than before, will produce records. ... Suppose Maris hits 61 with the help of those extra contests? Suppose after 154 games, Maris has 58 or 59 homers, then totals 61 over the rest of the season? Frick believes it would not be right to recognize the mark after 154 games. The commissioner has strong backing in this attitude. If Ruth had gone to 162 games, he would have hit seven more homers if he had continued at his current pace. In the last eight games of 1927, Babe hit seven.

Roger disagreed with Daniel's analysis. "How could anyone know that Ruth would have hit seven more home runs if he had played 162 games? He could have hit a couple more, or maybe none. I don't know how many he would have hit and neither does anyone else."

Dan Daniel, Roger Maris, and everyone else could only offer their opinions in the 154- vs. 162-game debate; Ford Frick's words would be law.

Frick's decision came on July 17, when Roger's thirty-five homers and Mantle's thirty-three were both well ahead of Ruth's pace: Roger by nineteen and Mantle by eight. Both lost homers in the rained-out night portion of a July 18 doubleheader in Baltimore, the first washed-out homer of Roger's career. "Suppose you hit fifty-nine, how will you feel about this?" the press queried Roger. Roger couldn't answer; he hadn't thought about it.

Roger would be forced to think about Frick's ruling. The *New York Times* report said that Frick "threw a protective screen" around Ruth's 1927 record by requiring that the record be broken within 154 games. If the record were broken after 154 games, a "distinctive mark" would reflect the fact that the record had not been broken in the first 154 games. How to handle possible record-setting scores other than the home-run mark was left unsaid.

Frick made a formal ruling "because of the unusual interest in the case." His ruling said:

> Any player who may hit more than sixty home runs during his club's first 154 games would be recognized as having established a new record. However, if the player does not hit more than sixty until after his club has played 154 games, there would have to be some distinctive mark in the record books to show that Babe Ruth's record was set under 154-game schedule and the total of more than sixty was compiled while a 162-game schedule was in effect.
>
> We also would apply the same reasoning if a player should equal Ruth's total of sixty in his first 154 games. He would be recognized as tying Ruth's record. If in more than 154 games, there would be a distinction in the record book.

Frick's proclamation does not mention an asterisk. Writer Dick Young, then of the New York *Daily News,* supposedly raised the question of an asterisk during the commissioner's press conference. Frick's answer, like his ruling, refers only vaguely to a "distinctive mark"; however, the press and public became attached to the idea of an asterisk. Countless baseball fans think of Roger Maris' achievements as only an asterisk in the record books.

The Frick edict had many immediate and long-term effects. It created an asterisk literature for baseball. Second, it intensified media interest in Roger's or Mantle's chances of breaking the Ruth record. Inevitably, this interest culminated in a series of comparisons between Babe Ruth and Roger Maris, between 1927 and 1961, and the like. The media suddenly gained the opportunity to speculate on a keen rivalry between the two contenders for the record. Consequently it increased the pressure on Roger and brought him to disparagement by much of the press and of the baseball public.

The *Sporting News* of July 19, 1961, carried an editorial clearly written before Frick's announcement that indicates that Dick Young had suggested the 154-game concept proclaimed by Frick:

> Dick Young of the *New York Daily News* has come up with the suggestion that pending some final decision, the American League or the commissioner could declare that records will be recognized only if they are established in the first 154 games each club plays.
>
> This is a lumpy solution and would require numerous asterisks and footnotes in the record books, but at least it is a step in the right direction.

The *Sporting News* sent to members of the Baseball Writers Association of America (BBWAA) a questionnaire asking: Should there be any limitation in terms of number of games? Should that limitation apply to other marks besides Ruth's home-run record? On August 9 the magazine reported the results of its poll. By a 2-1 margin, 37-18, the responding writers agreed with the Frick edict and with applying it to all records broken.

Asterisk specialist Dick Young sided with the commissioner: "I am 100 percent in accord with Commissioner Frick's ruling. I believe, as he, that we are in a transitory stage, and that eventually, perhaps in five more years, further expansion will produce 24 teams and a return to the 154-game sked. Therefore, all records should be preserved on the 154-game basis with a special section for these interim years of 162."

Shirley Povich of the *Washington Post* commented that if Ruth's record were broken in 162 games, "at best it would be artificial or synthetic."

Bob Broeg of the *St. Louis Post Dispatch* agreed with Frick and offered an analogy that the commissioner later used himself: "You can't compare times for a 100-yard dash or 100 meter dash because of different distances."

The August 9 article quoted these New York writers in support of Frick: Dan Parker, *New York Mirror;* Dick Young; Jack Butler, *Brooklyn Tablet;* Joe King, *New York World-Telegram and Sun;* Max Kase, *New York Journal-American.*

The writers who opposed the commissioner, although in the

minority, offered vigorous and spirited reasons for their points of view: A season is a season, records are made to be broken, rulings can't be made in the middle of a season, and double records would create confusion.

The poll presented only one New York-area reporter opposed to Frick. Jimmy Powers of the *New York Daily News* writes:

> I feel that the 154-game restriction is ridiculous. There have been so many changes through the years - playing habits, the physical layout of the parks, encroachments in space in so many ways - that the record book would be full of asterisks if we tried to reduce everything to a certain era and freeze it.
>
> ... Life does not consist of wallowing in the past or peering anxiously at the future. ... Mantle, Maris, et al. are the players who are in the parks now. Let us all back and enjoy them.

Bob Stevens of the *San Francisco Chronicle* noted, "Records are made to be broken, conditions to the contrary notwithstanding. And that includes Ruth's 60. I see nothing sacred."

George Davis, Los Angeles *Herald-Express,* believes that no player should be penalized because of baseball's expansion. "The A.L. promulgated the 162-game schedule in its zeal to expand, and it has no business trying to put a game limit on anybody," said John Carmichael, *Chicago Daily News.*

An especially vehement Larry Merchant of the *Philadelphia Daily News* threw down the gauntlet: "Commissioner Frick is out of order. He tries to change the tides. ... He cannot. ... What is a record? It is a recording of achievement. No amount of doctoring by asterisks, question marks, or exclamation points will alter the fact that when Ruth's record of 60 home runs is broken, it is broken."

Hy Hurwitz of the *Boston Globe* commented, "I don't think a rule should have been made in midseason when it seemed possible that Babe Ruth's record may be broken."

Having two sets of records will not work, remarked the *Washington Star's* Francis Stann. "Commissioner Frick is a nice man, but he is going to make blithering idiots of all of us if records are going to be departmentalized."

Much of the writers' criticism of Frick stems from their contention that they, not the commissioner, are guardians of the record. Dan

Daniel of the *New York World-Telegram and Sun* voted in support of Frick; nevertheless, Daniel questioned the commissioner's right to rule on the home-run record. As former president of BBWAA, Daniel stated, "in the matter of the Maris and Mantle threats to the Babe's record, I felt that the Records Committee should be reorganized and that it should be determined if it wanted to pass on the matter or refer it to the BWAA as a whole."

In Fargo Eugene Fitzgerald, who wrote about Maris for years in the *Forum,* stood against the ruling. To point out Frick's unfairness, Fitzgerald used the track analogy: "In fairness to Maris it must be recognized that Frick's ruling was untimely, coming as it did in July. A runner who goes after a dash record knows he is required to go 100 yards. He isn't told that the distance is only 90 yards or 110 yards as he hits the 50-yard mark."

In his "Keeping Posted" column for the *Syracuse Post-Standard* Bill Reddy extended the effects of a changed schedule to any standing record in sports:

> The fact that this year's schedule calls for 162 games, compared with 154 in Ruth's time, isn't really important. If it were, virtually all sports records now existing would have to be starred with asterisks because of changed conditions. National hockey league records were set at the outset in seasons which included 45 games. Now that the schedules stretch to 70 games, there's no quibbling. The man who scores the most points, gets the most goals, or racks up the most shut-outs in goal is a record-setter if he surpasses the previous high. Similarly in National Football League or National Basketball Association play, records continue to fall regularly as the number of league games are increased. They're still records.

After it had conducted the survey, *Sporting News* gave its own endorsement in an August 16 editorial entitled "Another Plus-Mark for Frick Ruling." The possibility of a 153-game schedule in 1962 "would mean that some records which might be set this year would never be broken. Hence, a nod once more for Commissioner Frick's ruling."

Even Pulitzer Prize-winning journalist James Reston, political columnist for the *New York Times,* entered the controversy over the

Frick ruling. After the 154-game restriction had passed, Reston wrote a column entitled "The Asterisk That Shook the Baseball World." Reston castigates Frick for reducing Roger "to an asterisk or footnote in baseball history." According to Reston, Frick put the asterisk in the wrong place. "He should have listed Maris with Ruth among the heroes and let the asterisk explain that it took Maris a little longer."

Reston feels that for Americans in a troubled age, sports heroes like Roger Maris are more concrete and definite than world politics. America empathizes with the slugger because "Maris is more than a ball player. He is a momentary antidote to the confusion of our times, a brief escape from frustration, and a particularly attractive figure as the symbol of bad luck."

Sporting News also surveyed participants in the All-Star game in Fenway Park on their reactions to the Frick ruling. Once again the commissioner won, 2-1.

Hall of Famers Stan Musial, Warren Spahn, and Eddie Matthews all agreed with Frick. "Eight additional games can make a big difference in the records," Musial commented. Spahn thought the ruling proper but of little import because "Personally I don't think it will be broken this year." Matthews agreed with the commissioner but faulted his timing: "The regulation should have been put in before the season started and not when a couple of guys get within reach of it."

In disagreeing with Frick, Roy Sievers echoed many others: "Records are made to be broken." Hall of Famer Al Kaline criticized the restriction by dealing directly with the changed schedule: "Whoever hits sixty-one home runs is entitled to the record, no matter how many games it takes. The owners and leagues made out the schedule and told us how many games we would have to play. So if a record is broken in the official number of games scheduled, it should be a record." Hall of Famer Ernie Banks also voiced his dissent: "Everything a player does in the season's schedule should be counted in his records. Don't forget, we've had playoff games to determine flag winners and those records counted."

The *Sporting News* did not overlook the Yankees playing in the All-Star contest. Yogi Berra simply said, "I can't comment on the subject." Roger Maris showed moderation in disagreeing with Frick and mentioned Mantle in his reply: "I think Mick [Mantle] has a good chance to break it. I think the commissioner shouldn't have made any 154-game ruling when he did. But if Mick breaks, it, I hope he does it in 154. The same goes for me."

Mantle, on the other hand, agreed with Frick and responded, "Ruth set it in 154 games and you should beat it in the same number of games. If I should break it in the 155th game, I wouldn't want the record." Whitey Ford did not equivocate: "I'm all for the commissioner's decision. Naturally, I'd like to see a Yankee player break Ruth's record, and I think the Babe would, too, if he were still living. But it's got to be done within 154 games or it won't mean anything."

In their memoirs written years later, Mantle and Ford do a surprising reversal and claim that they were opposed to Ford Frick all along.

In *The Mick* Mantle says,

> Commissioner Ford Frick attached an asterisk next to the 61 homers in the record book because Roger failed to hit them in the first 154 games, which happens to be the schedule when Ruth got the 60. I thought it was a ridiculous ruling. It made no sense at all. Check further and you'll note that the same year, 1961, Sandy Koufax broke Christy Mathewson's National League strikeout record. Mathewson set it in 1903, when they played a 140-game schedule. But you won't find an asterisk attached to Koufax.

In Ford's turnaround in *Slick,* he terms the ruling "absurd":

> Ford Frick ... let these old-timers influence him and got caught up in the nonsense of protecting Babe Ruth's record. ... Maris had the advantage of playing 8 more games than Ruth had. When this was pointed out to Frick, he made the absurd ruling that unless Maris broke the record within the 154-game span, his record would be notated with an asterisk.

When asked about the Frick controversy, manager Ralph Houk tersely told the press, "I hope they both break the record." George Weiss, who was instrumental in bringing Roger to the Yankees, firmly defended Frick. "Our records as they stand must be respected and honored for what they are, great performances within 154 games. It will be a sorry day for baseball when there is no excitement over records."

Babe Ruth's contemporaries also joined the continuing controversy. Hall of Famer Lefty Gomez, a teammate of the Bambino, did not want to see Ruth's mark broken, particularly not in more than 154 games: "I'd like to see Babe's record stand forever, personally," the pitcher said. "But if some young fellows come along and break it, more power to them. But they should do it in the same number of games the Babe did." The Philadelphia Athletics' Roger (Doc) Cramer saw things differently. "If somebody breaks the record," said Cramer, "it should count regardless of how many games they do it in."

The baseball world wondered how American League President Joe Cronin would respond. Although there were indications that Cronin would differ from Frick, the Hall of Famer stated his position only at the beginning of September:

I do not wish to become involved in a dispute with Ford. But I can see no logic in the ruling that if Ruth's record is to be topped it must be excelled inside 154 decisions.

After all, the Babe hit sixty in 1927 in 151 games. Therefore, if you want to be technical, you could say that Maris and Mantle would have to do it in 151.

I certainly respect the commissioner's feelings about the matter, but so far as I am concerned, it will be a new official record if either or both do it in 162 games.

Cronin, a contemporary of Ruth, found support for his stance in both the future and the past. If the home-run ruling were considered a precedent, the major leagues would have to compile new sets of records since the National League planned to move to a 162-game schedule in 1962. Cronin also used Hugh Duffy as a past example. In 1894 Duffy set a National League batting mark of .438 for 126 games. When the league went to a 154-game season years later, Cronin noted, no one spoke of a new 154-game record.

Frick quickly responded to Cronin in Chicago, where both were attending a meeting of officials planning the 1961 World Series. The commissioner snapped, "There will be two records if it happens: one will say most homers in a season (154 games) ... Babe Ruth ... and the other will say most homers in a season (162), etc." Frick supported his ruling with an analogy: "You don't break the one-hundred-meter record in the one-hundred-yard dash."

Frick maintained the record would not be depreciated. "As for that star or asterisk business," he said, "I don't know how that cropped up or was attributed to me, because I never said it. I certainly never meant to belittle Maris' feat should he wind up with more than sixty. Both names will appear in the book as having set records but under different conditions."

Frick unequivocally stated that the same differentiation would be made in all season records other than home runs: most hits, doubles, triples, strikeouts, wins, and the like.

While Frick and Cronin squabbled over the commissioner's ruling, others in the baseball world continued to express opinions on this matter. Dick Young pointed out that the press did little follow-up on Frick's July ruling until the writers realized how close Roger had come to the record. According to Young, only the New York *Post*'s Leonard Koppett challenged the ruling immediately. To Koppett "goes at least the credit of timely ridicule. The others lay in ambush, quietly." Young continued:

> Evidently, they did not possess the foresight of Frick. They attached no particular importance to the ruling at the time. Then, gradually as Maris closed in on the record, they opened fire at Frick. He had no right, they said, no authority to impose such a restriction.
>
> They machine-gunned Frick with asterisks. They whipped up sympathy for Maris with asterisks. Poor Rodg, they wept; all he would get for his noble effort would be an (*) in the record book. Double-entendre use of the word became stylish. Frick had made an asterisk of himself ... and so on.

The Ford Frick ruling and the controversy it engendered took its toll on Roger Maris. The open and seemingly never-ending debate made the public more aware of Roger's chances to break the homer record. The pressure on Roger was at times unendurable.

Once Frick had made the 154-game ruling, comparisons between Ruth and Roger Maris began to be drawn and circulated. Although Frick might have intended his edict to cover all records, he only referred to Ruth's at first. The Bambino's record — the most glamorous of all marks — was being challenged by a young Fargo slugger.

Roger Maris, Hank Greenberg and Joe DiMaggio.
(Bettman Archive photo)

Chapter VIII
The Babe versus Roger:
1927 versus 1961

Babe Ruth not only set the season home-run mark, but he also set the all-time record with 714 home runs in his career, a mark later topped by Hank Aaron. Ruth hit sixty homers in 1927 — more than any team hit that year. His .342 lifetime batting average earned Ruth the number-twelve ranking in that category. His 2,873 hits made him the twenty-seventh-ranking player in total hits. As Roger approached Ruth's season record, critics snapped that Maris had never even hit .300 — he was neither the batsman nor slugger that the Bambino was.

Joe King wrote in the *Sporting News,* "The stature of Ruth loomed like Everest to the older stars." King recalled Ruth's feats as a pitcher, including pitching the longest game in World Series history to beat Brooklyn 2-1 in fourteen innings in 1916. The Bambino pitched twenty-nine and two-thirds scoreless innings in series play, a mark unsurpassed until Whitey Ford in 1961. In 1916 Ruth won twenty-three games, with an earned run average of 1.75, the lowest in the league.

Roger couldn't match Ruth in statistics. Nor could he — or anyone else — equal the Sultan of Swat as a performer or baseball personality. "After all, there was only one Babe Ruth," wrote George Girsch for the *New York Daily Mirror.* Girsch asked:

> Wasn't the Babe Sir Lancelot riding down Broadway wearing a camel's hair coat with a big cigar stuck in his mouth? Didn't he pick baseball up by the boot straps when it was rocked to the very foundation by the Black Sox Scandal? ... People used to say they'd rather see him strike out with that tremendous flourish of his than see others knock the ball out of the park.

The *New York Times'* Arthur Daley marveled at the Babe's showmanship: "The Babe was a boisterous, big-hearted child of nature who exuded color out of every pore. He was a legend come to life. Paul Bunyan in the flesh. ... No one but Babe would have dared to point to the bleachers where he would then hit a home run off Charlie Root in the 1932 World Series."

Besides reiterating the greatness and unique stature of Babe Ruth, the media attempted to demonstrate that the difference in conditions between 1927 and 1961 made Ruth's feats even more remarkable. In his column in the *Forum,* Fitzgerald cites two umpires, George Hildebrand and Clarence (Pants) Rowland, who mention the 1927 regulation that allows umpires to rule a ball going into the stands as fair or foul according to how they last saw it. If the ball went into the stands fair and then curved foul, the 1927 ruling would be a foul ball; today, it would be a home run. These umpires and other so-called "experts" contend that Ruth might have had up to a dozen more home runs if 1927 games had been played under today's rules, but no one has offered any documentation to support the claim.

The Associated Press maintained that with the exception of Cleveland's old League Park, the average ballpark of 1927 had a greater distance between home plate and right field than every ballpark in which Roger played. The story did concede that Ruth had an advantage in Shibe Park, Philadelphia. There the home-plate-right-field distance measured 331 feet, while at the 1961 Athletics home in Kansas City, the distance was 353 feet. However, the story noted that every park in 1927 had a greater distance from home plate to center field.

The AP also presented the foul-line dimensions at Yankee Stadium. Some distances remained unchanged: 296 feet to the right-field foul pole and 301 feet to the left-field corner. However, the distance to the left-center wall was 445 feet for Ruth compared with 402 for Roger; to the right center-field wall, 395 feet in 1927 and 367 feet in 1961.

Sports Illustrated agreed with the Associated Press, at least in regard to old Cleveland Park. Even reporter James R. Harrison of the *New York Times* wrote that at the old Cleveland Park, Ruth hit ten homers so puny that "George actually blushed as he hopped around the bases." However, *Sports Illustrated* differed with the Associated Press's general evaluation. The magazine named two other ballparks where Ruth had the advantages: Sportsman's Park, home of the 1927 St. Louis Browns, and Fenway Park, where Ruth hit eight home runs. Both parks had easier right-field targets in 1927.

Some writers sought to prove that post-Ruth players endured more difficult playing conditions: night games, air travel, and contests as far away as California. Dan Parker dismissed this argument in the *New York Daily Mirror.*

Some, wrote Parker, "talk today about Babe (a night-leaguer of the old school) not having been handicapped as are Maris and Mantle by being required to play night games in dampness, under lights, which no matter how brilliant, can't approximate daylight." Such sentiments "do not take into account that today's players don't have to bat in semi-darkness when the late afternoon sun starts to throw lengthening shadows on the field or when there is a heavy overcast to help pitchers work their magic. In Babe's day there were no lighting systems to take care of such emergencies. Nor can those dreary day-and-a-half railroad trips to St. Louis that Babe had to put up with be used as an argument that they weren't subjected to the strain of air travel as are present players."

Another argument maintained not only that Babe Ruth was better than Roger, but also that hurlers of Ruth's day were in general superior to those in the Maris era. Because the expanded 1962 schedule accommodated two additional teams, the reasoning went, the quality of pitching must certainly have been emasculated. Needless to say, a collection of Hall of Fame pitchers did not serve Ruth his homers. In fact, the *Sporting News* presented the facts with the headline "Bambino Had His Share of Patsy Chuckers in '27." An Associated Press story concluded that the Babe "slammed a majority of his 60 home runs off mediocre pitchers." Joe King, *New York World-Telegram and Sun,* concluded that "there wasn't any law against palookas in '27, and if the M-boys are drawing some, so did the Babe."

The comparison of the grandeur of the Ruthian days with the mediocrity of the present did not sit well with many contemporary players, especially the pitchers. Tiger ace Frank Lary, winner of twenty-three games in 1961, showed his annoyance with the comparisons by publicly proclaiming that he rooted for Roger to topple Ruth's mark.

Writers and fans also continued to stress the advantages the hurlers of 1927 had over their modern counterparts. "In Babe's day,"

Dan Parker wrote, "the pitcher had the advantage of being permitted to 'push back' the batter without being warned of expulsion if they repeated it."

A fan from Freeport, N.Y., used Mike Lee's column in the *Long Island Press,* to explain that in Ruth's era teams played with dead balls and pitchers could throw spitballs. The Bambino supporter wondered, how many home runs would Maris score "against that kind of pitching, and a dead ball to boot?"

Scotty Reston expressed his opinion on whether Roger Maris was better than Babe Ruth in his *New York Times* column: "The essential difference between Ruth and Maris was not merely that Maris was a better all-around ball player, but that Maris had to worry about Ruth and Ruth didn't have to worry about Maris. The Babe swung with a free mind, and, as I remember it, often with an empty mind. The difference wasn't that Maris had a livelier ball or bat than Ruth had but that he had a livelier imagination — and that is no advantage to a ball player practicing his profession under savage pressure in a howling stadium."

Joe DiMaggio, the Yankee Clipper, expressed his unhappiness about the downplaying of present-day baseball. "I know how we older players and you veteran writers," he said, "feel about the records. I happen to hold one myself, the 56-game batting streak. ... But that will go, the home run record will go. The effort of some people, half of them biased, the other half old timers who think baseball died with Matty and Johnson, to give the impression that the game has made no progress is stupid."

DiMaggio commented on the impressive skill of pitchers like Whitey Ford who used the slider. "I certainly have no desire to say anything about the pitchers of 1927," the Yankee immortal added, "but I believe that the hurlers of today are throwing more varieties than the 1927 gang did."

Roger picked up on DiMaggio's reasoning: "Today a batter has to face a far greater variety of pitches than Babe did — or at least so I'm told. Every guy has six or seven kinds of pitches he can throw now. Take the knuckler. In Ruth's day, how many fellows used one? But today a Wilhelm comes along, extends his career with it, and the next thing you know three, four guys on every staff make it a part of their equipment."

Some of Ruth's teammates entered the argument. Earl Combs, centerfielder for the 1927 squad, calculated that Roger Maris hit 1 out of every 24 homers in a season that had seen more than 1,000 four baggers before August. "In 1927 there were only 439 home runs hit," Combs continued, "and the Babe got 60 of them. That's an average of 1 out of every 7." The obvious conclusion: the ball was livelier.

Former leftfielder Bob Meusel, another of the 1927 squad, insisted that Ruth "would have hit a lot more than 60 homers with the modern ball. The ball today is a lot livelier than the one we played with, so it makes a difference."

Babe Ruth's sometimes roommate during his Red Sox days, former pitcher Ernie Shore expressed his conviction that the balls of then and now differed: "To me the seams [stitches] are higher and wider. Then, too, everybody is hitting home runs this year. It must be livelier."

In a *Sporting News* article headlined "Bunnies in Balls? Nonsense, Says Spalding Prexy," Spalding president Edwin L. Parker said unequivocally, "The built-in characteristics of the ball haven't changed in 35 years." *Life*'s cover story on the home-run race asked, "Is it the ball?" After quoting Spalding personnel, *Life* noted, "Some say that the seams have been sewn tighter, making the ball smoother and harder to grip. The cover is also harder to loosen." Manufacture by machine definitely makes the ball different.

Veteran sportswriter Dan Daniel also responded to the ball question by accepting Spalding's assessment. Daniel said that comparing baseballs "is more than futile. It is thoroughly reliable and unfair. As the ball gets older, it gets deader. The horsehide loses its life, the yarn goes stale, and the rubber cores fail to respond the way they did when the ball left the Spalding hopper in Chicopee Falls, Mass. ... Believe me, gentlemen, it is not the ball."

Unconvinced, the *New York Times* commissioned the consulting chemists and engineers of Foster D. Snell, Inc., to test balls that had been manufactured between 1927 and 1961. The sophisticated project examined balls for "deformation measurements with a veneer caliper" and the balls' ability to withstand "surgical dissection and batterings by an explosive-driven Remington Arms Ram." The tests checked all aspects of the baseball: its "Compressibility," "Impact vs. Travel," "Rebound Coefficient," and "Rotational Stability." Foster D.

Snell also sought to determine how far a ball travels when hit on different parts of its surface.

The Snell Company's findings were inconclusive. A *New York Times* headline proclaimed: "Is the '61 Ball Livelier Than the Ruthian Variety? Maybe Yes and Maybe No." The story revealed that "The 1961 ball is slightly larger, slightly lighter, and slightly livelier than the 1927 ball." However, the *Times* continued, "The only valid conclusion which can be drawn from the data herein presented is that there are differences in the construction of balls between 1927 and 1961. The effect of these differences cannot be estimated in the absence of the quantity of test samples."

Dan Daniel had offered an explanation for the increase in homers — the baseball bats. A subhead in his column read, "Lighter bats help trigger hike in homers." Daniel continued: "The strike zone has been lowered off the shoulders. The bat is much lighter. ... Now the bat weighs thirty-four ounces, maybe thirty-two in hot weather. It is highly maneuverable. The free swingers get under the ball and send it far, and still farther."

The *Times* picked up on the idea and wrote: "It takes two to tango. It also takes a bat as well as a ball to bring in a home run." Ruth used a forty-two-ounce bat, while Roger Maris swung a thirty-three-ounce lumber. The *Times* quoted an executive at the bat-makers Hillerich and Bradsby who produced "an order slip from Ruth for a fifty-two ounce bat." However, the executive added: "I don't think he ever used it. Our records show he favored a forty-two-ounce bat and never used anything lighter than thirty-eight ounces."

All the comparisons drawn between Ruth and Maris and between the conditions of 1927 and the conditions of 1961 did not resolve the disparity between the number of games each played in their record-setting season. Some people — motivated as they said by a sense of fair play — looked for a plan that would allow the full 162 games to count but still account for Ruth's 154-game schedule. One solution involved determining a home-run hitting average and number of home runs per game. Thus, Ruth with his 60 runs in 154 games has a homer-hitting percentage of .3896. To top Ruth, Roger would need 63 homers in 162 games, which would give him an average of .395.

The result slightly differed for a comparison based on numbers of homers per game. Ruth had 1 four bagger in every 2.5666 games. If Roger were to hit 63 home runs, the statistics would show 1 homer per 2.571 games and he would fall a fraction short. A 64th homer — a homer in every 2.53 games — would do it.

Frick's ruling seemed to reflect a desire by many in the baseball world not to have the Babe eclipsed. Big Julie said, "The old-timers, especially the sportswriters who covered and loved Ruth, could not stand to have a modern kid like Roger breaking his record." Dr. Surprise agreed: "The writers resented Roger literally muscling in on Babe Ruth. They were personally hurt that Roger was threatening the Babe's record. The old timers felt they were part of the legend in the days they were covering the Babe. Now it would be all gone, destroyed."

Many players of Ruth's era, especially old-time Yankees, openly admitted their preference. They liked Roger and Mantle, but they sought to hold on to part of their heritage, their past. Joe Dugan, Yankee third baseman in the Ruth era, summarized their feelings: "The Babe was one of us. He was part of my generation and we don't like to let it go. When and if it does fall, it will be the end of more than a baseball record."

Members of the Ruth family, particularly his wife, Mrs. Claire Ruth, did not want the record broken. "The Babe loved that record," she said. "He wanted to be known as the king of home runs forever."

Dan Daniel believed that Mrs. Ruth had little reason to worry about the Babe's record. A telvision series about the Bambino was being put together under her supervision. "Even if Maris hits 61," Daniel wrote, "the 100,000 fans who visit the baseball museum and Hall of Fame at Cooperstown, N.Y., every year will continue to crowd about the displays having to do with Herman. But Mrs. Ruth will have to resign herself to the strong possibility of a new record. It would be no derogation of the Babe. Nor of her TV series."

Dave Anderson of the *New York Journal-American* interviewed the Babe's stepdaughter and adopted daughter on the great pursuit. "I hope it's preserved," commented stepdaughter Mrs. Julia Stevens, in Eaton Center, New Hampshire. "It's a question of sentiment. It has stood for thirty-four years. I hope it stands for at least forty years. But I know that if Maris does break it, Daddy wouldn't be jealous. He was too much of a sports fan." The Babe's adopted daughter Mrs. Dorothy Perone, in Wallingford, Connecticut, expressed similar sentiments: "If it is broken — and it looks pretty good for Maris at the moment — I know the Babe would be a good sport about it. He'd accept it gracefully. That's the kind of man he was."

That was in 1961; however, in 1988 Mrs. Perone was not such a good sport. Having authored *My Dad, the Babe*, she appeared on Bob Costas' "Coast to Coast" program to speak of her father. Roger "was cheated out of a lot of publicity" for his feat, she conceded, but insisted that the Babe is still the season homer champion because it took Roger eight games longer.

The furious debates spawned by Frick's pronouncement brought the Fargo slugger to a new stage of growth as a baseball player and as a man. His trade to the Yankees in 1960 and his Most Valuable Player season had received much copy from the press, yet Roger had never created much excitement in his brief major-league career. The events of 1961 would change all that.

Chapter IX
Roger and the Mick

To ensure that "Frick's asterisk," Babe Ruth, and baseball records remained "hot" topics, the media presented the public with a fantasy — the intense rivalry between Roger Maris and Mickey Mantle.

Since both chased the Ruth record, the press reasoned that Maris and Mantle had to be bitter rivals. As Dan Parker explained, "Nobody knows how the Yankees' two top bombers feel about each other deep down. But if they're human, each must have his flashes of envy or irritation with the other to such a nerve-racking competition as they are now engaged. They wouldn't be keen competitors if they didn't."

In a 1978 article for UPI, Milt Richman commented that in 1961 the press tried to manufacture a "falling out" between Maris and Mantle over the amount of publicity each was getting. According to the scenario the writers developed, Richman said, "At first, they stopped talking to each other, and then their silence hardened into full-blown mutual aversion."

While both sought to win the home-run crown, surpass the Babe if possible, and help the Yanks to a championship in the process, they were "friendly rivals." On the rivalry between the sluggers, Dan Daniel noted, "At least on the surface, it is the most amicable situation in the history of home run competition between team-mates." Their life situation attested to their relationship: they shared Julie Isaacson's apartment in Queens. As roommates and teammates they worked, ate, idled, shopped, and conversed together in an arrangement that promoted frequent exposure.

Maris believed he knew how the rumors of "bad blood" between the sluggers originated. After his retirement from baseball, Roger said that a writer — whom he knew but never identified, in typical Maris style — started the feud stories. According to Roger, the writer "didn't know more about me and Mickey than he did about the man in the moon. We were living in the same apartment together when this guy wrote the story, but he didn't know that either. I enjoyed playing with Mickey. You play with a fellow like him and it's a pleasure. He was a super player and he's a super individual."

Kubek relates his theory in *Pinstripe Power*. The contrived M-M rivalry had its roots in the "mythical rivalry" of Gehrig and Ruth, who didn't shake hands after hitting home runs. According to Dan Daniel, the resentment was only on the part of Gehrig, who felt that the Yankees did not treat him fairly in terms of salary. Daniel believes that Gehrig never received more than $40,000, whereas Ruth got as high as $80,000.

Obviously, the press was probing, searching, fishing for an enmity that wasn't there. Jack Lang reproduced in the *Long Island Press* this part of a Mantle interview with reporters:

> "It's a competition," he added, groping for the right word. "Anything you do you want to do better than anyone else."
>
> "It's rivalry?" another reporter queried.
>
> "That's it," Mickey answered. "A rivalry. But it's a friendly one."

Some writers saw the home-run race as the sports competition it was. Frank Eck, Associated Press news-features sports editor, described Mantle and Maris as "friendly rivals." Eck wrote, "Fans can't believe" that the sluggers "are buddy-buddy. ... Baseball writers traveling with the club have tried to find a hint of jealousy between the pair, but their observations (some call it snooping and prying) have been to no avail." Eck noted that the two even applauded each other's homers.

Maris and Mantle helped each other in their home-run chase. Since Mantle batted behind Maris, Roger received not one intentional walk all season. As Roger said, "I just want him [Mantle] to keep hitting 'em, too. The way he's going, they've got to pitch to me first."

A reporter asked Mantle if he thought he "would have hit as many homers this year if Roger was not on the team." Mantle admitted that he would have been in the lineup less often had Roger not given him the incentive to play harder: "I'll tell you the truth, I doubt if I'd have played as many games as I have. It's a competition."

The M & M boys left baseball matters at Yankee Stadium when they went home to the apartment. Roommate Bob Cerv said, "There's no bitterness or jealousy between them. They hardly talk about baseball and never about home runs. They're the best of friends, on and off the field."

In *The Mick,* Mantle leaves no doubt about the quality of his relationship with Roger throughout 1961. "Through it all," Mantle writes, "we remained close. There was never any jealousy. I rooted for him and definitely rooted for myself. ... All my feuds should be as nice as the one I had with Roger. Believe me, I'd have no enemies."

Their supposed antagonism became a "running gag." One version had Mantle reading the newspaper in the apartment, putting it down, and exclaiming to Roger, "I hate your guts." Another version had Roger scanning the paper and suddenly shouting at Mantle, "Hey, Mick, wake up, read this. We're fighting again."

The Mantle-Maris home-run chase fascinated the press. Even without stories of jealousy, the press delighted in reports of simple comparisons: musical tastes, food preferences, reading habits, and the like. Often, the press presented inaccuracies as facts, and its exasperating talk about the feud sometimes degenerated into outright poor taste.

The Maris-Mantle homer competition also focused media attention on the Yankees themselves. If the Babe's record were to be broken, did the Yankees want the player to be Roger Maris or Mickey Mantle? Roger felt that the media concentrated on him because he not only threatened the Babe's majesty, but also stood as an outsider. He was not part of the Yankee tradition, not an heir to the Babe like Mantle. In later years Roger said that "some" of the Yankees "even tried to rig the lineup" so that Mantle would have a better shot at the record.

Yankee second-baseman Bobby Richardson remarked in "Pinstripe Power" that "almost all" of the players rooted for Mantle to break the record. Whitey Ford commented in *Slick*: "At the time I was pulling for Mickey. Nothing against Roger, but I had known Mick for eleven or twelve years and we had been hanging around together for most of that time."

Yankee catcher John Blanchard explained the Yankees' sentiments: "It wasn't that anybody on the team resented Roger. But Mickey had been a veteran on the team, ten years in fact. Therefore the players felt that he had a better claim to breaking the record."

Skipper Ralph Houk remained above the competition and comparisons in 1961, before the bitter feelings aroused by his handling of a Maris injury. Houk's *Season of Glory* demonstrates an obvious bias in some of its gratuitous comparisons. Houk wrote that Mantle spoke with "an engaging charm, a pleasant voice." However, Roger had a "monotonous" manner of speaking — his "voice was not noticeably deep or warm." "Mantle was a much better looking man." The photo captions in *Season of Glory* commended Mantle for taking the "pressure gracefully" and castigated Maris, who "found it more and more difficult to keep his emotion under control."

Despite the preferences individual Yankees expressed for their competing teammates, Roger and Mickey shared an unshakeable friendship. "Mick and I have always been the best of friends," Roger said after he had taken off the pinstripes. Some of Roger's friends noted that Roger had a positive influence on Mantle during their playing days. As one friend said, "Mickey's words and actions were not always in the best of taste, but when Roger was there alongside him, you would see none of this."

Mantle remained very close to Maris throughout Roger's fatal illness and served as moderator for "Just for the Record," the tribute to his former roomate Roger. The Mick honored "my friend Roger" with the words, "There might have been better players, but no one was a better man. ... When Roger hit his sixty-first home run, I was the second happiest person in the world."

Chapter X
Days of Torment

Finally, the distracting and distressing asterisk debate quieted. For an interlude, Roger could direct his attention toward playing his best and advancing the Yankees through their grueling pennant race.

However, Roger soon began to feel harried by the press. His Kansas City friend Jim Cosentino told Roger, "You need a good public relations man," but Roger's North Dakotan openness refused to allow him to be cute, tactful, or diplomatic. He would typically answer day-after-day questions of little substance with a quick "That's stupid!"

Hardly a day passed without his fielding a Ruthian question, e.g., "Are you ever sorry that you ever heard of Babe Ruth?" Roger responded: "Don't ask me about that record. I don't want to talk about it. One guy wrote that I don't deserve to break the Babe's record. Now I admire Ruth. He was the greatest. But what am I supposed to do: stop hitting homers? They make it sound as if I'd be committing a sin if I broke the record."

Roger's first homer after the Frick ruling came in Boston off Bill Monbouquette and followed an 0 for 10. Roger had no sooner returned to the bench when Mantle hit his thirty-seventh, making him one up in the homer chase on July 21.

Mantle's advantage lasted only until Tuesday, July 25, when Roger experienced the doubleheader players dream of. On a hot, humid night at the stadium, Roger creamed four homers and drove in eight runs against the Chisox. He put himself twenty-four games ahead of Ruth's mark and led the Yanks to twin victories.

Ironically, Roger had planned to ask for the night off because he was feeling "lousy." "It was the heat or something I ate," he said. "I just felt washed out. I didn't want to play. ... I never had a good doubleheader even in the minors until this one. I don't know why."

Roger's joy at the successful doubleheader ended the next day when he felt something pop in his leg as he motored into second with a double. With a sense of deja vu, Roger fell victim to his second-half-of-the-season injury jinx. He sat out the game on old-timer's day and played only as pinch hitter in the first game of a Sunday doubleheader. The leg injury kept him out of the lineup for the second All-Star game in Boston.

During the July that followed his glorious doubleheader, Roger hit no other homers. As he wrote in *Roger Maris at Bat,* "My leg wasn't right and it would be a couple of weeks before it felt right again. Although I didn't know it at the time, I had run into one of those streaks every home-run hitter gets into now and then. I was off just enough that I stopped hitting balls into the air."

On August 4 in the stadium Roger finally broke his homer drought with his first-ever hit off a tough rightie, Minnesota's Cuban hurler Camilio Pascual. This four-bagger — his first in eight games — gave him 101 RBIs for the season and put him up on Mantle, forty-one to forty.

At about this time of the season, the "who do you prefer — Roger Maris or Mickey Mantle?" game caught the fans' interest. Manager Houk, who controlled the lineup, received strong advice from the fans, most of it favoring Mantle. Houk told the press: "You should read some of the letters I've been getting. They are demanding that I switch Mantle to hit third, while I should put Maris into the fourth slot for the rest of the season. They seem to think Rog has the edge by hitting ahead of Mickey."

The skipper disregarded the fan sentiment. "I'm only interested in the pennant race," he said, "and for that I believe the present batting order is my best. I want Mickey in between Rog and Yogi."

Yankee fans also voiced their preference at the stadium. "The fans began to get behind Mickey," Roger remarks in *Maris at Bat.* "Now he would be cheered all the time, while the fans began to get on me. It wasn't vicious, but they got off Mickey and on me. I guess they figured I was only a 'rookie' with the Yankees and didn't rate ahead of Mick."

The Minnesota series ended with a doubleheader. Roger played his typical twin bill, batting a meager 2 for 12. Meanwhile, an explosive Mantle hit three homers to pass Roger, 43-41.

In the opening game against Los Angeles on August 7, Roger made headlines for a surprise bunt that helped the Yankees beat the Angels in a tight game. The press could not understand why Roger had passed up a chance to add to his home-run total. Roger explained to the media with his usual honesty that he would be happy to get any hit that would lead the Yanks to a pennant. As Roger relates in his book, the reporters were "practically laughing in my face." Their laughter inasmuch as said, "Okay, you gave us the bull. But how do you really feel?"

Roger had only one homer in his last sixteen games, although he had one or more hits in twelve of them. He hoped that things would improve when the Yankees went to Washington and a park in which he had hit no runs so far in 1961. Roger finally tagged one there — his third of the season — against the lefty pitcher Pete Burnside. Mantle also put one into the stands, adjusting the count in the M-M race to 44-42. The four-game series proved very pleasant for Roger, who made one homer in each of the games. The home-run race stood deadlocked at 45-45. Both sluggers bested Ruth's 1927 schedule by sixteen games.

The writers noticed the pace being set by Maris and Mantle. At the end of the Washington series, a new phase of the 1961 season began — a period of unprecedented, unbearable pressure for the final six weeks of the campaign. The press conference after the series finale attracted not only the usual New York reporters, but also the press from outside the metropolitan area and the magazine writers. Roger told the press that he hoped either Mantle or he would break the Ruthian mark, although he did not expect to be the one.

Under continued questioning, Roger expounded on the Babe and his record, the old-timers versus the present-day players, the condition of today's balls and gloves, and varied playing conditions. He might have said too much, but Roger adhered to his credo: "I always believe that an honest question deserves an honest answer, but sometimes you get into trouble by saying the wrong thing."

When the Yanks returned to New York to face Chicago on August 15, they found that the home-run pursuit had electrified the fans. Fifty thousand gathered in the stadium to watch Roger hit number 46 off Juan Pizarro, giving Maris a one-homer advantage that Mantle would never overcome. Despite Roger's efforts, the Yanks lost 2-1, and Whitey Ford missed a chance at a record-breaking fifteenth consecutive victory. Because Detroit had won two, the Yanks' lead had dwindled to two games.

The team's loss tempered Roger's satisfaction at hitting a homer off a tough lefty. Maris had come up in the eighth with a chance to tie the game. At the first pitch he sent the ball a foot foul, and on his next swing he had to settle for a double. He was disappointed. He felt pretty low and somewhat drained from playing hurt, even though he had nearly recovered from his injury.

Joe Reichler covered the game for the Associated Press and wrote a story that typified the press's misinterpretations and distortions of Roger's words and actions. The Reichler article carried the headline, "Near Miss for No. 47 Angers Roger Maris," and its lead read, "Roger Maris was an angry man Tuesday night after hitting his 46th homer of the season for the Yankees." The story detailed the near-miss in the eighth inning and gave Roger's sentiments: "'It couldn't have been foul by more than this much,' growled Maris, holding his hands about three or four inches apart. 'It was fair all the way until the final second. Then the darn thing hooked behind the pole.'"

The story "recorded" Roger's disappointment at the eighth-inning shot that went foul. "'That makes about five or six near misses I've had this year — that I know of,' he complained. 'There might have been more. And don't forget that homer was washed out in Baltimore when we couldn't get in five innings.

"'They say those things even up. That's a lot of hogwash. They never do. All I know is they owe me about four because I got two homers this year on drives that hit the foul pole.'"

When the subject of fatigue arose, the reporter depicted Roger as a malcontent. "'Gosh, I'm tired,' he complained. 'Could use a good rest. This has been a real long season for me. Why don't they go back to the 154-game schedule. Playing 162 games is too tough — much too long.'"

At this point Roger had little to say about his ability to surpass Ruth. The reporter took a swipe at Roger for his noncooperation and used Maris' angry response to illustrate his stubbornness.

"Maris, as usual, refused to discuss his chances to break Ruth's record.

"'Every writer asks me the same question. Do I think I can break Ruth's record. How the heck do I know? They're the know-it-alls. Why don't they ask themselves?'"

After Roger's death Bob Fishel, the Yankee's public-relations official in 1961, executive vice-president of the American League, later lamented the actions of the press before his death in 1988. "I could have done much better by him," Fishel said. "Pete Rose held press conferences each day during his bid to break Ty Cobb's hit record, and I should have done the same for Roger when it appeared he might break Ruth's homer mark."

Fishel said that the novelty of the Roger Maris situation encouraged the press to keep the first watch of its kind in baseball history. Reporters conducted impromptu interviews at Roger's locker. With a press conference, "he could have gotten all the questions taken care of at once. ... Finally it got to him. That's why some people thought he had a bad attitude toward the press."

Roger's naked honesty and refusal to finesse at these inquisitions resulted in his bad press. Arthur Daley, writing for *Columbia,* a Catholic magazine, pinpointed the situation: "For those six weeks he went through an ordeal such as no athlete ever experienced before. He was harassed, heckled, tormented, tortured, bewitched, bothered, and bewildered. Day after day, he was mercilessly grilled by writers and radio-television inquisitors, probing for his secret thoughts. A few questions were sharp, penetrating. But most ranged from the inane to the insulting. He had to fence his way warily past the booby traps in the first category and suffer through the second."

Joe Williams also appreciated Roger's ordeal. Writing in the *New York World-Telegram and Sun,* Williams says, "Public adulation seems to conflict with his 'inner reticence.' Not all of the country boy has rubbed off. On the whole, though, he has accepted the irksome obligations of his sudden fame with dignity, patience, graciousness, and intelligence."

On August 16, Roger belted two round-trippers off lefty Billy Pierce. These four-baggers increased Roger's total to forty-eight homers, scored thirteen games ahead of the Babe. In addition, Roger had now hit home runs in six consecutive games, and seven runs in six days — an American League record. The holder of the major-league mark of eight was Pittsburgh's Dale Long, later to become Roger's friend when both were on the Yankees. Don Mattingly became the American League holder of the record in 1987, with homers in seven consecutive games.

Joe Reichler again covered the game and produced a story headlined "Sudden Fame Difficult to Cope With," with a subhead "'Angry Man' Hits Two to get 48 Total.'" The lead says nothing about the homers or the game; instead, Reichler offers his "findings" on Roger's personality:

Roger Maris is known as the "angry man." Even his own

teammates among the New York Yankees refer to him on occasions as "the red-necked Roger."

The man who today has the best chance ... to shatter Babe Ruth's most fantastic of all home run records ... admits he is not the easiest person in the world to get along with.

"I was born surly," he says through the lips that always seem to be snarling, "and I'm going to stay that way."

Reichler's report continues by quoting Roger on his difficulty in dealing with media: "'You fellows are tougher than some of these pitchers,' he *once* said *testily* [emphasis added]. 'Where do you think up these silly questions? How the heck do I know whether I'll break Ruth's record. Besides, you're the only guys thinking about it. I don't. All I'm interested in is having a good season and winning the pennant.'"

The journalist then focuses on what he perceives as Maris' mercenary nature. Reichler again quotes Roger: "'I'd rather have the dough than the record. And if I have a real good season, I'm going to ask for real dough next year, too.'" Reichler notes that Roger presently received a $32,500 salary. The reporter then predicts that Maris would soon ask for $75,000 — Mantle's current salary, as Reichler innocently adds.

Finally, Reichler returns to the two home runs Roger hit off the Chisox. The reporter observes that although the public wants Babe's record to stand, if someone must break it, the public would prefer him to be Mantle, not Maris.

With all this negative reporting, it might seem that the fans, especially New Yorkers, could never have accepted Roger, the quiet boy from the country. This was not true. Roger electrified the fans. He brought back a mood of excitement that had been missing from baseball for decades. The fans idolized Roger, but he would not pay the price of their adulation. He refused to act contrary to his personality or to engage in public relations gimmicks rhetorical games. Roger remained wary of the applause of the crowd: "I know there are a lot of nice people out there. But there are a lot who got on me pretty good when I wasn't going as well. A lot of those have stopped getting on me and are cheering me now, but I don't like people who go only for front runners. That's too easy."

Roger knew who his biggest fans were: his family and friends in North Dakota. After the two-home-run game, Rudy Maris called his son to congratulate him and encourage him to keep up the pace. All the attention Roger received after his twin homers thrilled his mom, even though she didn't understand the game of baseball too well. Senator Milton R. Young (R., N.D.) interrupted a United States Senate floor debate on a foreign aid bill to proclaim the "momentous announcement" that Roger Maris of Fargo had struck home runs numbers 47 and 48.

Roger could not keep up the torrid pace. He could do nothing against Frank Baumann and Russ Kemmerer in the series finale, but the Yanks won, 5-3. After the game, a thoughtless scribe asked Roger if he had hoped that the White Sox would tie to the score so that he would get another shot at a home run. As he says in *Roger Maris at Bat*, "I told him that the first time I felt like that it would be time for me to take off my uniform, hang it up, and go out to look for another job."

Roger's friends and acquaintances in Fargo and his roommates at the apartment saw a sharp wit and a keen sense of humor. Why didn't Roger use these to defuse the tension or to disarm an unfriendly press and, by extension, the fans? His friends could not come up with a substantive answer, but some authorities on the Great Plains offered some interesting thoughts.

Father Sherman observed: "In North Dakota and ... the Great Plains, one prefers not to make a public show or to be too demonstrative. An exhibition of wit or humor is not desirable. More important, in this part of the country, before one shows this wit or humor, a friendship has to be developed between the people involved."

Professor Warren Kress, professor of geography at North Dakota State University and an authority on the ethnic characteristics of North Dakotans, suspects that Maris' "attitude was, 'Just let me hit my home runs. I don't want to be in the spotlight.' When he was grilled by the press, he couldn't be effusive. He couldn't make a display in public. The entire questioning made him uncomfortable, put him in a situation alien to his nature."

Mike Jacobs, editor of the *Grand Forks Herald,* said: "Roger Maris could not let loose with a barrage of witticisms and explosive wit. That would have made him a smart aleck. All he could be in public was retiring, but, unfortunately, the New York fish bowl made him look surly, which he was not!"

The end of the White Sox series meant Roger could get away from the New York fish bowl, as the Yankees took to the road. In Cleveland excited fans crowded into the first two games. Neither Roger nor Mantle hit any homers. On August 20, the press interviewed legendary pitcher Satchel Paige in the Yankee dugout before the scheduled doubleheader. He said he would pitch to the M & M boys "low and outside. That's how you should pitch any power hitter — away from his power." Satch thought he could pitch to the sluggers and "get 'em out, too. But if one of 'em pulled my low outside fast ball for a home run, I'd throw up my glove and quit on the spot."

The Cleveland pitcher should have taken Satch's advice. The 55,000 fans at the twin bill later watched Roger hit number 49 off Jim Perry. Mantle also hit a homer, number 46, as the Yanks took both games.

The next challenge was in Wrigley Field designated as the "House of Thrills" by Irv Kaze, publicity man for the Los Angeles Angels, because of the many close games played there in 1961.

In the sixth inning of a game played on August 22, Roger tagged one to deep center off Ken McBride, making Maris' fiftieth home run for the season, thirteen games ahead of Ruth's 1927 pace.. Roger became the first slugger to reach that many home runs before September. He also joined Babe Ruth, Jimmie Foxx, Hank Greenberg, Hack Wilson, Ralph Kiner, Mickey Mantle, Johnny Mize and Willie Mays as only the ninth hitter to reach the fifty-homer plateau. The fiftieth blast eased the sting of the 4-3 Yankee loss and Maris' continuing slump — only three hits in the last twenty-four at bat.

Roger did not connect during the last two games of the Los Angeles series, but he looked forward to playing in Kansas City. The Athletics series would give him a chance to spend time with his family in Raytown and meet his new son Randy, who had been born on August 21. He did not know until arriving home that the paper had printed his address in the paper in the birth announcement story. Suddenly, traffic filled the streets of quiet, peaceful Raytown as curious fans flocked to see the Maris home.

On Roger's first day home, the tourists drove by all day long. The hesitant curiosity seekers just entered the driveway, while the bolder fans marched up to the door for autographs. Roger described his emotions in a *Look* article: "My feeling of relaxation and contentment at being home disappeared in the fire of my suddenly exploding temper. This was an invasion of privacy completely uncalled for."

In the second game of the series against Kansas City, on August 25, Roger broke an 0 for 9 by tagging number 51 off Jerry Walker. He was 10 games up on Babe, with 25 games left in Frick's 154-game season. While Roger did not boost his home-run total in the final game of the series, he said that the four days in Kansas City "had a lot to do with making it possible for me to go on and keep striving to reach the sixty home-run level. It was a good break in the pressure-packed season."

The Yankees went to Bloomington, Minnesota, for the last stop of their August schedule, with a very weary Roger Maris in the lineup. "I'm tired, plain old-fashioned tired if I may call it that," he said, "and the reason is the heavier schedule. They added games but compressed it into the same period of time as before. The result is fewer days off." Roger had played in all but one of the 129 Yankee games and would not request to be benched, because "The Tigers are right on our tail, only two games away, and all of us have to play every minute we can."

Each of the three games drew large crowds. The opener brought out 45,000 spectators and also reunited three one-time Fargoans: Roger Maris; Art Naftalin, then mayor of Minneapolis; and Fargo Mayor Herschel Lashkowitz. Roger's dad also rooted for the slugger at all three games.

Despite the hoopla, the Twins' opening hurler Camilio Pascual said, "I pitch to them [Maris and Mantle] just like I pitch to the other teams — throw everything at them." Pascual did just that and stopped Maris and the Yankees. Mantle hit two homers in the series, bringing his total to 48. Roger went homerless, making it four games straight in which he failed to up his total, but he still lead Ruth's pace by seven games. The Yanks' loss in the finale gave them a slim one-and-a-half-game edge over Detroit at the end of August.

Roger demonstrated his value to the Yankees in game two. He made no homers or important hits but made an important, intangible contribution to the Yanks' 4-0 triumph. In the fourth inning of a scoreless game, Roger slid hard into Minnesota's Billy Martin and broke up a possible double play. As a result, the Yanks got a run that inning, and the Twins never recovered.

Roger played to win in a tight pennant race. He later said: "I had to take my chances with an injury. ... We're out to win the pennant and any records will be incidental. I'm out to win each game."

Bill Martin, the personification of aggressiveness, commented on Roger's style. "He runs the bases and slides hard."

At the end of the trip. Roger had the numbers to prove how tough he was in the clutch. Twenty-seven of his fifty-one homers came in clutch situations: tieing the game, breaking a tie, overcoming a deficit, or adding to a one-run lead. On four occasions, Roger homered with men on to overcome a lead. He tied the score three times. Twice his homers added to a one-run advantage, and he broke a deadlocked game eighteen times. Maris' homers accounted for 86 RBIs: 17 with one man on, 9 with two men on, 25 with the bases empty, and 35 RBIs came on hits other than homers.

Houk praised his slugger: "He's got a lot more big hits than people realize. He and Mantle both do it regularly — but Mantle's been doing it longer and people who have followed the Yankees for years know how he comes through in the clutch. I don't think many people realize how true it is of Maris, too."

As August ended, the superexcitement of the homer pursuit grew to fever pitch. "M Boys Bask in Spotlight," said the headline of the *Sporting News* editorial of August 30. The editorial told of all the attention the sluggers received in the media and the almost overexploitation of their home runs. However, growing crowds swarmed to Yankee Stadium and to wherever the team played on the road, and this was good for baseball.

In fact, attendance figures rose dramatically because of the home-run battle. At the stadium, the Yankees outdrew the other nine teams by as much as 2 1/2 to 1. The games attracted the largest TV-viewing audience in the New York metropolitan area, and all road games were shown on the air.

Whitney Martin concluded his Associated Press analysis with the observation, "The home run derby obviously is bringing hundreds of thousands of dollars to the league."

The home-run chase also brought forecasts of economic windfalls for Maris and Mantle. Frank Scott, personal agent for the players, said, "The potential take is $500,000 over three years for the man who breaks the record. The home run record is the biggest plum in sports." Half of the money would come from merchandising arrangements involving such items as T-shirts, bats, and balls. In addition, Scott had already arranged for both sluggers to appear on the "Perry Como Show," for televising during the World Series.

In Fargo, Rudy Maris Sr. stayed on top of the home-run watch and expressed his excitement in the local press. He told Richard Rainbolt of the Associated Press that he was cheering for both his son and Mantle. Rudy said: "It's funny, but in 1957 I asked Rog if he ever thought about being the guy who would break Ruth's record. He just said, 'Maybe so' and dropped it there." Rudy took pride in his son's ability to handle the pressure. The proud father beamed: "The constant pressure on that guy — gee, I don't know how he does it."

Roger Maris, President Harry S Truman
and Mickey Mantle.
(Courtesy of Truman Library)

Chapter XI
The Roger Maris Watch

The scenario for September's opening game at the stadium had the M & M boys in contention for the Ruthian record, and a hot Detroit team, with eleven wins in its last fifteen games in competition with the Yankees.

The Yanks swept Detroit, going up by four-and-one-half games and virtually ending the pennant race. Roger also had a big series, hitting two homers off two tough hurlers, righty Frank Lary and lefty Hank Aguirre, in the second game. Maris found it especially satisfying to hit a four-bagger off Lary, a reputed Yankee killer.

Roger's two-out single in the first inning of game three, right before Mickey's first homer of the day, received scant attention. Those two important runs in the hard-fought game crushed Detroit's hopes for the flag.

Mantle's second homer in the finale really excited the media. The Yankees became the first team to have two players who had hit fifty or more homers in a season. Mantle's entry into the fifty-home-run club, for the second time in his career, meant that everyone could expect a thrilling Ruthian pursuit in the last few weeks of the season.

Washington followed Detroit to play a Labor Day doubleheader at the stadium. Roger had already hit eight round-trippers off Senator hurlers earlier in the season, with three coming off of Pete Burnside, Roger's chief victim. In the nightcap of the Labor Day twin bill, Burnside gave Roger a zero-for-four collar.

The Yankees swept the Senators, but Roger went zero-for-eight. A reporter noted that Roger's average had dropped below .270. Senator pitcher Burnside retorted: "'So what? With one hundred twenty-four RBIs and fifty-three homers, who needs averages?'"

Roger's frustration at his no-hit games peaked in the clubhouse, where reporters hounded the slugger about his reaction to the fans booing him. Roger's response appeared in the newspapers the following day:

They are a lousy bunch of front runners, that's what

they are. Hit a home run and they love you, but make an out and they start booing. Give me the fans in Kansas City any time. There's no place where the fans can compare to the people out there.

There are a few faces you see all the time. I know who they are ... the same ones always give me a hard time. As long as they leave me alone outside the park I don't care. They never say anything to you face to face.

The press reminded Roger that even the booers pay to come to the game. Roger's responded:

I didn't ask them to come. If they keep giving me a hard time, I'll do my job on the field and give them what they pay to see. But they better not come around after the game bothering me for autographs. I can walk through fifteen million of them and never look at one of them.

Again, Roger spoke openly, honestly, and truthfully, even though he realized that not all fans were as he had described. As he later reveals in *Roger Maris at Bat*: "I was very sorry that I had said it. I must admit that it wasn't the right thing to do. The way it came out it sounded as if I were talking about all the fans, but I most certainly wasn't. There are only a few fans that are really bad." On the following night at the park, Roger wished that he could apologize, but he could not. Worse, another hitless game only made the boos louder.

Although Roger's remarks were tactless, the fans had acted boorishly, directing verbally malicious insults at Roger both on and off the field. Even a policeman at one of the road games remarked: "Some of the fans' profanity even embarrassed me. I'd hate to be in Maris' shoes right now and have to listen to that kind of stuff."

As a columnist for the *New York Journal-American,* Jimmy Cannon closely and sympathetically followed Roger's pursuit of the record. A few days after the media published his remarks, Roger calmly told Cannon about the fans: "It's the other things they say. Not wisecracks. I can't tell you what it is. You wouldn't be able to print it. They stop at nothing. They even insult my family. I don't mean the majority. I mean the ones without good heads on their shoulders."

Away from the ballpark, Roger told Cannon, he had hardly a

moment of peace from the fans:

> I was in a restaurant in New York eating with my friends. I was just putting a bite into my mouth when this guy came up and said he wanted an autograph. I said I'd be glad as soon as I finished eating. I was right in the midst of a conversation with my friends.
>
> This guy said he wasn't going to wait. He wanted it right now. This is not once. It happens all the time.

Washington Senator manager Mickey Vernon wondered if Roger would "be able to fight the pressure. You hear about it all around the league."

Roger's zero-for-sixteen famine finally ended in the final game of the series. He hit one in the fourth, with two outs and Tom Cheney working on a no-hitter. The blast into the Yankee bullpen sparked a five-run rally and another victory for the home team. Number fifty-four moved Roger to seven games ahead of Ruth's pace. "I was beginning to wonder what I was doing up here in these high numbers ... with the Ruths, Greenbergs, Foxxes, Wilsons," Roger said in amazement and disbelief. "I never even dreamt in a fantasy that I was Babe Ruth. Hell, I just wanted to be a good ball player, have a good year, and help my club win flags."

After the Washington series, simple mathematics showed that Roger needed a homer every two-and-one-half games to tie Ruth within Frick's 154-game guideline. The opponents for the next fifteen games at the stadium were Cleveland, Chicago, Detroit, and Baltimore, then the Yankees would be on the road. Roger did well away from home; in fact, he had hit twenty-eight out of the fifty-four homers on the road.

Maris revealed that "Every homer I hit after forty I kept thinking might be my last one, so I figured I might as well save them." He had been giving some of the balls to friends, but from now he would keep them. When a reporter asked what he intended to write on number sixty, Roger answered, "I'll let you know when and if I ever get that one."

A reporter persisted, "How about number sixty-one?" Roger responded, "I'm not saying I'm going to hit it, but if I do, I'd like to have it, sure." Maris would reward the person returning the historic ball, "but he'd better be pretty darn sure it was the right one."

George Vecsey of *Newsday* presented another graphic example of the press bias against Roger in his story, "Secreted World of Roger Maris." Vecsey spoke to Bob Hale, a Yankee reserve outfielder who caught Roger's fifty-fourth homer in the bullpen and returned it to him. Hale said that the number-sixty-one homer ball is "too important to give away." After quoting Roger on recovering the record-homer balls, Vecsey reported on Roger's reaction to Hale's comment:

> That bit of information was relayed to Maris. Roger looked the informer up and down with an icy-blue-eyed stare. There was a long pause. "Hale is full of it," Maris finally pronounced. "Nobody on this team is gonna keep my number-sixty-one ball."

> Later it was decided that the only way Maris could be sure of keeping his number-sixty-one ball would be to hit an inside-the-park homer. Maris heard this comment and snickered. He was in mid-season form.

Vecsey missed the point that Hale, the comic of the 1961 team, obviously intended to put the press on. In *Sixty-One,* Kubek called him the "class clown." Kubek recalled, "Imagine hearing the national anthem. Then imagine hearing Porky Pig. Then put them together and you have Bob Hale in the Yankee dugout in 1961."

The ball retrieval incident again shows Roger's inability to make use of his refreshing but very private sense of humor in a situation that cried out for it.

Roger spent more time in the spotlight as media personnel gathered for the five-game series with Cleveland, the Yanks' last series before going on the road. The press anticipated that Roger would move very close to the record. Four of the scheduled Tribe hurlers, Gary Bell, Jim Perry, Mudcat Grant, and Barry Latman, had already surrendered one hundred gopher balls in 1961; and so far Roger had stroked three homers off Perry and two off Bell.

In the third inning of game one, Roger slammed number fifty-five into the bleachers, the twelfth homer he had hit off lefties in 1961. Roger drove in a run with a bunt single, added another single that knocked in a run, and brought in one more with a sacrifice fly.

After he failed to connect in the second game, Maris remained seven games ahead of Ruth. Mantle smashed number fifty-two, putting him only one game behind Ruth's 1927 pace. With their two hits, Maris and Mantle tied the two-man one-hundred-seven-homer record of Ruth and Gehrig in 1927.

The Ruth-Gehrig mark fell the next day in the seventh inning. Roger hit number fifty-six off Jim Mudcat Grant and into the right-field bleachers. Roger's homer put him six up on the Babe, but he still needed five more blasts in twelve games, or within 154. Roger also moved two runners into scoring position in the ninth inning, as the Yanks rallied to win their tenth straight game, 8-7.

The homer by the "Dakota Destroyer," as the *New York Journal-American's* Til Ferdenzi called Roger, undid the seemingly unbreakable Ruth-Gehrig record. "This record," Ferdenzi said, "seemed as inviolate as the one the incomparable Babe Ruth slashed away thirty-four years ago."

The Yankees prepared for a doubleheader on September 10, Roger's twenty-seventh birthday. The team celebrated with a sweep, but the birthday boy came up empty. Maris was now four games ahead of the Babe. Mantle managed a four-bagger that brought his total up to fifty-three.

Roger's birthday celebration in a Manhattan restaurant gave the media sharks something to gnaw on. Maris sat with Bob Cerv and Big Julie when the restaurateur brought Ava Gardner over for an introduction. Two columnists saw exciting possibilities and linked Roger with the movie goddess. The rumors persisted even when the team went to Baltimore, where Roger had his last chance to surpass Ruth.

The *Long Island Press* noted that one columnist "insisted Ava attended a Yankee game incognito and was invited to dinner by the home run slugger." Roger totally denied all stories and "called his wife to advise her not to believe what she reads in the gossip columns."

The Ava Gardner episode exemplified the media's reckless and malicious exploitation of Roger Maris. Roger charitably described as "weird" the following interview between him and a *Time* magazine reporter; certainly the questioning ranks as the most tasteless.

"Do you play around on the road?" the writer interrogated Roger.

"I'm a married man," Roger replied.

"I'm married myself," the writer persisted, "but I play around on the road."

"That's your business," Roger said, concluding the interrogation.

The media pressure that Roger had neither foreseen nor prepared for began to be more than Roger could handle. John Blanchard, the Yankee's valuable catcher-outfielder, remembers, "Writers that couldn't get to Roger would literally crowd into my locker and talk to Roger through the screen. I'm probably the only player that ever had a locker that was a confessional."

One day while standing at Mantle's locker, Roger confessed: "I'm going nuts, Mick. I can't stand much more of this."

Mantle had dealt with pressure situations over the years and sympathetically advised, "You'll just have to learn to take it, Rog. There's no escape."

Mantle often spoke to the press to take some pressure off his roommate and halt any further stories of a feud between them. Mantle told the media that Roger "deserves" to break the record. He added: "I'm rooting for him. Let's everybody root for him. I want to see him do it, and I am sure he will."

Roger received support and prayers from his friends and followers in Kansas City and Fargo. He told Jimmy Cannon, "One nice thing — the pastor back in my parish in Kansas City when he says prayers, ... he includes my name, too." At St. Mary's Catholic Cathedral, Roger's boyhood parish, Msgr. L. J. Arrell, the pastor, customarily asked congregants to say a prayer "for the sick of the parish and the boys in service." As the number of games approached the 154 deadline, the pastor added: "And for those who don't think it's too silly, for Roger Maris."

The city of Fargo provided its visible support by renaming a street "Roger Maris Road." Mayor Lashkowitz began distributing business cards that read "the home town of Roger Maris."

The road trip began in Chicago, an ideal spot. White Sox pitching had already given Roger thirteen round-trippers, one short of Gehrig's mark of fourteen against one team. To magnify Ruth's 1927 mark, reporter John P. Carmichael noted that the Babe had only six home runs against Chicago. But Carmichael neglected to mention that the Sox of 1927 were 70-83 for the season, finishing in fifth place. The 1961 White Sox were a winning team that finished with 86-76.

Rain, the effect of Hurricane Carla, dampened the excitement in Comiskey Park. Roger managed a single before the opener was called in the sixth. Not only did Roger lose a turn or two at bat, but the shortened game gave reporters more time for their daily grilling of Roger. Maris had a bad night at the plate and a worse evening in the clubhouse. The press focused on Roger's striking out in the second inning on a call by plate umpire Hank Soar. According to Roger, he started to swing and held back. As he reports in *Roger Maris at Bat:* "Umpire Hank Soar called me out on strikes. I discussed it at length, but didn't think I had said anything out of line."

On the following day the press in essence reported that Roger had lashed out at Soar and the umpire responded in kind.

The press reported these of Roger's comments on Soar's umpiring:

Soar called me out on a swing, which I didn't swing. I was going to wait for strikes, but they [Pierce and Baumann] weren't giving me any, so I didn't swing.

Soar is a better umpire than that. He just had a bad night, I guess. I was trying to lay off the bad pitches, but it didn't do any good. He called them strikes time after time. All I ask is a fair shake. I know they've got a tough job and I never argue with an umpire unless I'm sure I'm right.

I realize that people will say I'm a cry baby, but I can't help it ... not after the bad calls I got.

Stan Isaacs's *Newsday* article headlined "Red Neck Roger Flares at Ump" noted that the "prevailing opinion around Comiskey Park last night was that Roger Maris doesn't know enough to keep his mouth shut." Later in the story, the reporter acknowledged that Roger is "in the hottest pressure cooker any ball player has ever known." Isaacs asked Roger, "You haven't knocked the umpires all season. Why are you doing it now?" Maris responded: "I know I haven't knocked the umps all year. But tonight I made up my mind and then this happens. When it just keeps happening time after time you get fed up."

The *Newsday* reporter wondered if Roger realized how the public would react to his words. According to the story, Roger answered, "Tell them to go to Center Moriches."

One version of the strike-out story has Roger telling Soar, "You really shoved it to me on this one." In the "standard" version of the incident, Soar responded to Roger's comments:

"'Bad calls? What bad calls? He's so tight up there he can't breathe. He's trying so hard he thinks every pitch he leaves alone is a ball.

"'He's never said a word to me. I honestly like him very much. I try not to look at him when he's up. ... He's just another batter. I just look at the plate and the pitcher. I figure he's on the spot and the pressure is getting to him. They never give him a good pitch to hit. ... They keep throwing him junk, low and outside. I know what he's going through.'"

The reports claimed that Soar was astonished that Roger tried to bunt in the second inning before the strike-out. "'If he's going for a home run record, then why was he trying to bunt?'"

The newspaper reporting angered Roger, especially Soar's comments on his bunting. "I bunted," Roger explained, "because we might have needed that other run to win. ... I feel we've got it [the pennant], but I want to make sure. That's why we've been fighting." Roger always placed winning paramount, even with his own home-run glory on the line. The press thought the open and honest Roger naive for thinking the Yanks might lose an eleven-and-one-half-game lead. Leonard Schecter felt the pressure was getting to Roger. In Shecter's story headlined "Maris Starting to Feel the Strain," he reflected on Roger and his bunt: "That's his story, and he's stuck with it. No one can go inside his head and take pictures. You can guess he's naive enough to mean it. Or you can guess it's all getting to be a little too much for him."

Roger spoke to Soar after his remarks had appeared in the papers. In *Roger Maris at Bat* Roger reveals, "He [Soar] told me that he had never said the things that were in the papers." Roger emphatically stated that what the press printed often did not coincide with what he had said:

> Too often, however, writers are trying to create excite-
> ment and juggle words to make a better story. Things don't
> always come out the way I say them. Many times I would
> be answering a question, but another writer would come
> in about halfway through the answer. He'll only hear part
> of it, yet he'll base his story on that. I have never regretted
> anything I have said, provided that it was written as I said
> it. Many times, however, a word or two gets twisted and
> then it comes out bad.

Roger went into the second game of the Chicago series three games ahead of the Babe. The raw and miserable weather did not bother him. Roger told the media, "The only pressure is from the press and photographers." He vowed to use caution when speaking to them. He could only respond to questions "that weren't loaded." Before he had answered "questions that I had already answered hundreds of times." Now Roger had a new policy: "there would be no answers that could be twisted."

In the third inning of the game, the rains came. Then, after an hour-and-a-half wait, the game was called. During the long interval, the press observed and questioned Roger. After the Soar episode, the press remained critical but tried to look for the positive in Roger.

Stan Isaacs watched Roger during the rain delay. Although he described the slugger as "the first angry man ever," he admired Roger, a "fun-loving kid." Isaacs saw Roger as "an incomparable, brash broth of a boy who can say all the wrong things, but come out all right."

Leonard Schecter of the *New York Post* spent "A Rainy Night with Maris." Roger wasn't talking to reporters, Schecter observed, because one of them had made an uncalled-for comment about Pat Maris' coming to New York for the Yanks' final games. However, Schecter clearly respected Roger for staying outside the club house "thoroughly available to the full complement of reporters" and "in full sight of the general public."

After the season, Schecter paid Roger even more compliments in a story describing that rainy night. Roger signed autographs and "bantered with the fans." Schecter wrote: "When I remember Roger Maris, I'll remember how he made a difficult job a little easier. I'll remember his grousing with fondness, his friendly little rages with glee. And I'll remember how much I liked him because he was the kind of ball player you could walk up to and say, 'What's new?' and come away with a story."

Jack Lang rapped Roger for his response to the pestering reporters, giving one exchange as an example. When asked if he thought he would break the record, Roger responded: "Okay, if you guys want me to concede, I'll concede." Lang concluded his story with this advice: "No, Roger. No one wants you to concede. Just act like a man."

On that rainy night, Roger's teammates also thought about the Soar matter. "He just shouldn't say things like that," catcher Elston Howard remarked. Roomie Bob Cerv, who knew Roger better, observed: "You know Roger. He says what he thinks. I think he might have calmed down if the reporters hadn't gotten to him while they were still waiting for the game to be called. But what the hell? He was right. Soar did call some bad pitches, didn't he?"

The Chicago rain made it necessary to play two doubleheaders in twenty-four hours. Roger had hit more than one homer in only two of the doubleheaders the Yanks had played that year.

The Chicago doubleheader proved no different. A strong wind with gusts up to thirty miles per hour whistled towards right field, Roger's home-run corner. "If I ever saw a wind," Roger observed, "which could help a guy hit ordinary flies into the seats, that wind ... was the one." Yank announcer Rizzuto anticipated a Maris round-tripper: "Boy, that wind! If he gets one up in the air, it's gone." Roger couldn't take advantage of the gale to right field; he made three hits, but none flew into the seats. The Yanks dropped both games. Roger remained one game ahead of Ruth, but had only seven games (within 154) to hit five round-trippers.

Mantle had not added to his home-run total during the series. Roger's ailing roommate, playing with an abscess on his hip, felt "about ready to give up. I haven't got a chance now — even in 162 games." Roger tried to project optimism: "I think I've still got a chance if I can get hot in Detroit. I haven't given up. I like to hit in Detroit. Maybe I'll get hot there."

Roger felt relieved to leave Chicago for Detroit after the no-homer games, the Soar incident, the distorted press reports, and Rogers Hornsby's remarks. Hornsby agreed with Chicago's CBS sports editor announcement "I am rooting for Babe Ruth's memory." The great right-handed hitter said, "It would be a shame if Ruth's record got broken by a .270 hitter." Hornsby's words would ring in Roger Maris' ears long after the 1961 season.

Roger had no protection from the hordes of media personnel that inundated Detroit. *Sports Illustrated* visited Lindell's bar in Motown and found the fans grimly determined to keep Roger from breaking Ruth's record in Tiger Stadium: "We'll be busting ourselves in half to keep from giving up the record home run. ... Maris will have to have a junk dealer's license to get into the ball park."

A frenzy had gripped the fans in Detroit and other cities nation-wide. Even bridegrooms supposedly went to the altar to say "I do" clutching their transistor radios to find out first if Roger did.

Roger approached the series with his "winning-comes-first" at-titude. The Yanks' double loss in Chicago bothered Roger more than not hitting home runs. Roger told the press: "I don't care what anyone says. We still haven't got this thing won. Sure, we have a pretty comfortable 10½-game lead. But I don't see any asterisks in the standings that we've clinched the pennant, do you?"

On the eve of the series, Houk admitted that he had thought of moving Roger to the lead-off position with Mantle following, once the Yanks had clinched the pennant. Houk wanted to give them some additional at bats, but he quickly dismissed the idea. The skipper said: "Nobody is more anxious than I for them to break the record. By the same token, I don't think they should receive any special favors to make the job easier for them. Ruth's record probably is the most glamorous and highly regarded of any ever made. The fellow who breaks it must do it fairly and honestly. There should be no taint to it. He should receive no special help."

Ron Kline and Don Mossi pitched in the opening twi-night doubleheader. Mossi, the left-hander, insisted there would be no help or sympathy from him. "I don't want anybody to hit a homer off me," he said. "Not Maris, not Mantle, nobody."

Neither Roger nor Mantle hit a home run off Mossi, but Moose Skowron tagged him for the Yanks' two-hundred-twenty-second homer of the year, a major-league mark. Roger had yet another dismal doubleheader, managing one for nine as the teams split. The Babe and Roger were now deadlocked. Maris began thinking in terms of 162 games. Roger admitted: "I'm not even thinking of 154 games. As far as I'm concerned, Ruth hit his 60 home runs in a season. I'll not consider myself out of it until we have played the final game."

After the game the press waited to converge on Roger, but he was not be found. He had sought a few moments of privacy after a frustrating day at the plate and vicious outbursts from the stands — an understandable reaction, but a judgmental error.

The trainer's room was off limits to writers. Throughout his major-league career, Roger liked to sit in the trainer's room when playing in Detroit and Baltimore. "It is just a habit," he said. On that particular night, Roger's brother, Rudy, who had driven from Cincinnati to see the games, joined Maris in the trainer's room. The brothers hadn't seen each other for a while, Roger explained, and they had business matters to discuss, since Rudy handled his brother's financial affairs, particularly the product endorsements.

Roger later called the ensuing post-game incident "the biggest rhubarb of the season." He was not avoiding the press. "I thought they knew me well enough to know that I wasn't hiding from them or anyone else," relates the slugger in *Roger Maris at Bat*. "Under different circumstances, if I had not wanted to see them, I would have come out and told them right to their face."

Rudy Maris' presence in the trainer's room provided a red flag for the press. "Get him out," roared one reporter to Bob Fishel, the Yankee's public relations director. Fishel tried to convince Roger to face the press, but Maris rebuffed him twice. "After this," Roger reportedly told Fishel, "I'm going into the trainer's room every day. They've been ripping me in almost every city we've been in."

Dissatisfied with the results of Fishel's intervention, the press went in search of Houk. "Rog won't come out," a reporter fumed. "That's his business," the manager responded angrily.

"How come we can't go in and talk to him, and his brother can?" demanded one correspondent.

The usually calm Houk became enraged. "Are you trying to tell me how to run my clubhouse? It's my clubhouse, and I'll run it any way I want."

"But his brother ..." an obstinate writer retorted.

Growing calmer, Houk explained that Roger had only one brother. "What do you want me to do, stop a man from talking to his brother or family? If that isn't the funniest thing all year."

The press agreed, but they still wanted to speak to Roger too. Houk sarcastically told them: "He didn't hit a homer tonight. He hit one single, wore the same pair of shoes, the same glove, broke one bat, and cussed out one fan. There's the whole story. I give it to you."

Houk's commentary didn't pacify the media. A thoughtful newsman said to the manager, "The important thing for him is to make an appearance."

Houk found this acceptable but said: "I know that, and I know Maris, and now is not the time to talk to him. We'll all be more relaxed later on."

Roger finally did emerge to answer some innocuous questions from the few persevering correspondents who waited until the evening's end.

Neither the Detroit press nor the New York reporters treated Roger well. The Detroit writers emphasized that Roger was determined not to talk because of the fans' taunts, much of it "obscene."

Jack Lang led off his article for the *Long Island Press* with "Roger Maris began the big sulk today."

Joe Trimble of the *New York Daily News* chided: "If there is a slight sound of triumphant laughter from above, Babe's ghost is chortling. ... Maris secured himself in the trainer's quarters of Tiger Stadium ... looking like a culprit trying to hide."

The *New York Times* ran a story by Louis Effrat headlined, "Maris Sulks in Trainer's Room as Futile Night Changes Mood." Effrat wondered at the change in the slugger: "How does Maris feel? Well, he didn't say. In fact, Maris wouldn't say anything. Often, it has been difficult to get him to stop talking. But here it was different."

Before game two of the series, Roger and Houk had a meeting unrelated to Roger's conduct with the press. Roger discusses the pre-game meeting in *Roger Maris at Bat* and reveals: "We discussed the whole thing. Some of the writers were spreading rumors that Houk had given me orders to talk to the press and not hide. What a lot of bull! ... Ralph actually told me that whatever I did was my business. He wouldn't interfere in my business. That would have surprised a lot of writers if they had really known what happened."

Roger would have more to say following game two of the series. The Yanks lost, delaying the pennant clincher, but Roger hit his fifty-seventh home run off a Frank Lary fastball in the third. The awesome smash hit the facade in the stands and bounced back on the field. Rightfielder Al Kaline retrieved the ball and threw it into the visiting team's dugout.

His first homer in eight games was "a big one for Roger," said Houk. "Psychologically, it should do him a world of good He hadn't hit one since last Saturday, and he was aware of that, too. Maybe that was getting him down." "He got it," Mantle said, "and I think it will give him a big lift. I also think he has a helluva shot at the record." Roger was now one up on Ruth.

When the press descended on Roger after the game, a reporter asked a tactless question: "Wasn't it nice of Kaline to throw the ball back in?" With prairie frankness and artlessness, Roger simply answered, "It was nice for Al to have done that, but I guess anyone would have done it." The local press seized on Roger's answer as "ungrateful." The *New York Times* headlines stressed the slugger's silence and bitterness: "Maris' Big Bat Speaks Louder Than He Does;" "57th Homer Gets Ace Talking again, but Not Effusively;" "Abusive Crowd, 'Bad Press' Embitter Yank Slugger."

Roger's latest homer excited not only the press and the fans following the home-run chase, but also activated Casey the computer, which set the odds. The electronic brain programmed by the Statistical Tabulating Corporation gave twenty-to-one odds against Roger breaking the mark in 154 games, predicting instead 62 home runs in 162 games.

Casey went to work again after the series finale when Roger stroked number fifty-eight. With two out in the Yankee sixth, Roger took a Jim Bunning pitch to the deepest part of Tiger Stadium. The ball hit the screen, and what would have been number fifty-eight became a triple instead The Yankees had a 4-2 lead in the eighth. They seemed certain to take the game, but Roger would be homerless. However, the usually reliable Moose Skowron made a throwing error that led to a 4-4 tie in regulation time, which gave Roger two more opportunities to hit.

In the twelfth, with two outs, the count went to 1-1 on Tony Kubek. He smacked a hit through the middle, bringing Roger up to the plate. Terry Fox, the pitcher, had only been victimized for five homers during the season.

An unidentified correspondent claimed that the Detroit bench cheered for Roger to belt number fifty-eight. Roger didn't disappoint them, putting the ball between the first and second decks. Roger knew he had number fifty-eight when he crossed home plate, but "after the game," he said, "I realized only Babe Ruth has hit more homers than me. That means an awful lot."

The Yankee bench exploded when the ball landed in the seats. "It was one of the warmest things I've seen all year," Bob Cerv said. "We all knew how tough it's been for Rog, and I guess we all decided right then, all at once, that we wanted him to know how much we were for him."

The excitement carried over to the clubhouse where Roger called number fifty-eight "The Greatest Thrill of the Year." Maris now needed three runs to surpass Babe Ruth's homer record — and only three games remained before Frick's 154-game limit.

Skipper Ralph Houk expressed his opinion on the 154-game deadline. "It's got to be an official record if he does it in 162," the manager remarked. "He'll have sixty-one in one season, won't he? He'll have more than anybody else ever had, won't he?"

Chapter XII
Countdown to 154

The Yankees met their next challenge in a three-game series against Baltimore. For Roger, the arithmetic was simple: he needed two to tie, three to overcome Ruth according to Frick's 154-game rule. Appropriately, the greatest challenge to the Babe's record would come in Ruth's native city. Baltimore's Memorial Stadium posed an especially difficult problem, for Roger had made only one hit there all year, and it had been nullified by a rain-out. Sluggers had hit only 101 homers in Baltimore in the 1961 season, and visiting teams made only 42 of those runs.

In addition to the daily abuse from the stands, Roger received an avalanche of hostile letters and telegrams. "A lot of people in this country must think it's a crime to have anyone break Ruth's record," Roger said. One telegram "wanted me to know I was a lousy hitter and shouldn't be hitting this many home runs." "I'm learning a lot about people, that's for sure," the Fargo athlete observed.

On the eve of the showdown series, Roger startled the baseball world by revealing that he was considering asking Houk to give him a day off. A day off would leave only two games in which to hit two or three homers. "I'm bushed," Roger said. "This has been a long, tiresome season. I can't wait for it to end."

Roger had practical reasons for wanting the time off. He had a poor hitting record in doubleheaders and a feeble mark in the Orioles' park: two for 15 or .133. Maris also wanted to sit out during the game pitched by lefty Steve Barber. "He's rough on me," Roger said. However, Houk had no plans to let Roger rest. The manager stood firm: "I'm thinking of just one thing,the pennant. If the pennant was clinched and he asked me, I would probably let him out of it."

Several weeks before the Yanks came to town, pitcher Barber admitted that he "wouldn't feel too bad if either [Maris or Mantle] hit number 60 off me, unless it cost me a ball game."

The other Birds' hurler in Roger's upcoming twin bill, Skinny Brown, the right-handed knuckleballer, revealed: "Personally, I would like to see Maris break Babe Ruth's record of 60 homers, but I'd hate to be the one to throw the ball. I won't walk him on purpose. I'll just throw them and pray just like everyone else."

Yanks' catcher Elston Howard, an expert on first-rate pitching, saw a tough road for Roger. "The pitching they've got here is pretty darn good," Howard said. "That Barber is one of the best left-handers in the business. He can blister you with that hard stuff, and when you get too set for that, he can come in there with a good slider. Skinny Brown throws knuckleballs....When Brown's got it, you aren't hitting him very much."

The computers gave neither Roger nor Mantle much chance of breaking Ruth's record. According to the IBM 1400 digital computer, Mantle's odds were zero out of 100, and Roger's, nine out of 100. The computer predicted that Maris would make his sixty-first homer in game 159.

The weather complicated the situation. Hurricane Esther threatened to force the cancellation of the doubleheader. The Yankees next played in Boston, another city potentially in the hurricane's path up the Atlantic Coast.

While the baseball world engaged in endless debates and emotional diatribes on Roger's chances of and ability to surpass Ruth, the slugger had his mind on other matters. In the hours before the game, Roger went to Johns Hopkins Hospital and the bedside of Frank Sliwka, the gravely ill four-year-old son of a former Senator farmhand. "It took my mind completely off my problems and the ball game," Roger told Baltimore's Lou Grasmick.

"What have I got to lose?" Roger said. "This kid was so sick. It shook me up to see the little fellow lying there with so many big problems." Roger visited the youngster once more; he died a week after the Yanks left Baltimore.

Roger did not care to publicize the visit. When the writers heard about it and tried to "exploit" the story, Maris prevailed upon them to drop the matter.

"This visit was typical of Roger," said Big Julie. "What he did, he did because it was the decent thing to do, not because it would look good in print."

Herschel Lashkowitz also remembers the unnoticed kindnesses of his fellow Fargoan. Lashkowitz served on the national board of the Multiple Sclerosis Society and enlisted Roger's assistance in fundraising. With the approval of Yankee management, Roger became society co-chairperson along with Shirley Temple Black. "He was by no means a token co-chairperson," said the former mayor. "He visited hospitals, nurseries, and spoke whenever asked to advance the cause of patient care and research."

Lashkowitz added: "Roger did many such good deeds during his life. All he asked was anonymity for his participation."

Roger's involvement in charitable work sometimes resulted in misunderstandings with the press. On one occasion Roger did not keep a luncheon date with a writer, reportedly because he was visiting children at a nearby hospital.

Roger's hospital visits took his mind off the immense challenge that awaited him at the ball park, but near game time, Roger remembered the media crush that awaited him before the game and after. In the twin bill at Baltimore, the force of Hurricane Esther joined with the pitching of Barber and Brown to stymie Roger. In the words of Dick Young, "The chauvinistic wind whipped up its proud fury" to safeguard the Babe's record in his native town. "The misty advance gusts of Hurricane Esther blew hard from right field into the face of Roger Maris."

Roger did nothing against Barber in the opener, not even a long foul. Following a zero-for-three opener, Roger managed one for five against the knuckleballers Brown and Hoyt Wilhelm.

The excitement in the nightcap came when Roger slammed one into the right-field seats, but the ball went foul by a wide margin. Roger faced Wilhelm in the ninth, swung, and missed. The Yanks, however, took a 3-1 nightcap victory to clinch a tie for the pennant.

The simple homer mathematics had now become sobering: two to tie, three to overcome in 154 games. Could he do it? Roger answered with a slight smile, "You'd almost have to be a Houdini to do it."

A reporter asked an obvious question about the pressure. "Pressure, what pressure?" Roger responded. "The only pressure I have is before and after a game. I'm relaxed during a game. It's a relief to get out there."

Game 154 attracted more media, press, and photographers than at any other time during the pursuit of the record. More than seventy newsmen covered the Yankees. "Most of the writers left me alone," Roger said. "They would come up, mutter a few words of encouragement, and walk away. It was as if they were afraid to break the spell that seemed to be encircling the whole field."

Roger's name appeared on the lineup card without his usual follow-up. Mantle's abscessed hip had sidelined him. Yogi Berra took Mantle's slot, and Berra offered some sage advice: "Pick out three good balls and swing from the butt. That's three homers and ... the record in 154 games."

Pappas, the Orioles' pitcher, had the lowest earned run average of the Baltimore starters. The accomplished hurler was not an easy opponent. In his career he had chalked up more than two hundred wins.

Only slightly more than 21,000 people sat in the stands, 10,000 fewer than turned out for the doubleheader. The Oriole fans, never very sympathetic to the Yankees, came to the park viewing Roger as an infidel who did not believe the Babe's record sacrosanct. "People all looked at me in a funny way," Roger remarked. "It was as if they were studying me to see if I were cracking up. It was as if a mysterious pressure was pushing down on the whole park."

Roger walked around the locker room, picking up objects and studying them, trying to find something to do with his hands. "I looked at all the newspapers lying around and smoked a few cigarettes," Roger related to the press. "I knew that if I just sat down in front of my locker I'd tighten up in a hundred knots."

Meanwhile, two hopeful wives prepared to view the game: Mrs. Claire Ruth, from her apartment on Manhattan's Riverside Drive and Mrs. Pat Maris, from the KMBC-TV studio in Kansas City.

As he went to bat in the first inning, Roger heard the Yankee bench urging him on: "C'mon, Rog, let's see you get one!" "Hey, Rog, let's have our party tonight!" He put good wood on the ball, but it did not get up high enough in the air. Earl Robinson snared the line drive in right.

While Roger waited in the box in the third inning, he spoke to Oriole catcher Gus Triandos. "Roger, quit talking to me," the catcher teased, "or people will think I'm getting you good pitches." After ball one, Roger swung and missed, and then took another ball. Then it came. "I knew it was gone as soon as I hit it," Roger said. The ball cleared a fifteen-foot wall at the 380-foot mark. Roger had number 59, his first homer in Memorial Stadium in 1961.

Roger thought he had three more chances possibly.

Pappas didn't appear when Roger came up for his third turn.

Instead, Dick (Turkey Neck) Hall, the 34-year-old veteran from St. Louis, confronted Roger Maris, the 27-year-old from Fargo. In coming up against Hall in the fourth, Roger faced a quality hurler, who ended the season with a 3.06 ERA and 79 strikeouts in 94 innings.

Hall used a tough side-arming motion to deliver an inside pitch, as the count was one and one. Roger's hit reached the right-field seats but had gone foul. Hall struck out Roger on a two-and-two fastball. Roger later commented: "That pitch wasn't close to being a strike. I never should have swung."

Roger had one more shot at Hall in the seventh, perhaps his last chance of the day. Everyone in the Yank bullpen came to the fence. "Come on, Roger baby," shouted pitcher Jim Coates. "Hit it to me. If I have to go fifteen rows into the stands, I'll catch that Number 60 for you."

The umpire called "strike" at the first pitch; at the next pitch, Roger struck. The crowd rose to its feet, but the ball went into the right-field bleachers, foul by ten to twenty feet. "From the second I hit it, I knew it didn't have a chance," said Roger. He hit on the next pitch. It looked like a homer as it soared toward right field, but then the wind caught it. The ball died when Robinson snared it about ten feet from the right-field wall.

"The way Hall was getting us out, with that screwy wind-up of his I figured then I was dead — that I wouldn't get another bat," Roger said. Instead, the Yankee batters gave Maris one more chance: he came to bat in the ninth inning, feeling an atmosphere of pressure to get Number 60. "After that fly ball," Arthur Daley wrote in the *New York Times,* "the screws were tightening on the rack that was torturing him. It was a slow torture because he had belted a beauty that was just foul."

Hoyt Wilhelm topped the list of pitchers Roger did not want to face. Baseball's premiere knuckleballer, Hall of Famer Wilhelm maintained the lowest ERA — 2.52 — after twenty years of playing. Wilhelm had more wins, more saves, more innings pitched, and more strikeouts than any other reliever in the history of baseball. In addition, the talented pitcher had given up only 5 homers in 112 innings. Roger had struck out against Wilhelm on four pitches the previous evening.

"When we came in to bat in the ninth," Roger said, "absolutely the last guy in the world I wanted to see came walking in from the Oriole bull pen: Hoyt Wilhelm. ... He kills you with that knuckle ball. It's hard to describe and hard to hit. It sort of floats up to the plate and then does a little dance, as though someone is holding it on a string."

Manager Luman Harris sent in Wilhelm when the Yankees led 4-2 and the game's outcome seemed hardly in doubt. Whitey Herzog, then outfielder for Baltimore, comments in *Sixty-One* on Harris's controversial decision: "The game was pretty much over. There was just no reason to use Hoyt other than to make it tough on Roger personally. ... They just didn't want Roger to set the record in Ruth's hometown."

Peter Golenbock in the Spring 1978 *Baseball Quarterly* files an illuminating report on the instructions Hoyt Wilhelm received from the Baltimore manager. The controversial Golenbock quotes Paul Richards, who had managed the Orioles for most of the season, but not for game 154. "Wilhelm, a quiet man, was more than willing to throw Maris a fast ball or two to give him a chance, but Paul Richards, the crusty manager told Wilhelm, 'If you throw him anything but knuckleballs, it will cost you $5,000.'"

As Roger stepped up to home plate, he flashed some of his Fargo humor. Home plate umpire Ed Runge recalled the anecdote during the 1987 Roger Maris Celebrity Benefit Golf Tournament. "In the last days of the season, when new players were coming up from the farm teams, players would run to me and ask about the hurlers: 'what's this guy throw?' Well, Roger Maris steps up in this building pressure, and then looks at me, with a straight face and asks, 'Hey, what does that guy out there throw?'"

Catcher Triandos's briefing had no humor: "Well, this is your last shot." "Don't think my collar isn't tight," Roger said to the backstop. The first pitch, a knuckleball, came as no surprise and was a called strike. Wilhelm served the second low, as Roger, checking his swing, fouled it back. Roger never had a chance to swing on the third pitch. Maris turned his body to hit what he thought would be an inside offering. However, the ball accidentally hit the bat and squirted down the first base line. There Wilhelm personally preserved Ruth's record by tagging Roger out.

Roger's four masterful, powerful swings in four of his five at bats had yielded only one homer. Still, the fans had seen a remarkable, gutsy performance under unprecedented pressure. Even the Baltimore fans appreciated the effort. Wrote Bob Considine for the

Hearst Headline Service: "The quiet young man was given one of the warmest and most encouraging ovations I've ever heard."

After the inning, umpire Charlie Berry stopped Roger, who was headed to the outfield, to say, "Son, you've had a fine year. Just keep up the good work."

Locker-room buddy John Blanchard remembered: "I came running out with Roger's glove as we headed for the outfield. I told him, 'I'm very sorry that you didn't make it. But I just want to tell you that I'm a proud ball player to be playing on the same team as you.' Roger just smiled. Praise from a teammate meant a lot to him."

Game 154 had three final outs left, as the Yankees marched to another pennant. Ralph Houk had earned a select honor: he became the twelfth rookie manager to win a flag.

During the locker-room celebration, Roger expressed relief that the pressure was off. "I could start learning to live like a human being again," he told the assembled media. "During the last couple of weeks, I was half nuts. I had splitting headaches. I was smoking twice as much as I normally do, and the crowds, the tensions, the same questions over and over were driving me out of my mind."

An Associated Press story reported that Pat Maris in Kansas City appeared "on the verge of tears" after watching her husband's gallant assault on Ruth's record. Pat plaintively wondered, "Rog, why did you swing at that one?" when Maris missed the ninth-inning knuckler. However, at the end of the game she smiled, "There's always next year."

The Associated Press also reported that during the game Pat exchanged seats with another viewer in the Kansas City TV studio. The release continued, "She remembered she and Roger have a superstition that whenever she leaves her seat while watching a game, it puts a hex on him. 'I knew I shouldn't have moved out of that chair.'"

Pat Maris later scoffed at the report. "Many of the ball players' wives are superstitious," she observed, "but I am not." However, she admitted in a 1962 *Look* article that she had arrived at KMBC-TV a "little too late" to see Roger's fifty-ninth, but she had pledged to be there in person for number 60.

Mrs. Babe Ruth, watching from Riverside Drive, liked what she saw. She told the *New York Journal-American:* "That was one record I didn't want broken. I have the highest regard for Roger Maris. He is a fine hitter. But the Babe loved that record and he wanted to be known as the king of home runs forever."

Roger's inability to match Babe's record spelled the defeat of the computers. The *New York Times* ran a story headlined "There Is No Joy at IBM For Casey Has Struck Out." The IBM 1481 electronics computer named Casey had predicted on August 30 that Roger had a 55 percent chance of hitting 61 within 154.

The Statistical Tabulating Corporation of New York had also made predictions, twenty different ones, beginning on August 29. Its computer failed to predict Roger's 59-homer finish in 154 games. Its last calculations gave Roger only 58.

Roger tried his best to tie Babe's record. Kubek praised Roger's efforts: "He gave it everything a man could give. ... [Wilhelm's ball] was almost impossible to hit. ... It wriggled like a snake, and it was fast." Bobby Richardson agreed that Baltimore "made it rough" for Roger. Richardson's first strike had come on a Wilhelm throw "so fast and unusual I didn't know for sure whether it was a knuckle ball or maybe some kind of crazy fast ball."

Sportswriters had varied opinions on Roger's inability to break the record in 154 games. Old-guard writers were understandably pleased; however, they gave Roger plaudits for his heroic effort.

Oliver Kuechle of the *Milwaukee Journal* gloated over the defeat of an unexceptional player with little color. Wrote Kuechle, Roger "has never hit 300 in the majors. He has little of the particularly imposing physique commonly associated with the true slugger. He has been only average in the field. He is often surly. There just isn't anything deeply heroic about the man."

Writers like Frank Gibbons of the *Cleveland Press* resorted to poor humor. According to Gibbons, "Among the many things Roger Maris has accomplished this year was to teach a number of players the definition of the word 'asterisk.' An asterisk is singularly appropriate for the boy from Dakota. ... I still can't understand the resentment throughout the land over Commissioner Ford Frick's ruling that he had to break Babe Ruth's record in 154 decisions or settle for the asterisk if he did it in more. Why, even Mrs. Maris said it wouldn't be the same as Ruth, and I have it from solid sources that she is his best fan."

Still, new admirers in the press recognized what Roger had done under the existing conditions that existed. Al Abrams of the *Pit-*

tsburgh Post-Gazette wrote: "No one ... will take away from him the glory, the glitter, the publicity, and the pressure, all of which engulfed him. ... Maris went down fighting to gain the respect and admiration of even those fans who didn't want to see the exalted Ruth's record broken. I know he provided me with a memorable thrill which will take its place alongside the best I have ever witnessed."

Bob Maisel of the *Baltimore Sun* applauded Roger and offered the feelings of fans from Babe Ruth's city: "One man [at game 154] seemed to express the crowd when, while leaving the stadium, he said, 'I came in here hoping the guy would never hit another home run, and I left pulling for him to tie Ruth. ... He gave it such a try that he converted me.'" Maisel added, "Nobody will ever be able to accuse Roger Maris of not having the stomach to battle the tensest of situations right down to the end."

The *Sporting News* expressed happiness that "Babe Ruth is still the king," but it also observed that in game 154 Roger "probably won himself more friends and admirers than he had all season. ... In this final game, Roger Maris was a tremendous competitor."

Jimmie Foxx congratulated Roger in a telegram: "You have broken my record and Hank's [Greenberg]. May God give you strength to break all records." Foxx signed Greenberg's name to the wire. Greenberg, the Tiger great responsible for signing Roger, had done game 154 for national television.

The Yankees' dressing room buzzed with the obvious question: now that game 154 was history, did Roger agree with Frick's ruling? Roger responded: "He's making the rules. I've got nothing to say about it. I'd like to have had it in 154, but that's the breaks of the game."

Although Roger fell short in 154 games, he left no doubt that the season was 162 games. "I'll keep playing," he promised. "I want to give myself every chance. I'd like to see what happens. It would be nice if I could hit a couple more."

Roger also wanted the ball he had hit to make number 59. Robert Reitz, the 32-year-old Baltimorean who caught the ball, was reluctant to surrender the memento. "I'd like to have it," Roger said, as he offered Reitz an autographed ball in return. Reitz posed with Roger between innings and then asked for two World Series tickets. Roger held out two autographed balls, but Reitz didn't budge. Surprised, Roger asked, "You gonna keep that?" Reitz nodded.

Ducky Casseres, an attendant in the umpires' room, tried to

negotiate. He would see that Reitz received two tickets to each of the first two games of the World Series if Reitz showed up with the ball at Yankee Stadium. Reitz and a friend listened and started to return to the bleachers. "Just a minute," said Ducky. "Let me mark that ball, just to make sure you show up with the right one."

"Reitz went as far to ask Roger to come to a press conference at his cousin's store," Fargo's Bill Weaver related. "Roger agreed, but when he got out there, Reitz asked for money. Roger told him to keep the ball."

Reitz announced: "There is a lot of rumors around that it might be worth $25 or even $2,500. That's a lot of money for a man who's unemployed."

"I'd like to have it," said Roger, "but I'm not looking to get rid of that kind of money for it."

Lou Grasmick even drove Roger to Reitz's home, negotiating with Reitz while Roger waited in the car. When Reitz insisted on a fixed $2,500 price, Roger told Grasmick, "No dice. Let's go."

Reitz soon admitted that after he had caught the ball, the pressure of still having it kept him from sleeping at night. He began smoking six packs of cigarettes daily. Offers for the ball came in: $1,000 from a Maryland resident who wanted the ball for his private collection, and a $500 bid from a Miami fan. However, Reitz remained adamant: "That ball's the best thing that ever happened in my life. The Yankees have everything, but I have the ball."

Six days after Reitz caught the ball, the Sports Boosters of Maryland retrieved it. They gave Reitz $500 for the ball, then turned it over to Roger. Reitz donated his money to the Associated Catholic Charities of Baltimore.

Before he resumed his quest for the home run record, he had a "confession," a revelation to be more precise. He had been losing patches of hair on the back of his head. "I was worried," he admitted. "I thought I had a disease or something. But the doctor told me that it was a case of nerves from the tension and pressure I've been under." The hair would continue to fall out, however there was no need to worry, "because when it's all over and I'm calmed down again, the hair will grow back."

One reporter tried to cheer Roger up by telling him that his case was not unique in baseball. Marshall Samuels, a former publicity director for the Cleveland Indians, also lost hair during the pennant chase of 1954. "How is he now?" asked an interested Roger Maris. "He's almost bald," replied the journalist. "That's a helluva thing to be telling me," the slugger said.

Marshall Samuels notwithstanding, a more relaxed Roger reported to the ballpark for the Yanks' final game in Baltimore.

Roger Maris with Mrs. Babe Ruth, 1962.
(Courtesy of New York Yankees)

Chapter XIII
Three for Number 61:
Maris, Stallard, Durante

With the pressure of the 154-game deadline now history, Roger Maris seemed more at ease. Still, all the player's tension had not dissipated. Newsman Jack Lang observed, "Throughout any conversation, whether it be a period of post-game questioning or merely a relaxed conversation in a hotel lobby, Roger's right leg jiggles nervously. ... Maris is and probably will always remain a nervous man."

Despite his nervousness, the slugger enjoyed a pleasant day before playing game 155. For the second successive year, Roger Maris received the Sultan of Swat award. Presented annually by the Maryland Professional Baseball Players Association, the $2,500 jeweled crown honored a player who "came closest to doing the things Babe Ruth as a player was noted for ... overall performance, and not necessarily leading home run hitter."

An additional honor came later that evening, before Roger replaced the still-injured Mantle in center field. The Oriole Advocates, a civic booster group, surprised Maris with a three-foot trophy, "not for hitting 59 home runs, but for his sportsmanship." The trophy inscription praised him for earning "the ultimate respect and admiration of Oriole Fans."

At bat Maris countered Jack Fisher's pitches with a strikeout, a fly to short center, a rollout to first, and a fly to left. His two hits excited the fans, but each time the ball sailed foul as it went into the stands. After the game, the slugger commented: "I had good pitches to hit. It's nice to know that the 154 games are over, and that you don't have to push for anything."

Some observers speculated that a pitcher might groove one for Roger to gain press coverage for himself as the "lucky" hurler. When asked if he ever discussed this problem with members of the opposing team, Roger responded, "I don't want anybody to see me talking with a pitcher. They'll think I am setting him up."

Roger had little hope of breaking the Babe's record in Boston's

Fenway Park, the last stop on the road. Earl Torgensen, a member of the Yanks' coaching staff, had played in Boston and recalled the winds' ferocity: "Some days up here, it was enough to make you sit down and cry." Fenway had a relatively distant wall in right center — not an easy target for lefty swingers. Although he had made four round-trippers there and had victimized scheduled pitcher Bill Monbouquette twice that year, Roger noted that if the wind "blows at all in this series, I hope it's blowing out. I can use all the help I can get."

In the opener, Mantle returned to the lineup against the Red Sox ace rookie Don Schwall and hit number 54, his last home run of the season. Roger only managed a single and two walks against right-hander Schwall. Maris' offense against righty Monbo — the Bosox's second most winning pitcher — consisted of a walk and a single. For the third straight game, Roger failed to make a homer.

Bill Monboquette had no qualms about being the pitcher of the record-breaking homer. "I wouldn't mind it if it didn't hurt me. If I were leading by a big margin, let him do it and I would say good luck to him. He's a helluva hitter and he's hit them off a lot of people."

Roger's three walks in the Bosox series came from Boston hurlers who were just trying to win the game. Monbo also had one big concern: "I don't want to walk him in a close game if I think it's going to hurt me. I also don't want to give him anything good to hit at."

Frustration gripped Roger during the two-game set. "The way this is going," Roger said, "I don't think I'll hit 60 by the end of the season." He admitted that he swung at bad pitches but only because "they pitch me high, they pitch me low, but mostly they pitch me outside. They're going to keep making it difficult for me by not giving me anything good to hit at." Maris' opponents seemed to avoid serving him good pitches; they dreaded being labeled as "the pitcher who gave Maris number 60 or 61." Maris believed that even at Yankee Stadium only a series of pitcher mistakes would allow him the hits needed to break the record.

Leonard Schecter showed little empathy for Maris in his coverage of the Red Sox series for the New York Post. "This latest cry of Maris is an old one," wrote Schecter, "that there is a conspiracy abroad in the land to prevent him from hitting home runs. ... Once poor Maris dreamed that when he reached 59 the pitchers' union would capitulate and collaborate in the artistic construction of a home run record. Alas, this was not to be."

Following the Boston series, the Yankees returned home to New York for the rest of the season. Pat joined Roger there for the final week of ball playing, and as his wife noted, "The only thing that we didn't talk about was baseball." The Marises and Mantles moved into Loew's Midtown Hotel in Manhattan, while Bob Cerv recuperated from a knee operation in the hospital. The roommates gave up Big Julie's apartment as they pursued their separate lives. However, one gossip columnist alleged that a final eruption in the Mantle-Maris feud led Mickey to walk out and so terminate the living arrangements.

Pat's presence seemed to reduce Roger's stress level, with observable results. In the opener, Roger reached Baltimore pitcher Jack Fisher for a line-drive single to center in the first inning, setting the stage for the second at bat in the third inning.

With two out and the count two and two, Roger sent the right-hander's high curve into the upper right field stands, about three feet fair. The ball slammed into the back of a seat and bounced back onto the field. Oriole rightfielder Earl Robinson picked it up and tossed it to first-base umpire Ed Hurley, who lobbed it to Walley Moses, the Yankee first-base coach. Moses rolled it to the Yankee bench as Maris arrived there amid a tumultuous roar from the crowd.

Joe Trimble called the blast "the Golden Gopher" in the *New York Daily News*. The Yanks applauded Roger and his historic homer. Over 19,000 fans stood in ovation, clapping wildly until Maris came out of the dugout and waved his cap to them. "The guys kept urging me out," Roger said. "I didn't know if it was the right thing to do or not. I thought I might feel silly. They [the crowd] was very nice."

After the game an ecstatic Roger confessed: "It's the greatest thing that has happened to me, probably the greatest thing that will ever happen to me ... now that I've got it, I'd like to get one more, just one more."

On the post-game Red Barber show, Mrs. Ruth, gracious now that the 154-game limit had passed, told Roger, "The Babe would have wished you well. If the Babe were here, he'd be just as thrilled as I am. Congratulations on a great year and good luck in the series."

Kissing Mrs. Ruth, Roger shyly admitted to her, "I'm glad I didn't break Babe Ruth's record in 154 games. This record is enough for me." When Maris later recalled this statement in *Roger Maris at Bat,* he emphasized his sincerity: "I meant it then. I mean it now."

In the after-game celebration, Roger complimented the Baltimore pitcher. "Fisher wasn't fishing around. He tried to get me out. He was moving the ball in and out. I think he was trying to hit the outside corner with that pitch, but it slipped." Baltimore catcher Gus Triandos remarked that Fisher's surrendered eighteenth homer of the season "was a helluva curve. It broke big — just right for Roger."

Pat, the other members of the Maris family, and all the citizens of Fargo shared in the joy of Roger's sixtieth home run. "He hit 60 for me," exalted Pat Maris. "I was just kind of hoping he would hit one because I just arrived from Raytown, and he said he would hit one for me. When he did I just thanked God, that's all." Roger's thrilled father reported, "I feel great. I hope he gets another one." Mrs. Corrine Maris revealed her emotional reaction to her son's feat: "Whenever he'd hit a homer, it brought tears to my eyes. I was overjoyed by the sixtieth."

The Associated Press recorded the sentiments of some Fargoans. Monsignor L.J. Arrell, pastor of St. Mary's, Roger's boyhood parish, thought it "great [that] Roger could do it." Bill Ross, president of the Fargo-Moorhead Twins and an avid Yankee fan, remarked, "I sure feel good about it. Why not? I'm glad a Fargo Yankee did it."

Baseball Commissioner Frick watched the game in his Bronxville, New York, home. He called the Maris blast "a marvelous thing" and added: "It will go into the books as a record for a 162-game season while Ruth's record stands as the mark for 154 games."

In a report on the Cincinnati Reds' clinching of the National League flag, the Associated Press reiterated Frick. Both the Reds and Maris had reached their "goals," but Cincinnati made it "in plenty of time," while Roger came in a "little late." So, according to the Frick edict, Roger's achievement "will be listed in a separate category from Ruth's."

Frick's adamant refusal to recognize Maris' accomplishment angered Fargoans. Roger's former coach Sid Cichy hoped the slugger would smack number 61 "because of the curbs put on him by Frick." As Cichy observed, "Roger could have hit 70 home runs if he had played only day games, as Ruth did."

Roger's dad still felt that the Frick ruling "was fair, but it should have been made when the 162-game schedule was adopted, not in July when Roger was well in front."

Ignoring the controversy, Fargo Mayor Lashkowitz proclaimed

Roger Maris Day. The city's favorite son had "put on the cloak of baseball immortality. By his actions, on and off the field, [Maris has] reflected great credit on his home town of Fargo and has become an inspiration to all generations."

In anticipation of Roger's hitting one more home run, two attractive offers heightened the excitement surrounding game 158. A Sacramento, California, restaurateur had promised $5,000 and an expense-free trip out West to the fan who caught the record-breaking sixty-first homer. Officials of the 1962 Seattle World's Fair offered transportation to the fair in exchange for the historic baseball.

Roger chose to take the next day off and avoided a confrontation with the tough pitcher Steve Barber. The Yankees had a free day after the Oriole series and before their final competition with the Red Sox. Maris "figured taking two days off in a row would set me up for the final weekend and the World Series." Houk agreed: the slugger was "completely bushed, mentally and physically. He had never a moment of peace in the last month. It's all new to him. He hasn't been trained for it."

A reporter asked Houk, "Why's he bushed?" The skipper retorted, "You'd be bushed too if you had 40 guys asking you questions every day."

The press hounded him for taking a day off when he was only one homer away from a record. "I can't win for losing with you guys," Roger told them. "First, you say I've played too many games to break the record. Then I don't play, and you ask how I could miss a game when I'm going for the record."

Even skipper Houk's insistence that "It was my decision, not his" did not satisfy the press. Disgruntled newspaperman Leonard Schecter of the *New York Post* called Roger "stubborn" because "he had taken it into his head that he needed a day off and yesterday was it." The reporter cited an unnamed Yankee who had told him, "I don't think I would have done that. Seems to me if you got a chance at a record like that, you do everything you can to get it."

According to Schecter, by taking a day off Roger might have missed the opportunity to make "the record a lot more elusive by hitting 62 or 63."

Houk repeated his approval of Roger's action during the Oriole finale as Maris suited up for the Red Sox series opener. "He'll be a refreshed player as a result of his rest," the skipper remarked. "I think he did the right thing passing up Wednesday's game. The pressure really was building up on him."

Red Sox pitcher Monboquette kept up the pressure on Roger in a tough, well-pitched 2-1 game. The home run king walked in the ninth, stole second, and came in on John Blanchard's single. Roger had only another walk from the right-hander that game.

Leonard Schecter's strange report on the game focused on Roger's reply when questioned about his "changed" personality in the last few weeks of the season: "Which way can you go. Bad. You get irritated quickly. Let's face it. It gets a little tough." Schecter editorialized on Maris' answer: "Success makes people change, and money. Slowly, inevitably, Roger Maris has become less the charming grouch he used to be and more the busy, harried, far less personable grouch. There's been less desire to sit around and chew the fat, less effort to explain himself, more eagerness to be off, to be some place else, preferably where nobody knows him."

On Saturday afternoon, more than 19,000 fans came to the stadium in the hope of seeing number 61 and perhaps being fortunate enough to catch the ball. Bosox rookie Don Schwall provided tough opposition by handling Roger with a low fast ball. Maris walked in the first inning, grounded out in the third and fifth, and singled in the eighth. Schwall later commented on Roger's game 161: "My best pitch is my fast ball, which can be kept low and away from these left-handed sluggers. I was lucky enough to do just this most of the day and keep him from making me the guy who gave up his 61st homer. ... No one really wants to be the fellow to give up that record homer."

Roger sounded enthusiastic as he prepared for game number 162 and his last chance at the record. "I've got four cracks at it," he told the press, "and I'm going to try to take advantage of every one of them. I'm going to start swinging the first moment I leave the dugout."

Before the big game, Maris had a baloney and eggs breakfast at the Stage Deli. "Roger hardly said anything," Big Julie recalled. "He was nervous. He did not say anything about that 61st homer, but I had no doubt that he was thinking about it. In fact, we never, ever discussed the homer race. We'd speak about our kids. But I thought I'd break the rule on the last day. It might break the pressure a little."

Pat Maris spent the pregame hours with the other players' wives.

"I also prayed to my favorite, St. Jude," she said, "as I had done all season. He is the patron saint for lost causes. ... I had felt all along that Roger's chances of beating the record were nearly hopeless. I prayed the hardest that Roger would be protected from injuries. He had had so many. Above all, I have always prayed for what Roger and I believe in most — to do your level best no matter what you do."

The cool fall day of October 1, 1961, drew only 23,154 people to the historic game. Fans packed the right-field seats, hoping to catch the ball and win the prize money.

Press consensus had Roger facing rookie pitcher Tracy Stallard, a 23-year-old, 6 foot 5 rightie, with a 2-6 record and an ERA in the high fours. "There was not much tension as far as I was concerned," said Stallard. "My mind was not preoccupied with the homer record. What I wanted was a win so that the Red Sox would remember me on a positive note for 1962. I had faced Maris before and he had not damaged me."

Stallard won the battle in the first inning as a change-up produced a weak flyball to left. In the fourth inning of a still scoreless game, the first pitch curved and sailed high. Home-plate umpire Bill Kinnaman called Stallard's fastball ball two. The crowd sensed a walk, and the stadium resounded with boos,

Trying to ignore the crowd, Stallard threw a fastball that came in low but directly across the plate. Roger was ready for it. He sent a towering drive 380 feet from home plate and into the lower right-field seats, about 10 rows in, sailing over the head of Boston's Lu Clinton.

Roger ran his typical homer,head down as he rounded the bases, with no showboating. He said later,

> I saw it was a good fastball. I was ready and I connected. As soon as I hit it, I knew it was number 61; it was the only time that the number of the homer ever flashed into my mind as I hit it. Then I heard the tremendous roar of the crowd. I could see them all standing. Then my mind went blank.
>
> I couldn't even think as I went around the bases. I couldn't tell you what crossed my mind. I don't think anything did. I was in a fog. I was all fogged out from a very, very hectic season and an extremely difficult month.

When Roger connected at 2:43 p.m. and the ball left the park, John Blanchard noticed that one of the spectators, Mrs. Babe Ruth, had tears in her eyes. Ironically, the Roger's sixty-first home run landed near the spot where Ruth had hit his sixtieth on September 30, 1927.

The Yankees' Scooter Phil Rizutto held the mike for the historic homer and announced a record number of "Holy Cows." The entire Yankee dugout shook Roger's hand and then pushed him out to take a bow. After he returned to the bench, Hector Lopez and Moose Skowron pushed him out for another bow. More cheers rang out as he trotted out to center field after the inning.

As he stepped up to the plate again in the sixth, Roger told former Tribe teammate and current Red Sox catcher Russ Nixon, "It would be great to hit another homer." Roger did not get his wish: he fanned on a three-and-two pitch. When he faced lefty Chet Nichols in the eighth, he popped up to the second baseman.

Roger Maris hit home run number 61 on his 588th official trip to the plate. His first homer had come in game 11; in actuality, Roger made 61 homers in 152 games, counting the tie game.

After the game, Roger paid tribute to Tracy Stallard, who "was man enough to pitch to me to get me out. When he got behind me, he came in with the pitch to try to get me out."

Stallard graciously applauded the new home-run champion. "I knew he hit the stuff out of it," the pitcher said, "but I didn't think it was going to be a home run. I turned around and then saw the thing going way up. I give Roger all the credit in the world. I gave him what I feel was my best fast ball and he hit it."

Twenty-five years later, Stallard recalled his feelings as Roger rounded the bases after hitting his 61st. "I just stood there. I didn't want to interfere with any of the celebrating that was taking place. But, no, I was not sad or depressed. I was happy for Roger. I gave it 100 percent, and so did he. He made it, and I didn't. I was happy he came through because it was something he wanted."

On the twenty-fifth anniversary of Maris' homer, Stallard appeared on the NBC "Today" show. Host Bryant Gumbel asked him if the Maris blast had been a source of "embarrassment" for the pitcher. Stallard replied that he took a " measure of pride" in the record-breaking hit that has kept the baseball world "from forgetting me."

From his strip-mining company in Coeburn, Virginia, Stallard admits that he lost contact with Roger in 1962 after meeting during spring training in 1962. "We never reminisced about that home run," Stallard said. "But I did get to learn about Roger and have always admired him as an individual who conducted himself admirably on the field and off. He was that type of family man that you have to think highly of."

Sal Durante still speaks with pride about catching the lucky ball on October 1, 1961. The 19-year-old truck driver and mechanic from Brooklyn's Coney Island section had chosen his seats carefully. During the first game, he and his fiancee Rosemarie had noticed that "all the hitters including Maris, seemed to hit the practice balls in Section 33." For the second game, Rosemarie and Sal had seats 3 and 4 in box 163D, section 33 — eight rows back of the right-field wall and about ten feet from the edge of the Yankee right-field bull pen. Even the bull pen players stood gloved and ready. As reliever Hal Reniff said, "I don't know about the others. I just feel it would be a big thrill to say I caught the 61st homer. I'd be proud to present the ball to my teammate."

Sal describes his impression of the homer: "I saw that ball coming — round, white, and beautiful. It wasn't flat or oval-shaped, like a ball that has a spin on it. That ball was hit clean and true."

Many hands reached out to snatch a bit of glory and the $5,000 bounty. No one in the stands surrounding him intended to lose the prize without a fight, but Durante was ready. Sal jumped onto his seat and caught the ball one-handed. "I fell backward over my seat and landed in the one above me," Sal said. "Everybody charged me then. I could feel hands all over me. Somebody had me by the arm, another had me by the leg, and one guy grabbed me around the neck. My right elbow was bruised. But I never let go of that apple."

Tod Wolkiewicz of Flushing sat in seat 5, box 153d. He claims that he had made a clean catch of the ball, but someone had wrestled it away from him. He said, "I had my hands on the ball and then suddenly I was on the ground. If you look at the film clips, you can see my brother, Tom, right near the ball."

Stadium personnel helped Sal escape from the battling fans and escorted him toward the Yankee bull pen for interviews and pictures.

To everyone's amazement, Sal seemed uninterested in the $5,000 promised for the ball. Durante exchanged congratulations with Maris, then astounded the home-run king by announcing: "Rog, this is your ball. You hit it and it belongs to you and every baseball fan. It's going to the Hall of Fame."

Sal's generosity overwhelmed Roger. "What do you think of that kid?" Roger said to backstop Russ Nixon during the eighth. "The boy is planning to get married and he can use the money, but he still wanted to give the ball back to me for nothing. It shows there's some good people left in this world after all."

Roger insisted that Sal "keep" the ball, collect his $5,000, and then return the historic ball. "Get what you can," Maris told Sal in Houk's presence, "and then give it to me."

Roger's "a real nice guy," said an ecstatic Sal. "I think God meant that ball for me. My family is in a financial hole at the moment and part of this $5,000 is going to help square them away."

In addition to the promised money, Yankee President Dan Topping offered Sal two season passes for the 1962 home games. Several days later, the instant celebrity and eleven of his relatives appeared on CBS-TV's "Calendar" program. On camera Sam and his brother Al Gordon staged a ceremony in which they "presented" Sal with his check. In reality, Sal would receive the check in Sacramento in November, when Sam Gordon promised a parade.

The media spotlight gave Sal a sample of what Roger Maris had undergone. Sal reflected years later, "I had some day with the press after I caught the ball. They would jump in with a new question before I had fully answered the previous one. They can put words in your mouth. For example, one reporter said that Sal Durante would write about the World Series. That was something I never said."

The press asked him if he would invite Roger Maris to his wedding. Sal remembers, "I said, 'Sure, why not?' Before I knew about it, the press told Roger he was invited to my wedding."

Twenty-nine years later, the "fame" has meant little to Sal Durante, but October 1 will always have a special significance for him. "Every year we talk about the game and relive the excitement," he said. "After all, $5,000 was a fortune for a kid who was making $60 a week."

While media attention apparently focused on Sal Durante, the press clamored for Roger Maris. The Yankee front office had issued a directive barring the press from contact with Roger until at least twenty minutes after the game. Big Julie describes the scene once the Yankees allowed the press to enter: "In all my days, I have never seen so many media people on one story. There were more writers after him than President Kennedy. It took almost five hours after the game before Pat Maris and I could see Roger. All the time he was giving out interviews."

Many of the interview questions dealt with the meaningfulness of Maris' record, since it had come after the 154-game limit. "Whether I beat Ruth's record or not is for others to say," Roger responded. "But it gives me a wonderful feeling to know that I'm the only man in history to hit 61 home runs. Nobody can take that away from me. Babe Ruth was a big man in baseball, maybe the biggest ever. I'm not saying I am of his caliber, but I'm glad to say I hit more than he did in a season."

Roger did not challenge anyone to break his record, unlike Ruth, who reportedly announced "Now let's see some son of a gun go out and match that" after he hit his sixtieth run. Instead Roger answered "no comment" when a reporter asked, "Do you think you can break your own record?"

Reporters also questioned Roger about the pressures he had endured on the way to his sixty-first home run. A relieved Roger confessed, "A thing like this can make a nervous wreck of you. The pressure was terrific, mentally much more than physically. You have no idea what it is to put up with something like this for two months. People are around you all the time. You can't eat, you can't sleep — you can't even think."

The five-hour media marathon ended when a reporter again asked Roger, "Hey, Rog, what did you hit?" Roger had heard and answered that question ad nauseam. He retorted, "A baseball. Yeah, I hit a baseball."

Pat Maris had waited for Roger for what seemed an eternity. She remembers that "Every last person had left the stadium before I got to see Roger."

The Marises met Selma and Big Julie Isaacson. In Pat's words, "We are not very big on celebrations and whooping it up," so the couples had planned on having a quiet postgame dinner at Joe Marsh's Spindle Top on West 47th Street.

As they were leaving the stadium, Big Julie noticed *New York Post* writer Milton Gross, who had scheduled an interview with Roger during the Yankees' last trip to Baltimore in 1961. Maris never appeared for the session; instead he visited a hospitalized child who died from cancer two days later. Because Roger never wanted any publicity about his hospital visits, he never told Gross why he had stood him up. Furious, the journalist wrote a scathing article tearing Roger apart. Big Julie eventually explained the situation to Gross.

Now, to make amends, Big Julie invited him to join the party and offered him an exclusive on the evening's festivities. Gross's October 2 article carried the headline "With Roger Maris, Victory Dinner."

The group stopped at St. Malachy's on West 49th Street before dinner. The Marises intended to hear evening mass but came out about two minutes later. A surprised Big Julie asked about the "quick service." Roger explained that a priest who had spotted Roger began talking about him to the congregation. "Roger had his fill of attention," said Big Julie, "and, therefore, the Marises made a quiet exit."

At the restaurant, Roger explained that his tension had not fully subsided. Big Julie remembers Roger saying, "I haven't unwound yet. I'm just beginning to unwind. A lot of it is still hazy."

The warm, relaxed dinner atmosphere and sumptuous spread helped Maris to relax. Milton Gross recorded the details of Roger's meal: "Shrimp cocktail, a steak medium, a mixed salad with French dressing, a baked potato, two glasses of wine, a sliver of cheese cake, two cups of coffee, and three cigarettes."

Big Julie proposed a toast: "To many more healthy and successful happy years like this one." In thanking his friend, Roger alluded to the rigors of the season: "This was the greatest experience of my life. It had to be, but I wouldn't want to go through it again for anything."

Roger even encountered harassment during his quiet and intimate celebration. Big Julie recalled that someone in the restaurant shouted, "Hey, Maris, I don't particularly care for you, but my son wants your autograph." Roger gave the man his autograph.

Another autograph seeker, a shy teenage girl, approached Roger as the victory dinner party ended. She asked if in addition he would put the date on the autograph. "The date?" Roger asked. "What is today's date?" Big Julie reminded him, "The date is the one you did what nobody else ever did."

Roger and Big Julie returned to the teammates' former apartment, where they leafed through the approximately seven hundred telegrams that had arrived. A congratulatory cable had come from Fargo mayor Herschel Lashkowitz, on tour with the Conference of Mayors. The mayor received news of Roger's feat while in Berlin, on a visit to the Berlin Wall. Columnist and television host Ed Sullivan, also in Berlin, had chided the Fargo official, "Roger will never make it. No one will ever break Ruth's record." As Lashkowitz jubilantly remembers, "Roger proved Sullivan wrong!"

The mayor of America's largest city, New York City's Robert F. Wagner, wired: "Our city is indeed proud of you, and I am sure every fan in the country is equally so. We're particularly glad that a Yankee player was the first to hit sixty-one homers in a season."

Mrs. Babe Ruth and Mrs. Lou Gehrig sent their congratulations. The Old Professor, Casey Stengel, heard the news before flying from Los Angeles for New York to take over the reins of the new New York Mets. "I'm happy for him," said Roger's former skipper. "He's a great player. He hit thirty-nine for me last year in only half a season. He played more than that, but he was hurt a lot of the time and couldn't swing right."

Big Julie handed Maris a distinctive-looking message that had come from President John F. Kennedy. Roger treasured the words the President had written: "The American people will always admire a man who overcomes great pressures to achieve an outstanding goal."

New York newspaper editorials praised Roger for his accomplishment. In a piece entitled "Aggression in the Bronx," the *New York Times* tipped its editorial hat to Roger for topping the Babe. The article noted that the United Nations could enter the debate and decide the validity of the new record set. According to the *Times*, Maris' "act of aggression has increased the urgency of assuring the efficient functioning of the United Nations .... Since baseball is no longer the sole property of the United States, it is folly to believe that other nations will stay out of the debate. Obviously, the U.N. is the only appropriate forum if the rule of law is to prevail and reason be substituted for brute strength. In the meantime, we salute Roger Maris. His has been a mighty performance, a great hitter on a great team."

The *Long Island Press* ran its laudatory article under a headline proclaiming "Roger Maris for President." The story noted with pleasure that both sides had won: Roger had set a new record and Babe Ruth loyalists retained their 154-game mark. The newspaper staff wished Roger well and hoped "he goes on to make a million bucks and that he saves some."

Kubek in *Sixty-One* offers a final, provocative observation on how a city and its fans assisted Roger in his record-breaking drive during the 1961 regular season: "I don't think he could have done it anywhere else but in New York. The more attention he received from the fans and media, the more stubborn he became. Not only was Roger determined to pass Ruth, he was going to prove himself to all the doubters."

As the World Series opened, the press, often hostile to Roger in the past, warmed up to him. Ken Smith of the *New York Daily Mirror* wrote a four-page section of an insert devoted to the slugger and his career. The *New York World-Telegram*'s Joe Williams remarked, "As the first man to hit 61 home runs in a Major-League season, Roger Maris' position in baseball history is secure. There can be only one first. Even more resplendent heroics may be in store for him." "What Next for Maris?" asked a friendly *Post* column on the eve of the series.

The *Mirror's* Dan Parker lavished praise on Roger while attempting to correct the popular image of the slugger: "The picture of Roger Eugene Maris is 100 percent untrue. If some wrong impressions of Maris were obtained by some baseball writers, while he was attacking Babe Ruth's record of 60 homers, they can be traced to tremendous tensions under which he labored.... Maris is a quiet, humble, soft-spoken family man, with four kids and a happy wife. Maris is a devout man religiously."

The series started inauspiciously for Roger and the Yanks as they split the first two with the Reds. Puzzled by his series performance, Roger admitted, "I hadn't even hit one out of the park either here or in New York in practice since the Series started." After going hitless in ten at bats, Roger made up his mind "to go for the first pitch when I noticed Bob Purkey had been getting most of them in, and, furthermore, he wasn't throwing the knuckleball on the first pitch." Maris turned the slider into a tremendous four bagger in the ninth inning of game three, leading the Yanks to a 3-2 victory.

The Yanks took the World Series in five, but Roger had a paltry .105 batting average with only two hits. Despite Maris' poor standing, Cincinnati skipper Fred Hutchinson called Roger's third-game home run the pivotal point: the play unknotted the series' tie on the Reds' own ballfield.

Roger had earned his first World Series ring and, more importantly, a sense of the satisfaction and relief that the season was finally over. As Roger relates in *Roger Maris at Bat,* when the plane left Cincinnati, "I felt all the pressures, tensions, and caged-up feelings dropping back to the ground. I knew it was all over. At long last, I had reached the end of it all. Definitely, completely, and surely it was over. I had been going in such a mad, crazy whirl for more than a month that I had just wanted to get away ... as far as possible, to leave it all behind."

Sam Gordon, Roger Maris and Sal Durante, 1961.
(Courtesy of Sal Durante)

Chapter XIV
'Pull Down the Curtains ...
Shut Out the Crazy World'

Maris' one wish expressed his relief at the end of the 1961 baseball season: "I just wanted to pull down the curtains and shut out the crazy world I'd just been through."

Unfortunately, his status as a full-blown celebrity required a second season of him – one beyond the stadium walls and playing fields. Requests poured in for him to endorse products, to make guest appearances, to present speeches. In addition, he faced the challenge of negotiating a new contract with the Yankees.

The statistics of the 1961 season made it easier to assess Roger Maris' achievements calmly and dispassionately. His 61 homers established a new baseball record. In addition, he ranked tops in the American League for the second straight year for his 140 runs batted in. He led the league with 366 total bases . For the second consecutive year Maris won both the "Sultan of Swat" award and a place on the *Sporting News's* All-Star Major League Team. His other awards included the Hickok Belt as Top Professional Athlete of the Year, the A.P. Professional Athlete of the Year, the *Sporting News* Player of the Year, *Sports Illustrated* Sportsman of the Year, Catholic Athlete of the Year, the B'nai B'rith Award, and *Sport Magazine*'s Man of the Year.

Roger's Most Valuable Player of the Year award gave him special pride. Only a handful of players have achieved the special honor of back-to-back MVPs: Jimmie Foxx, Hal Newhouser, Yogi Berra, and Mickey Mantle in the A.L.; and Ernie Banks, Joe Morgan, Mike Schmidt and Dale Murphy in the N.L.

Sportswriters voted on who was to receive these awards. Even though the press had more fondness for Mickey Mantle and Yogi Berra, for example, the media as a whole had no particular hostility toward Roger. As Pat Maris said, "You cannot deny that Roger had many writers who liked him, and he liked them. However, certain writers and their reports got blown up and the public got a false picture."

Maris had some insights into his relationships with the press. In 1975 he remarked, "Maybe I was unfair to group everyone under a label of 'writers' when talking of my complaints. Many New York writers were good to me, especially the more veteran ones." In 1977 Roger categorized the troublesome sportswriters. "I think of the two kinds of sportswriters," he said. "There were a lot of old guys who had known Ruth. And there were young guys who were just breaking in. They kept trying to write something new each day, something different. The guys who had known Ruth didn't want me to break the record. The others were trying to get enough of a story to be read."

The press also fed the public a misconception in regard to the asterisk designation. While Roger was preparing to play in the World Series, reports indicated that the Baseball Records Committee leaned toward accepting the home-run feat without requiring any special distinctions. According to these stories, the committee would issue their ruling on the matter at the winter meetings in Tampa, Florida. However, Ford Frick quickly discounted committee sentiments and made its ruling academic when he unequivocally announced that he would not recognize any possible ruling.

Regardless, the Baseball Writers Association of America convened its annual World Series gathering on October 3 and approved a resolution calling on the Baseball Records Committee to protest strongly the commissioner's stand. Among those spearheading the fight to sponsor the resolution and empower the Records Committee to communicate its thoughts to Frick were the *New York Post*'s Leonard Koppett and the Associated Press's Joe Reichler. Although Reichler may have criticized the approach and personality Roger Maris displayed during the pressure-cooker weeks preceding victory, Reichler never demeaned Maris' baseball talents. Despite the journalist's personal perceptions and sentiments, as a sportswriter Reichler wanted Maris' accomplishments to receive their proper recognition.

Frick himself never mentioned the asterisk as a "designation," and an asterisk never appeared in the official records. Seymour Siwoff, member of the Records Committee and publisher of *The Little Red Book* (now, *The Book of Baseball Records*) made the immediate decision. He told Frick that the *Red Book* would contain this statement:

... Each performance will be judged on its own merit and if the accomplishment was directly benefited by an increase of scheduled games, the record will be annotated with the phrase [162-game schedule].

For example, the most singular record of the 1961 season was Roger Maris' 61 home runs. It is a fact that he benefited from the expanded schedule of the American League, and it will in no way detract from his accomplishment to list his record as having been made during a 162-game schedule.

On the other hand, it would be a gross inequity to delete Babe Ruth's record of 60 home runs in a season, hit during a 154-game schedule. Therefore, Ruth's record will be retained along with Maris'.

In 1969 the Baseball Records Committee ruled that "Major League Baseball shall have one set of records, starting in 1876," and "no asterisk or official sign shall be used to indicate the number of games scheduled."

Thus, neither the *Book of Baseball Records* nor the *Sporting News Record Book* has ever used an asterisk. The *Book of Baseball Records* lists the home-run records: "Most Home Runs, season, 61-Roger E. Maris, A.L., N.Y., 1961 (162-game season); 60-George H. Ruth, A.L., N.Y., 1927." It lists those having 50-home run seasons with Roger Maris at the top, with no mention of the 162-game season.

Under the "Most Home Runs" category, the *Sporting News Record Book* shows that Roger Maris had 61 in a 162-game season and that Babe Ruth had the most in a 154-game schedule.

Roger Maris' record does not carry the "taint" of an asterisk, despite the popular conviction that such a designation does or did exist. Even so-called experts who should know better persist in the error. George Vecsey in a *Times*'s story inaccurately reported that Frick "affixed" the "infamous asterisk" to the home run champ.

Joseph Durso, the *New York Times* reporter, wrote in Roger's obituary: "The asterisk was inserted to distinguish Maris' home run record from the one set in 1927 by ... Babe Ruth, who hit 60 in the days of the 154-game season. It was inserted into the record books by Ford C. Frick, the Commissioner of Baseball, who apparently reflected the traditionalist view of many fans that the Olympian feats of Ruth must be defended against long seasons, short fences, and newly arrived sluggers." Durso added that fans will remember Roger Maris "as the man with the asterisk in the record books."

The asterisk "problem" affects not only bleacher fans and writers, but also national sports announcers like Al Michaels. In his TV commentary about the 1987 professional football players' strike, Michaels said that record books will list the games played with replacements in the same manner as Roger Maris' home-run record – with an asterisk.

Ford Frick reiterated his satisfaction years later in his 1973 autobiography, *Games, Asterisks and People,*. The former commissioner writes, "A lot of my newspaper friends have enjoyed kidding me about the Asterisk Incident. ... As a matter of fact, no asterisk has appeared in the official record in connection with the Maris feat. Roger hit 61 home runs that season to set an all-time record, and he is given full recognition for that accomplishment. But his record was set in a 162-game season. The Ruth record of 60 home runs was set in 1927 in a 154-game season."

Even though no asterisk appears next to Roger's name, the record books still note that Maris achieved his home-run mark in 162 games, while the Babe accomplished his feat in 154 games. Only Maris is so cited: the records make no such distinction for other marks established after the league extended the season by eight games. A writer for the *Fargo Forum* called this discriminatory treatment a "subtle stigma" that still remains.

But no one can doubt that in postseason 1961 Roger Maris was a star, not an asterisk. He made personal appearances, including one on the Perry Como show that netted him $10,000. His sports achievements had made his name a household word: advertisers sought to use him in commercials, and Maris endorsed a handful of food products. A line of Maris and Mantle men's and boy's clothes earned him a $45,000 income annually for three years. Roger appeared in Columbia Pictures' *Safe at Home*, a movie in which a runaway Little Leaguer meets Maris and Mantle who, in perfect Tinseltown fashion, return the youngster to the right path. Thanks to Maris and Mantle, the movie also featured Big Julie and Whitey Ford.

Despite the potentially lucrative demands for his time, Roger set limits. John Blanchard explained:

> Roger turned down appearances that would have given
> him much in excess of $500,000. Roger had no hesitation

in saying no. There was no temptation. He did not want to be away from home. Family always came first.

Rog wasn't a politician. He wanted to be with Patty and the young family he had at the time. He could have gotten a lot more publicity and endorsements if he had wanted to pay the price. But that's the way he was. He didn't care to go into all this appearance stuff.

Roger also placed loyalty and friendship over the acquisition of money. Big Julie remembers discussing a prospective Roger Maris biography "with a lot of big names out there. ... Everybody wanted to do his story. But Roger stuck with Jim Ogle, who had been loyal to him. He was a sportswriter and, more important, Roger's friend."

Maris' choice of biographer did not sit well with New York journalists. Jim Ogle wrote for the *Newark Star-Ledger*, and as Big Julie notes, "The Yankee writers were not pleased. The least he [Maris] could have done was to pick a writer from New York, not Jersey."

Ironically, Ogle's book was not widely read and merited only a handful of reviews. Today the book has become almost a collector's item. The Roger Maris Museum in Fargo displays a copy, but the public library has none in circulation.

Roger had little fondness for the rubber chicken circuit. When he received the Associated Press's Athlete of the Year Award in Milwaukee, he told a private luncheon at the Miller Inn: "The banquet circuit is okay except for four things – speeches, newspapermen, cameramen, and traveling."

He told Dan Daniel, "I have had a lot of bids to dinners and the like for pay, but speechifying scares me to death, and I don't like the menus at those affairs. I have seen what the chicken circuit can do to a ballplayer, and I don't care to risk a similar experience." Perhaps Maris made superstitious reference to the Yanks' Bob Turley. In 1958 Turley had won the Cy Young award; in 1959, after a postseason of dinner appearances, Turley's record plummeted to eight wins.

Maris became uneasy when he found himself surrounded by local bigwigs, businessmen, or politicians. The slugger preferred the slacks, sports coats, and tee-shirts of casual get-togethers to the tuxedos and ties required at formal affairs. During these seemingly interminable events, Roger frequently consulted his watch, anxiously anticipating the tedium's end.

The press at the Milwaukee awards' banquet mistook Roger's

boredom for rudeness and reported that he took his award and went into the back room to shoot pool. Jim Ogle's 1967 article, "Fact and Legend of Roger Maris," for *The Sporting News,* shatters that report. Ogle reports that Roger stayed until the end of the banquet and signed autographs, even though he had to keep his friend, sports editor Charlie Johnson, waiting.

Without knowing the circumstances, the press also rapped Roger for rushing from the New York B'nai B'rith dinner after accepting his award. Roger had intended to take the next day's early-morning flight to the Hickok Award Dinner in Rochester, New York, but a public relations man for the affair insisted that Roger board a 10:30 train that evening. According to Big Julie, "He was forced to leave, but was attacked for it. ... The press jumped all over Roger for exiting that dinner."

The press continued to pose repetitive questions into the postseason. When asked to cite the most annoying of them, Roger answered, "During the season they kept asking me if I thought I could beat Ruth. The one that is getting a little irritating right now is, 'Are you going to hit 62 in '62?'"

Roger had stock answers to other irksome questions: "What are the advantages of playing in New York?"

"The money is there."

"What pitcher would you like most to see out of the league?"

"Camilio Pascual of the Twins."

Other tiresome rehashes concerned the expanded schedule, his relationship with Mantle, the Frick decision, and the comments Mrs. Ruth made after game 154. Roger's responses coalesced into an image that the press imprinted in the public mind: Roger Maris was a dull, humorless individual who didn't like baseball, didn't like Ruth, and didn't like Mantle.

Roger's awkwardness at a podium could have stemmed from his preference for private conversations with close and trusted friends, rather than public speeches to curious and distant onlookers. After receiving the home-run crown for the second consecutive year, Roger spoke at the Maryland Professional Baseball Players Association banquet. In reporting on his speech, John Steadman of the *Baltimore News-Post* mistook the public Roger Maris for the private Roger Maris:

As a public speaker, Roger Maris is much better as a home-run hitter. ... The truth of the matter is, Maris doesn't talk much of a game. He's stoic, unemotional and doesn't come crashing through as a conversationalist. ...

> Maris, by actual count, was interrupted 97 times from the moment he started his fruit cup and worked his way through dessert. There was an endless parade of greeters, hand-shakers and autograph seekers. This qualifies as a record that won't have to carry an asterisk. It's a wonder he was able to contain himself, but this is the price of fame. ... His patience was tested to the breaking point, but he acted the perfect guest.

The slugger's postseason press entanglements began on his trip to Sacramento to pick up the historic 61st home-run ball. Roger had little enthusiasm for flying across country in November, only a little more than a month after the World Series. He wanted no publicity and no speeches: Roger merely intended to help Sal Durante get the promised $5,000 bounty.

According to Sal Durante, already honeymooning with Rosemarie when Roger arrived, "There was a lot of hoopla, with a Brink's truck and a mass of reporters. But I tell you one thing: Roger Maris is friendly. Without Roger Maris, I would not have gotten the $5,000. Roger Maris only went to Sacramento so that I could get the money."

According to Jim Ogle, an unnamed New York columnist who hardly knew Maris "did one of the finest 'rip' jobs on record." His contrived story said that Roger and his brother, Rudy, stormed into Sacramento and made ridiculous demands, among them that the Maris brothers get a piece of the business at Sam Gordon's Ranch Wagon restaurant.

In actuality, Gordon did not keep his word. He invited a circus of reporters with their questions to greet Roger. Maris repeatedly insisted that he would not make a speech at the ceremonies marking the presentation of the ball. Gordon sought Maris' permission to use his name for a restaurant chain. Roger refused. In the confusion, a television lamp fell on Roger's head and nearly knocked him out.

Despite the reality of the situation, the Sacramento media coverage reflected the hardened anti-Roger Maris bias of the press.

Wilbur Adams's story for *Sporting News*, datelined November 15, 1961, Sacramento, presented a fairer picture, even though it did not receive wide circulation. It reported that Roger did not make a speech, but that he did make some brief comments and answered questions. The article noted that Roger, when asked his opinion of the reception, responded with a blunt, "I don't think much of this promotion."

Nor did the Eastern press mention an item covered by Adams: Roger spoke to twelve-year-old muscular dystrophy victim Kenny Bing from Carmichael, California. From his wheelchair, the youngster smiled, thanked Roger for giving him an autographed ball, and urged, "Next time you come here, don't forget to bring Mickey Mantle with you."

When the press in Sacramento asked Roger what he planned to do with the home-run ball, Roger replied, "I haven't made up my mind." After twelve years the baseball – and bat – became part of the Hall of Fame collection, acquired through the efforts of former Baseball Hall of Fame Director Ken Smith. Peter Clark, registrar for the Baseball Hall of Fame and curator of the shrine's holdings, reports that Cooperstown received the bat and ball in the spring of 1973. Associate Director William J. Guilfoile confirmed this.

Sal Durante states, "Several years later, after 1961, Roger told me that he was playing with his son in the backyard and lost the historic ball. I initialed the ball right after catching it so that there would be no substitution. If it's in the Hall of Fame, it must have my signature."

Durante's remarks have some credibility. A June 12, 1967, story carried by the *St. Louis Post Dispatch* wire services revealed that Roger had lost or misplaced the historic ball. "I have no idea where that ball is," he said. "It might be around my house, but I doubt it. For all I know my kids might have played with it."

Although unaware of the *Post-Dispatch* story, Clark insisted that Cooperstown has the "real" ball: the Hall of Fame exhibits are kept under lock and key, except for occasional cleaning.

On December 2, 1987, after maintenance personnel cleaned the case containing the bat and ball, Clark reported that there was "no 'S.D.' signature on the ball, nor any other inscription."

Still, the correspondence between Smith and Roger confirms that the bat and ball are in Cooperstown. On February 16, 1973, Smith wrote Maris that he would be in Florida in March and would like to assist in securing the bat that hit the 61st for the shrine. "Now that the event is twelve years past, the tremendous feat looms more wonderful with the passing of each year."

Roger phoned on March 12 to affirm that Smith could pick up the bat. The following day Smith arranged to pick up the 35-inch, 33-ounce Louisville Slugger.

An April 9 letter to Roger from Smith confirmed that "The bat that knocked home run No. 61 on October 1, 1961, also numbers 59 and 60, was delivered to the Hall of Fame, April 7, 1973, by Ken Smith personally. Also the sixty-first home-run ball that had been retrieved by Sal Durante."

Just as the celebrated bat and ball of number 61 fame found a home in Cooperstown's Hall of Fame Shrine, Roger Maris found what seemed like the perfect place for "a quiet home base." Raytown, Missouri, seemed like an oasis of peace after a hectic season in New York. As Roger told the *Kansas City Star,* "It's just a darn friendly place. The people here are nice, and I like Kansas City, too. In New York there's too many people and no privacy."

Jack Rice of the *St. Louis Post-Dispatch* found that while Raytown "may be proud of him," it "takes him in stride." Ken Clayton, editor of the *Raytown News,* clearly stated the relationship between hero and adopted hometown:

> ... Raytown, so far, is to be commended for taking his sports achievements in stride. After all, Raytown really doesn't have to toot; Roger does have his home here.
>
> The Marises have been good neighbors. Roger and his wife, Patricia, have a pleasant suburban home ... They have displayed interest in community activities. They have helped in the work of their church. They have avoided rather than courted the limelight.
>
> Maris has treated his home community with respect. When interviewed he has not reported he is from "Kansas City" or "a suburb of Kansas City"; he has said ... he lives in Raytown. ... Regardless of how many home runs he hits, we've a hunch he'd just as soon be treated as the pleasant neighbor that he's been in his home town rather than displayed like a captive refugee from a sideshow.

Raytown provided Roger with an ideal retreat from New York. The slugger's unassuming nature, wrote Rice, helped Raytown be "bigger than baseball and Maris." For example, Roger's home-run number 61 became a modest story for the record that took a back seat to "more important" local news.

"We've gone along with Roger in line with his request," said Clayton. "We try to play down his residence here. He's a very modest guy."

The lack of adulation suited Roger perfectly, as he went about his private life in his reasonably modest home on Blue Ridge Boulevard. He made lifetime friends in Raytown, like Jim and Jerry Cosentino, who ran the town family supermarket. Jim, who had done a short stint as a St. Louis Cardinal farmhand, befriended Roger because he knew how lonely a baseball player's life can be. "I remember what it was like, being in a strange town and not knowing anybody." Cosentino had been impressed with Roger at first sight, when Maris played with the A's against the White Sox. "He's the greatest natural ball player I ever saw, and when I saw Roger in my store I told him that."

The baseball connection grew into a relationship between the Maris and Cosentino families that has survived Roger's and Jim's deaths.

In Raytown the Marises became part of the "baseball gang" who resided in the Independence-Kansas City area. This group included Bob Cerv, Ed Rakow, and those especially close to the Maris family, Norm Siebern, Bill Tuttle, and Whitey Herzog. The families hunted, golfed, bowled, and partied together, often sharing steaming portions of chili, Roger's number-one weakness. A housewives' bowling league included Mrs. Pat Maris, Mrs. Mary Lou Herzog, Mrs. Lucille Tuttle, and Mrs. Liz Sieburn.

Frances and Jim Cosentino soon became part of the circle, and often invited the gang for hunting at Cosentino's lodge at Mound City, Missouri.

Raytown native and former Washington Senator and Minnesota Twin slugger Bob Allison often returned to his home town to see his father. After Roger moved into the area, Allison would occasionally spend time with him, playing golf or simply chatting. "I would call Roger a person who liked to be with the people he liked and trusted," Allison said. "He would spend hours with the players from the area. He shied away from talking about himself and in particular he had little to say about the 1961 season." As the *Kansas City Star*, noted, "The guy hasn't changed a bit" because of his 1961 stardom.

Maris' next-door neighbor on Blue Ridge Boulevard, retired dentist Dr. Marlon Steinert, vividly recalls the 1961 off-season. "Roger felt it difficult," Steinert said, "to differentiate between those who came to his door in honest and true friendship and those who were seeking to inherit his glory and publicity. And Roger would try to be as courteous as he could be to those who came by."

Roger was a very civic-minded person, and he and Pat loved those events that allowed them to have fun and not attract attention. Pat Maris remembers that although Roger would decline nearly all invitations "because he didn't want to hurt anybody's feelings by playing favorites. ... There was one Halloween party we attended after the 1961 season. Roger enjoyed it very much because he wore a mask."

According to Steinert, Roger was the type of person "who functioned best when he had a day-to-day routine" that included get-togethers with baseball friends, carpentry in the house (making a cedar chest, for example), and, most important, quiet times together with the family. "The Marises were very family oriented," Steinert said. "Roger did not go anywhere without the children, even if it was just a trip to the grocery store."

Mrs. Mary Steinert remembers that "family life meant everything to Pat and Roger. They wanted very much to be left alone. Pat hated the media intrusions in their private life."

Still, even in the off-season the media came to observe the Maris family. Steinert recalled a particular occasion at "about seven in the morning, when the press barged into my office and began clicking pictures of Pat as she sat in the dental chair."

The dentist thought he understood why the public never became entirely "fascinated" with the slugger. "Roger was a man of impeccable integrity," Steinert said. "A person like Roger who has integrity cannot pretend because he will be caught. He believed in things that counted most: religion, friendship, and family. You can say he lived a life that was ... highly commendable, free from criticism. But this is the type of life, the type of person, that people don't get excited about. It has little interest for them."

However, the media remained interested in the Marises. Deirdre Budge, wife of tennis champion Don Budge, visited Raytown – "practically moving in on the Marises" – to get a story for *Look* magazine. Her "firsthand glimpse of a living legend" afforded her such insights as Roger was absent-minded and conscientious and that his favorite meal was kidney stew followed by raisin pie.

Pat confided to Deirdre Budge that some of Pat's girlfriends envied her marriage to a famous baseball player. Said Pat, "I think to myself that I love being in my shoes, too, but I wonder if they would, knowing some of the social difficulties that being a baseball wife entails." Roger's extended absences during the year forced Pat to develop a variety of skills, "like fixing furnaces and leaky faucets, running the house, paying the bills."

In her article, Mrs. Budge gave her impressions of the couple: "In all my talks with Pat and Roger, I found them to be free of all artifice. They both have a level-headedness that I admire. They worry about their children before themselves and about their friends and neighbors more than public opinion. ... Their biggest fear is losing their identity as private persons."

Although Roger could maintain his privacy in Raytown, he could not escape the deluge of mail. An amazed local mailman observed, "I guess I'm going to have to get a special cart marked 'Maris' because your mail won't fit into my pouch any more."

The postman carried letters requesting autographs, participation at events, and money for charity. He also brought hate mail, *e.g.*, "You'll never be another Babe Ruth, no matter how many home runs you hit." On occasion, the mailman would bring hilarious communications. One pen pal "reminded" Roger of their marriage and splendid honeymoon in Coney Island. "You were only a struggling player then," she wrote, "and I often wondered whatever happened to you. Now look how far you've come in the world."

Roger eagerly anticipated mail from Fargo. He maintained a correspondence with Sister Bertha, who remembers "the first large picture he sent of himself. When he sent that autographed picture, I had the students eating out of my hand."

With Don Gooselaw, Roger shared his worry that his fame would affect his relationship with the people back home. Gooselaw recalled, "It was very important to Roger that these long-lasting relationships not be severed."

Chapter XV
1962: 'Sour from the Start'

On New Year's Day, 1962, Roger and Pat Maris went to Los Angeles to watch the Rose Bowl from the private box of their host, comedian Bob Hope. Not long after they had sung the last "Auld Lang Syne" of 1961, Roger faced the troublesome prospect of contract negotiation. The issue was money.

Roger had earned $42,000 in 1961. The press had quoted him as looking for a "hefty raise" and it seemed a reasonable request. Maris' 61 homers had brought the Yankees millions of dollars. His MVP award proved his value to the team – if there were any doubt about it. Roger wanted a top salary not for glory's sake, but because his family had grown to include four children. He planned to build a bigger house. As he often told Dr. Surprise, "I'm a professional baseball player for my family. When I can provide for them in a better way, I will leave baseball."

With no agreement in the offing, Roger made a surprise visit to New York in January and met for ten minutes with Yankee general manager Roy Hamey. A United Press International story reported that Maris asked for $70,000 and the Yankees countered with $60,000. At the end of their contract discussion, the slugger told the press, "We were friends when I went in and still friends when I came out. I'm not going to discuss my salary publicly. Whatever comes out will come from the Yankees."

The Yankee publicity department responded: "Roger Maris just visited me [Hamey] and talked with me. No agreement was reached."

That winter the Yankees were never very serious about signing Roger, according to Big Julie. They wouldn't budge from that $60,000 figure, and Roger went to camp without a contract. You should know that Mickey made $75,000 in 1961; the Yankees raised him to $100,000 for '62. But the Yanks never announced his salary, so people thought he was making $85,000.

... Roger came over to me after one of those fruitless

meetings and said, "I am not going to get $100,000." I said, "What are they offering?" "Nothing. Something like a $15,000 raise," Roger said. "They told me they gave Mickey $100,000 but I wouldn't get it because no one on the Yankees would make more than Mickey."

Roger's meetings with Dan Topping and Roy Hamey had brought him only frustration and anger. Maris returned to Florida without a contract to wait for some breakthrough. According to Big Julie, Roger offered to compromise at $90,000 but the Yanks wouldn't listen. Houk and Big Julie argued over Roger's ability to draw thousands more people to the park. The manager reiterated that the Yankees would not give Roger what they gave Mantle and rejected Big Julie's $90,000 proposal.

Roger lowered his demands: first to $85,000 and then $80,000. The Yankees would go no higher than $67,000. Without the ability to use arbitration or free agency as inducements, Roger was at the mercy of the Yankee management. Big Julie convinced Roger to continue bargaining. As a result, the Yankees promised Roger $72,500, with another $5,000 for living expenses.

Roger barely disguised his resentment at his treatment during those preseason maneuverings. He announced to the media, "I got almost what I asked for. The main thing is that I'm happy and satisfied and want to go to work."

Hamey applauded Roger's capitulation: "We're very happy he's signed. We're most appreciative of what Roger meant to the ball club last year."

A February 25 Associated Press story from Fort Lauderdale, Florida, reported that Roger had become the fourth-highest-paid player in Yank history. DiMaggio led the list with $100,000, followed by Mantle at $82,000 – not $100,000 – and Ruth at $80,000.

In terms of club history, Roger did receive the "hefty raise" he sought. His $32,000 contract hike set a club record.

However, the entire negotiation process embittered Roger. After he retired, Roger remembered, "It was very difficult to get that raise. In fact, it was so tough that I never wanted to bargain for a contract again. I decided, 'This is the last time.'"

Dr. Surprise maintains that the Yankees would have paid Roger the $100,000 salary he wanted, if he had accepted the team's accompanying proviso: "The deal was that Roger would have to 'cooperate'" with the press. No deal would be made by Roger, who would not compromise his principles."

Shortly after Maris had signed his contract, DiMaggio offered his thoughts on Roger's prospects for another superseason. "He'll have to be able to handle the pressure," DiMaggio said, "because he's going to have plenty of it. He'll have more pressure on him this year than he did last summer when he was closing in on the Bambino's home-run record."

Media pressure began early, during the preseason in Fort Lauderdale. A youth with a ball approached Roger at the Yankee Clipper Motel and asked him, "Mr. X, will you sign this?" Playing along with the lad's game, Roger signed the ball "Mr. X." Maris later inscribed a ball and personally affixed his signature.

The youngster's father – the mayor of Fort Lauderdale – had friends on the local newspaper. The next day, Oscar Fraley attacked Roger for his lack of courtesy in a lead sports-page story, carried by U.P.I. Fraley, creator of the TV program "The Untouchables," had never had any contact with Roger, but perceived Roger as hostile toward the press. Fraley concluded his article: "If either of my two sons has a hero, I hope it's a modest fellow named John Glenn, who went for the circuit when it really counted. Because guys like Maris bat around zero with me."

In retaliation for the story, Roger publicly leveled a barrage of insults to Fraley's face. "If you weren't so old," Roger roared, "I'd knock you right on your ass."

The accumulated tension between Roger and the media reached its peak with the Fraley story. Roger announced to the press that from then on he would have three words for them: "I don't know." In an Associated Press story Roger answered all questions – "What kind of year do you expect?" "Do you think you'll reach 61 home runs this year?" "How many home runs will you be satisfied to hit?" etc. – with the same response, "I don't know."

The Associated Press presented a fair explanation of Roger's position: "Maris hasn't been treated kindly by the fans here. He's been booed and jeered. He blames a bad press and has reciprocated by clamming up."

The same story quoted Roger telling a friend his side of the story: "Look, I'm not going to change. I can't even if I wanted to. And I don't want to. I'm me, Roger Maris. I could have fed him a whole lot of baloney. But I'm no politician. I can't say things I don't mean. And when I've got nothing to say, I say nothing. If the guy wants to get sore, let him. I can't help that."

Roger next caught the wrath of Jimmy Cannon. According to Big Julie, Cannon wanted to speak to Roger during infield practice. "Roger and Jimmy Cannon had been good friends," Big Julie said. "But Roger was still mad about the Fraley story and so he told Cannon, 'I'm not talking to anyone, and that includes you.'" As Big Julie tells it, after the practice when Roger felt a "little more composed," he agreed to speak to the writer. At that point, Cannon refused a meeting.

In Maury Allen's version of the incident, Cannon, with the assistance of the Yanks' Bob Fishel, had scheduled an interview with Roger before the practice and Roger did not show up.

Yankee teammate John Blanchard remembers it differently: "Roger came off the field tired, drenched, and certainly emotionally weary. Cannon comes over and says, 'Roger can I have some of your time?' And Roger answers, 'I'm too tired now, some other time.' This was too much for Cannon. 'Who do you think you are?' he snapped at Roger. 'I interviewed Gene Tunney and other sports greats.'"

Jimmy Cannon revealed his side of the story in the *New York Journal-American*. According to the sportswriter, the slugger had told him that it was his "policy not to grant interviews."

"I've been ripped too much," he said.

"By me?" I asked.

"Oh, no," he said. "You've never hurt me. But I have a new policy."

Cannon's first column was entitled "Maris ... 'The Whiner'... a Threat to Yank Pennant." In his opening, Cannon observes:

> Success has made Roger Maris the most unpopular player on the Yankees. Their boredom with him has assumed aspects which conceivably could place the team's pennant chances in jeopardy.
>
> The distrust isn't confined to his companions in the dressing room where the right-fielder describes his fictitious martyrdom in incessant monologues.
>
> ... It has long been the policy of the people who run the Yankees to select ball players with the care of men picking a son-in-law. It has been a club known for the affability of its help. But Maris violates all the laws of protocol estab-

lished by Joe DiMaggio and Babe Ruth.

Cannon concludes his column with an apology for not reporting about Roger more carefully during the season, for "not turning it on him then for his treacherous smallness. The absence of stress does not diminish his capacity of self-worship." The journalist promises to continue his assault on Roger in a second column.

Cannon's second column, "Maris Envies Mantle's Prestige Among Yankees," reports on the supposed disharmony Roger created on the team. The article centers on Mantle's role as a Yankee and Roger's envy: "Obviously, Maris considers Mantle a competitor instead of a partner on a team. It might be a dangerous situation to the club's prized harmony if Maris could appeal to more of the players. But his personality limits his cult to a dwindling few. Only Bob Cerv is constantly in his company."

In a bitter summary Cannon states that Roger threatened the morale of the Yankees, envied Mantle's high regard among team-mates, and was an ingrate in his relations with the front office. In short, said Cannon, Roger Maris was an embarrassment to the Yankees and out of tune with the sterling Yankee tradition.

The excoriating columns end with Cannon's parting shot: "One fact is clear. Maris isn't a Ruth or a DiMaggio. He isn't a Mantle either. That's what seems to annoy Roger the Whiner most."

Maury Allen felt that because of the Cannon incident Roger "would be left so battered and bruised that, for the rest of his life, " he "never fully trusted any reporter." Yet while a Cardinal, Roger revealed his version of the Cannon dispute story in a Red Barber column: "Jimmy Cannon came along right then. He'd always been a good friend of mine, or so I thought. I was so burned about Fraley I told Jimmy I didn't want to talk. He cursed me. I cursed him back. He wrote two stories and called me everything."

Despite the anger Roger felt about the *Journal-American* series and toward Cannon personally, his Fargo friends never heard about it. "I never heard a bad word from Roger about anybody," said Don Gooselaw, "even if it were crude sportswriters." According to Bob Wood, this reticence was consistent with Roger's motto, "If you can't say something nice about someone, then say nothing."

Even though Roger would not speak ill of the journalist, he would long remember the Cannon episode in sorrow and disappointment. "I really thought our friendship was worth more than that," the retired player said to a reporter in 1978.

The Cannon series was read across America. Picking up on Cannon's tone, other writers started referring to the slugger as "rude Roger." The Fraley piece paled in comparison. As Golenbock writes in *Baseball Quarterly,* in the Cannon columns Roger's "character had suffered such assassination that if he had discovered a cure for cancer he still would be thought of as an arrogant and aloof scientist."

On the day Cannon concluded his diatribes, the Yanks and the newly born Mets arrived in St. Petersburg, Florida, for an exhibition game. United Press International photographer Joel Schrenk suggested that Hall of Famer Mets' coach Rogers Hornsby, who had a second-to-Cobb career .358 batting average, pose with home-run king Roger Maris. A surprisingly agreeable Hornsby said, "Yeah, I'll pose with him. Bring him over."

The unwitting photographer never knew, and a biased press never admitted, that during the 1961 session Hornsby had publicly insulted Maris. The Mets' coach had said that the only thing Roger could do as well as the Babe was running. The Hall of Famer added that Roger "couldn't carry Ruth's jock."

Smoldering from the journalistic torches of Fraley, Cannon, et al., and still reverberating with the taunts of Hornsby, Roger had no response to the request for a picture. He simply turned his back and walked away. Fargo's Bill Weaver remembers that incident: "Roger felt, If Hornsby wants a picture, let him come to him. Roger told me, 'I can't pick my relatives, but I sure can pick my friends. When I pick my friends, they are friends for life.'"

Roger's rebuff stunned Hornsby. "How the hell do you like that!" he thundered. The headlines reported the rest of his comments: "Hornsby Calls Maris Little Punk Ball Player!" Stories read: "That bush leaguer. I've posed for pictures with Major League hitters – not bush Leaguers like he is."

Maris calmly explained his actions: "During the winter, Mr. Hornsby said I was a lousy hitter who had to be awfully lucky to hit 61 homers. I didn't want to embarrass a great hitter like Mr. Hornsby by having him pose with a lousy hitter like me. He might have forgotten what he said, but I didn't."

No one championed Hornsby's case better than Jimmy Cannon's paper, the *New York Journal-American.* Barney Kremenko's story carried the headline "Hornsby: Maris Couldn't Carry My Bat." The newspaper also ran a comparison of the lifetime records of both players, a picture of Hornsby with his arm around Kremenko, and a quote of the sportswriter saying, "It was a thrill to pose with the Hall of Famer." Within the article, Hornsby not only downplayed Roger's home runs, but also assailed Roger's personality: "This fellow's behavior off the field is unforgiveable. I just can't imagine anyone refusing to sign autographs. As for having good relations with newspapermen, that's basic for a ballplayer. I always cooperated with them and most of the players I know did the same."

Hornsby obliquely contrasted himself and Maris by relating another incident in St. Petersburg. Yankee first-baseman Moose Skowron approached Stengel for permission to talk to Hall of Famer Hornsby about hitting. Hornsby said, "There were a few things he thought I could straighten out for him. I was glad to help. ... That shows you the difference between a class fellow and a swelled-up guy."

Bob Stewart, who profiled Roger for *Baseball's Greatest Players Today,* saw the Hornsby incident as part of the slugger's disdain for diplomacy. More important, Roger acted toward Hornsby as he would have at any other time:

> There was no reason why Maris should have posed for pictures with Hornsby, if anyone wants to argue. Hornsby was not always the easiest man to get along with. His records, not the man, earned him admiration. ...
>
> Maris would have shrugged off Hornsby in 1959 just the way he did in 1962. The records have changed, and Maris changed them, but Maris hadn't changed. He spoke up before he made it big; he continued to speak up.

Striving to repeat the 1961 on-field Maris-Yankee success, Houk acted to defuse an explosive situation. On March 23 in Sarasota, prior to an exhibition game with the White Sox, Houk convened an emergency press conference. He affirmed that his slugger Roger Maris ranked "A-1 with me and players." Houk added: "I've never seen him hustle so hard in any training camp I've ever seen him in. He's doing everything possible to get himself in shape. At the moment, that's what interests me most."

The Major rejected any suggestions of reprimand or counseling sessions: "I have no plans to talk to him. If ever I do talk to him, none of you fellows will ever know about it."

Moreover, Houk felt that the turbulence had had no effect: "If it had been some others on the club, " Houk said, "it might have folded them right up. Not Maris, he's got a hard nose. He'll probably have his greatest year."

Houk had overcome his reservations about commenting at all on the brouhaha because of eager press people and their early A.M. calls: "I got calls from the damnedest places, from writers I never heard of in places like Pensacola, New Orleans, Denver, and towns like that. They all wanted the manager's version of the Maris situation."

His manager's vote of confidence gave Roger an emotional lift. In Tampa he gladly posed for a pregame photo with Cincinnati Reds' slugger Frank Robinson. On March 25, he slammed his first roundtripper of the spring. Next at bat, hitter John Blanchard greeted Roger as he crossed home plate and noticed, "Roger looked relaxed and confident. Good times were ahead."

Maris' euphoria vanished as the press again made him its target. Tommy Devine, for example, took his pot shot in *The Miami News:* "If it weren't for sportswriters, Roger Maris would probably be an $18-a-week clerk at the A & P back in Missouri."

A beleaguered Roger Maris even lashed out at Dan Daniel, who had solidly backed Roger and earned wide respect as the dean of the sportswriting profession. After receiving a barb from Roger, Daniel responded with grandfatherly concern: "Maris will have to learn to laugh even while bleeding internally. If he continues to be the Angry Man, may the Lord have mercy on him. The customer won't."

The Yankee front office indicated its concern for Maris and the 1962 season by sending Big Julie to Florida. He said,

> Every paper I opened had a story ripping Roger. He was being abused, being called a redneck and worse by people who never even met him or spoke to him. Roger explained everything to me, chapter and verse. What can you expect? I have been in restaurants when he would be approached by grubby middle-aged men who would say in a nasty way, "Hey, Maris, I personally don't care for you, but my boy wants your autograph." So, when Roger tells them to go to hell, they have it coming to them.

Although Roger felt like cleaning his locker and heading back to Missouri, he would not let the criticism frustrate his determination to excel in 1962. In mid-September 1961 he realistically appraised his chances of topping his "61 in '61" season: "Ever since I've been in baseball, I've tried to do better the next year. But I'm on the spot for '62, no matter what happens."

According to Pat Maris, "The 1962 season was sour from the start because of his relationship with the sportswriters. Nobody respected him, not the fans. They wanted more. The boos increased."

The season started positively when Roger hit a three-run blast that put the Yanks ahead of the Orioles and him ahead of his own record. In 1961, home-run number one had not come until the eleventh game.

However, when the Yanks came to Tiger Stadium for Detroit's opener on April 13, an unpleasant incident marred Maris' early optimism. Once before, someone had hurled a seat slat protruding metal at Maris; now, a soda bottle thrown from the right-field stands struck Roger on the arm. The broken glass barely missed him. Detroit's owner John E. Fetzer pledged: "We'll prosecute if we catch them in the act."

As April came to a close, Roger had hit only 1 homer, with a .152 average, but he rallied quickly in a four-game set in Washington. With 10 for 19, he raised his average to the .262 mark; in addition, he put three into the seats.

Almost as Roger mouthed, "It's one of the best starts I ever had in baseball. Everything's wonderful now," the injury hex struck, the first of many to plague him after the 1961 season. On May 16, while leaning against Fenway's right-field bullpen wall trying to snatch a Carl Yastrzemski home run, Roger strained a groin muscle in his left side. Maris had been hitting .309 and had six homers when forced to the sidelines. Fan support for Roger ran high: he showed a reporter a stack of some seventy-five letters – the majority, favorable.

Roger returned to the lineup and set a record in the May 22 game against the Los Angeles Angels. In the Yanks' 2-1, 12-inning victory, Roger drew five bases on balls – the last four intentional – a mark for deliberate free passes. Roger phoned Mantle, disabled with a leg injury, at Lenox Hill Hospital: "Hey, Mick, you'd better get back here," "I'm tired of getting all those walks. Now I know how it feels."

Although Roger continued to produce, his performance could not satisfy the fans. "The boos came along," Pat Maris recalls. Mickey Mantle thought that "Nobody respected him [Roger]. They wanted more." As Mantle emphasizes in *Just for the Record*, Maris was "never treated as a champion because he challenged the immortals and won."

Roger suffered all sorts of abuse from fans who could not be pleased. In the second game of a July 29 doubleheader against the White Sox, for example, fans bombarded Roger with two golf balls and a beer can. Blanchard, who witnessed the scene from the bull pen in Yankee Stadium, said: "Some of the things those fans yelled at Roger were enough to make your skin crawl. Much of it was the personal variety that couldn't be printed in a newspaper. I never understood how he absorbed it all without blowing his stack."

Mantle also chronicles the fans' treatment of Roger in *The Mick*: "As for Roger, in 1962, the fans gave him the worst beating any ballplayer ever took. From April straight through September they stayed on his back. I guess they expected him to hit 62 home runs."

While Roger may have received supportive fan mail in early spring, as the season rolled on, the fans – for whatever reason – showed their resentment toward him. Between the jousts with the press and the rancor of the fans, Roger's on-field accomplishments received little notice.

Amid all the turbulence, Roger could find some peace in the placid existence at the apartment, which he now shared with former Pittsburgh slugger Dale Long. Big Julie told *Sports Illustrated* that the writers depicted the wrong Roger: "He's a good kid, a real nice kid. He's got a nice wife, a nice family. ... Writers have written things about him that were wrong. They make him out to be a bum who wouldn't talk to anybody. I tell you there's nothing he'd rather do than just sit around and throw the bull with anybody."

In 1962, Maris played in 157 games and finished with a .256 average and 100 RBIs. He had hit 33 homers and scored 92 runs and 34 doubles. He made the roster of both All-Star games. In reality, Roger had had an excellent year, but not in the eyes of the fans and other so-called "experts."

According to Mantle in *Just for the Record,* a season such as Maris' in 1962 would merit a ballplayer a salary of $1 million in today's dealings.

Eugene Fitzgerald of the *Fargo Forum* overheard a reporter in the Yank clubhouse ask Roger if he were unhappy about his "bad" season. Roger replied sharply, "I didn't figure I had a bad season. I'd take it every year."

Beyond his 1962 statistics, Maris played an important role in the Yanks' third straight World Series. He achieved a .174 batting average against San Francisco but made decisive contributions in games one, three, and seven. Roger's double drove in two first-inning runs for a Yank 6-2 victory in the opener. He drove in two runs to break a scoreless tie in the seventh inning of game three. Roger took second on the throw home, raced to third, as Willie Mays nonchalantly caught a ball in medium center, and then scored on an infield out. The final score was 3-2.

People remember Willie McCovey lining out to Richardson for the final out in the 1-0 deciding game seven. However, in that same ninth inning, when the Giants had a man on first and two down and Mays sliced what looked like a game-tying hit, Roger cut the ball off and made a superb off-balance throw to preserve the victory.

Whitey Ford in *Slick* recalls that fielding gem: "Roger Maris made one of the greatest plays I've ever seen by an outfielder in the clutch. It was why Roger was such a great all-around player and why those who watched him play every day appreciated him not only for his bat, but for his fielding as well."

Pitcher Ralph Terry, the beneficiary of Roger's fielding in game seven, was named the outstanding player in the series. However, after considering Roger Maris' performance – the hits, the 5 RBIs, and the fielding – Jim Ogle stated in the *Sporting News:* "There was no question as to the star.... It was Maris, who had had a big hand in each of the four Yankee victories."

Despite Maris' all-round excellent performance, Mickey Mantle, in 123 games, with 30 homers, and 89 RBIs, took the MVP crown. Roger did not even merit a tenth place vote. Worse, a United Press International poll of 254 baseball mavens voted Roger "flop of the year," in a close vote over the Detroit Tigers, the St. Louis Cardinals, Norm Cash, Don Schwall, and Jim Piersall.

If the Roger's 1962 season turned out less "glamorous" a season than his 1961 year, Roger could at least look forward to an off-season in which there were few demands on his private time. He spent treasured days with his family and friends in his new home in Independence, Missouri. As Dick Savageau in Fargo recalls, "Roger was really worried that his friends might believe all those horrible stories that were being written about him. Of course, we never believed them."

Don Gooselaw spoke for Roger's Fargo friends who never thought Roger had a bad year: "I remember Roger telling us how important the luck factor was in hitting home runs. The difference between a line drive out and one over the fence was only a friction. You hit it a little on top and it's merely a line drive."

The Yankee skipper felt confident that Roger would have a fine season in 1963, particularly because he had not been on the banquet trail. "Maris had a rough winter last year," the skipper said. "He hit those 61 some runs and that put him on the treadmill. The banquet league got to be something out of this world. ... By the time he got to training camp, he was worn out, and there was no way you could blame him for that. He was paying the price of the winter he spent."

Chapter XVI
Summers That Were Bummers

Yankee manager Houk thought that Roger would have a solid year: "He won't be starting out with the pressure he had a year ago. Folks won't be around him so much and that alone ought to get him off to a better start than he had last year in Florida."

The Yankee management, however, upset by the booing, had little confidence in Roger's future. Golenbock wrote, "If manager Houk had not insisted that Maris remain with the Yankees, general manager Roy Hamey would have traded him at the end of '62."

Roger himself believed that the booing would continue: "As long as I stay in New York, it's going to keep on. They're on my back and they're never going to get off."

Despite management reservations, Roger stayed a Yankee. He even avoided a contract hassle like the one that marred the post-1961 season by accepting a salary frozen at the 1962 level.

A series of ten injuries pockmarked Roger's 1963 season. On April 1, a tear of the left hamstring muscle left Roger sidelined for the first seven games of the season. A reinjury to the same muscle on April 24 forced Maris to miss three games.

On May 3 the Yanks played in Minnesota, the closest big-league park to Fargo, before many fans from Roger's hometown. In the ninth inning, Roger's injuries kept him from running out a grounder. The fans booed loudly and a nasty exchange ensued. Houk defended Roger by explaining that medical personnel had given Roger "strict orders" not to do any unnecessary running and risk further damage to an already twice-injured leg.

On May 14, a muscular strain on the lower back again sidelined Roger for three games. Roger suffered a contusion of the left big toe on June 9, but he continued to play. For about a month, a healthy Maris helped carry the Yanks. By mid-July Roger's average had climbed to .300 on the strength of a 12-game .444 pace, highlighted by 13 RBIs and 5 home runs. His batting average had benefitted from the opposition's use of a "stacked defense" with overshifting shortstops in the infield. The shift attempted to jam the right side and block Roger's hits that naturally veered right.

The overshift left a wide gap between second and third and Roger soon began aiming for it. "I've changed my thinking," he said. "I'm sick and tired of seeing those infields jammed to one side the way they've been. I'd be silly not to take advantage of the situation."

Roger's hitting was winning games. In a game against Boston, with first and third and two out, Roger bunted against Dick "Monster" Radatz, leaving no one a chance to field the game-winning hit.

In the series finale Roger demonstrated his versatile hitting with his fourteenth round-tripper and a run-scoring single to the opposite field. By mid-July Roger had 15 homers and Yankee management, especially Houk, wore grins. Said skipper Houk: "Maris is playing as good a brand of ball as I've seen him play. He meant a lot to us in that good winning streak we had in the last three weeks or so. It's given us a lift when we needed it most."

Maris' hopes for an impressive season collapsed on July 7. Rectal surgery and the recuperative period following forced him to miss 17 games. Worse, he failed to make the 1963 All-Star squad, after participating in 7 consecutive all-star games over four years.

Roger never regained his pre-July 7 form. His injuries mounted: on July 24, a bruised left heel and a muscle spasm; on July 26, a strained left hand; on August 27, a back strain; on September 12, a sore lower back. In total, Maris played in only 90 games in 1963. His final statistics showed a .269 batting average, 23 homers, and 53 RBIs.

Despite the meager numbers, Maris' contributions before the July surgery gave the Yanks vital assistance in winning their fourth consecutive flag. In the total disappointment of the World Series, the Yanks bowed humbly before the Los Angeles Dodgers in four games, whose hurlers kept the Yankee batters to only four runs.

Roger, again plagued by injuries, made no hits in five times at bat. In game two he crashed into the right-field railing at Yankee Stadium. Roger continued to chase the ball in the Maris style of hustle, even though he had grabbed his left biceps and his knees buckled. Manager Houk spoke up to the loud-mouth critics who called Roger a "slacker." Houk had never had any doubt that Roger had been injured, and the World Series film proved it: "He gave it a helluva try, and nobody can tell me now, after I've seen the pictures, that he wasn't badly hurt."

The injury Maris suffered on Tommy Davis's looping triple led Roger to exhibit the humor of his Fargo adolescence: "I guess you might say I was pretty well ripped up from one end to the other."

Before the World Series had passed into history, the press cornered the sidelined slugger about "reports" of his impending trade or his planned retirement. Roger said, "You might call me a well-traveled man," referring to his days with Cleveland and Kansas City, but in regard to being traded, "I don't know a thing about that nor is it anything I have any control over."

However, he had total control over his retirement, and "I've never heard anything more ridiculous in my life," he said. "If I had any such idea, I wouldn't just tell one person. I'd tell everyone."

Roger neither retired nor was traded after the 1963 season; instead, throughout another grueling season, Roger depended on his friend, Big Julie. "I got to know Roger when he first came to New York," Big Julie said. "I was with him at the beginning, not just when he began his '61 homer season. Roger was always loyal to those who were with him from the start. When everybody wanted to dump and hang Roger after 1961, I was still there with him."

Although still allowed to wear the Yankee pinstripes, Roger took a cut from the salaries of 1962 and 1963. A week before Christmas, Roger and now-general manager Houk met at the Hotel Muehlebach in Kansas City, where Houk relayed news of the $10,000 slash. Houk later announced: "It didn't take us long to shake hands on the new terms. Roger was good about everything. He realized he had been able to play in only 90 games because of injuries."

Most sources cited $72,000 as Maris' set salary; others reported $75,000. The press quoted Maris on his reaction: "After the year I had, I couldn't see how I could ask for a raise or even the same salary," Roger remarked on his first pay cut in baseball.

During the off-season, Roger enjoyed tranquil good times with his family and friends. It was when he was home for long periods of time that he realized how difficult was the responsibility of raising a family. "You're playing a boy's game," Mrs. Margaret Surprise once told Roger, "while Pat is home taking care of the kids."

Bill Campbell, a friend of Roger's from Independence, will not forget the slugger's off-season friendship: "Once we went duck hunting in Sqaw Creek, the finest hunting in the St. Joseph's area. When we arrived at the inn, Roger asked the manager, 'How many accomodations?' 'Only one' was his reply. 'Well,' said Roger, 'if my friend can't stay, neither can I.'"

Another historically prominent citizen of Independence was President Harry S. Truman. President Truman and Maris were two stubborn, "give 'em hell" individuals. The Truman Library records their only meeting in Independence on November 7, 1963. During that visit, Roger posed with Mr. Truman, museum curator Milton Perry, library director Philip Brooks, and Ken White, a neighbor of Roger's. As a fellow outdoorsman, Roger was present at the ceremonies honoring White, a world champion freshwater fisherman.

As the 1964 season approached, Maris looked forward to obliterating the memories of the "nightmare" 1963 season. He gave the press his philosophy for the new season: "I try my very best every time up there. You give 100 percent, and that's all you can do."

The Yankee front office had selected Yogi Berra as manager for 1964. As Dr Surprise noted, "Roger liked Yogi and enjoyed playing for him." Maris approached the 1964 season with good humor. He relied on the fact that "They have finally forgotten 1961," as Roger said in spring training. "I had two ordinary years and they have forgotten the homers. This year, I'm going to enjoy playing. I hope no one bothers me."

Although the fans continued to boo, the pressure on Maris had eased tremendously. The popular Berra began to fall into disfavor. Team discipline flagged as Yogi managed an aging squad that included the ailing Mantle, 32, and Ford, 35. In August the sluggish Yanks fell to third place behind Baltimore and Chicago.

In September it became obvious that Mantle with his injured legs could no longer cover center field. Yogi replaced the Mick with Roger, and things began to happen in center field. Roger shored up the outfield defenses and during the last month of the season hit over .300, consistently delivering the key hits.

On September 4 in an exciting 9-7, 11-inning victory over Kansas City, Roger went two for four and contributed to the winning rally with a bunt single. The Yanks moved to three behind Baltimore.

The next day the Yanks again beat KC, 9-7, while Roger had two for five, one-RBI day. His two-out single in the fourth helped produce a three-run rally that put the game out of reach.

The Yanks tasted victory once more on September 6. Mantle drove in the winning run in the 3-2 game and Richardson scored in the eighth. Maris' ability to move Richardson to third on a grounder enabled the runner to score on Mantle's swinging bunt.

An 11-inning, 5-4 win over Minnesota on September 7 brought the Yanks to one and one-half games behind Baltimore. Roger's double down the right-field line with two outs off Red Worthington gave the Yanks their margin of victory. His three other hits that day included his twenty-first homer, rapped in the fifth with a man on.

The next day the Yanks faced the overpowering Camilio Pascual, who struck out ten batters in seven innings and allowed only three hits. However, Roger made two of the three hits and so helped manufacture a 2-1 squeaker. In the first Roger singled Kubek to third, and Mantle's sacrifice fly brought him in. Roger scored the decisive run after opening the seventh with a double, being sacrificed to third, and scooting home on Elston Howard's single.

Roger had no hits in the Yanks 5-2 triumph over Detroit on September 10, but he started the three-run, two-out rally in the first by being hit with a pitch. The victory kept the Yanks even in the loss column, one and one-half games behind first-place Baltimore.

On September 16 Angels' Aubrey Gatewood served Roger his twenty-second homer of the year and the 1,000th hit of his career. Earlier in the game his single keyed a three-run rally. Roger's homer became the game-winner in the 9-4 triumph.

The Yanks regained first place on September 17 with a 6-2 victory over the Angels, after a comeback from six games behind Baltimore on August 22. Roger, with three hits against the Angels, hit a bunt single that made him the table-setter for the three-run rally in the fourth.

The Yanks held on to their one and a half game lead over Baltimore with an 8-3 triumph over Kansas City on September 19, as Roger batted in two runs, featuring his 23rd homer.

No lead seemed safe in the season's final days: the Phillies' six-and-one-half-game lead had started to slip with two weeks left. Roger again became the star on September 25. His first homer, in the seventh with two on, brought the Yankees to one run behind the apparently victorious Buz Narum. Maris clinched the game with his second homer of the day, in the ninth inning, The Yanks held on to their four game lead, increasing their winning streak to 10 with a 6-5 victory over the Washington Senators.

The Yanks closed September with a sweep of the Tigers at Yankee Stadium, giving them a 3 1/2-game lead over the White Sox with five games to play. Roger had three hits and three RBIs in the nightcap. His single in the first brought in the first of four runs in the first, and the Yanks never lost their lead in the 11-8 win.

Maris led the Yanks to victory in 22 of 28 games that September. The team secured the flag, their last until 1976 on the next-to-last day of the season, by finishing one up on the White Sox and two on the Orioles.

As a player on a contending team, Maris had one hundred World Series tickets that he could dispense at will. He talked about what to do with them with his friend George Surprise. "Don't sell them, George," Roger advised. "Give them away to baseball fans." Surprise remembers, "As he said this, we noticed an older man with a crippled kid who had come from Memphis, hoping to see the game in St. Louis. Roger nodded to me. 'Here's three tickets,' I told the man. 'Are they good tickets? What do you want for them?' he asked. 'You bet they're good,' I said. 'But maybe you can root for the Yankee rightfielder to get a hit.'"

Despite his charitable act, Roger's only RBI in the World Series against the St. Louis Cardinals came with his one home run. Soon after the Yanks' loss, the Yankee front office fired manager Yogi Berra.

Roger felt pleased with his performance during the 1964 season. His .281 batting average almost matched his 1960 mark of .283. Maris hit 26 homers and 71 RBIs, 24 of which came in the last 41 games for a .464 slugging average that was second only to Mantle's.

As a "reward" for Maris' 1964 contributions, the Yankees reinstated the top salary he had earned in 1962 and 1963. The press made no comment on the $7-10,000 raise.

Maris' received his greatest honor of 1964 and perhaps of his life not on the ballfield, but at the North Dakota state capitol. North Dakota Governor William Guy presided over ceremonies in which Roger received the Teddy Roosevelt Rough Rider Award, a commendation accorded to those who have distinguished themselves in their various careers.

Previous Rough Rider Award recipients came from the worlds of art and letters: musician Lawrence Welk, singer Peggy Lee, actress

Dorothy Stickney, photographer Ivan Dmitri, and journalist Eric Sevareid. Roger was the only North Dakotan honored for his achievement in sports. In his report for the *Fargo Forum* Del Johnson writes, "Roger Maris, a New York Yankee, who speaks softly and carries a big stick, received North Dakota's most notable achievement recognition."

Roger anticipated the 1965 season, watching with fatherly pride as his older boys, Roger, Jr., and Kevin, began to wear baseball mitts, swing bats, and fight over which ballplayers they would pretend to be. The innocent feuding of the Maris boys seemed to portend a much more serious brawl involving their father in the spring of 1965.

On April Fool's Day, Jerry Modzelewski, a Chicago male model, filed a complaint against Roger for assault and battery following an incident in a local Fort Lauderdale bar. Roger denied the charge, claiming that and he and other players had returned from Bradenton and entered Nick's Cocktail Lounge. An altercation had occurred between Yankee third-baseman Clete Boyer and Modzelewski.

According to Maris, he had tried to act as peacemaker "when I noticed Clete was getting mad. I said nothing to him [Modzelewski] and he said nothing to me. The first I ever saw him was when I nearly tripped over him while he was down. Somebody in the bar hit him, I guess, but it wasn't me and anyone who says so in court will be making himself liable to perjury."

Manager Johnny Keane supported Roger, as did Joe DiMaggio, a frequent visitor to the bar. The Yankee Clipper phoned Yankee Vice President Houk to say, "I want you to know that Roger most certainly did not hit anybody."

Police charged both Maris and Boyer as the Yankees left Fort Lauderdale to play in Puerto Rico.

Municipal Judge Arnold Grievior acquitted Roger on April 7, ruling that "There is a reasonable doubt as to what happened." Maris then sued the model for $310,000: $10,000 in compensatory damages and $300,000 in punitive damages. The episode prompted numerous Associated Press and United Press International stories; suddenly, the incident disappeared from the press. Pat Maris claims the suit was "dropped."

On April 17, Roger cleared both right field walls at Kansas City's Municipal Stadium. In accomplishing this feat, Maris joined a select group of power hitters: Mantle (who did it twice), Larry Doby, Harry

Simpson, Norm Cash, and Fred Whitfield.

In the seventh inning of a game against Kansas City on April 28, Roger made a stunning, rally-killing catch . As Bert Campaneris lined a drive to right center, Roger sped to his right and made a backhanded catch. As he caught the ball, Roger's right leg collapsed under him. He lay motionless on the grass while his teammates rushed to him. Finally Roger got to his feet, but he had to be helped off the field.

Team physician Dr. Sidney Gaynor reported that the slugger had pulled the medial muscle on his right thigh. He had aggravated an injury sustained in a spring 1963 exhibition game against the Tigers at Lakeland, Florida. That injury meant three weeks on the shelf.

Even though Roger's catch might have saved the game and evened the Yanks' 1965 record, the Yankees paid a heavy price: Roger sat out 26 games.

Roger came back to a team mired in the second division in pursuit of an unprecedented sixth-straight flag. After a slow start, and despite having missed all those games, Maris had 8 homers and 25 RBIs. Roger's home run in the opener of a twin bill against the Twins gave him an 11-game hitting streak: 4 homers, 14 RBIs, and a .340 mark. Unfortunately, while sliding home, he jammed his pinky and ring finger against umpire Bill Haller's shoe. After that twin bill, he sat out five games. In the last week of June Maris had 138 at bats, 8 homers, 25 RBIs, and an average of .232.

On June 28, the Yanks on a five-game winning streak took two from Washington and stood within two games of the .500 mark. Roger had returned to the lineup that day even though he was still unable to grip the bat handle. In the second game Roger faced leftie Mike McCormick. On McCormick's first pitch, the slugger lost the bat as he swung. Maris said later: "There was a real sharp pop in my hand, loud enough that I could hear it. It was just like you snap a pencil. The hand swelled up right away, double its size. I ended up taking a pitch right down the middle to strike out."

Three doctors one each in New York, Washington, and Minnesota examined Roger's many X-rays for the Yanks. After he retired, Roger revealed that despite the medical consultations, "There was never any mention of a break." The Yanks just accepted the injury as one of those day-to-day occurrences. Their growing roster of injured in 1965 included Maris, Mantle, Howard, and Stafford. Roger and the

Mick particularly had been so physically battered by July 4 that two New York Met heroes, Ron Swoboda and Ed Kranepool, had more home runs, more runs batted in, and a higher combined batting average than the Yankee duo.

Clete Boyer in *Just for the Record* observes that because the Yankees were an "old" team, many people, including Roger's fellow players, looked at him in a "funny" way. Some thought he was "jaking", players' terminology for laying down on the job, even though Mrs. Margaret Surprise still vividly recalls the Roger of the 1965 season as "constantly in pain, bent over in great torment."

According to Pat Maris, the Yankees believed Roger was only "sloughing off, that he was not interested in playing anymore." Maris himself described his herculean efforts to play:

> At first I could go out in the field and take infield practice, throw the baseball. Then the ball club every four or five days asked me to take batting practice, or I'd go ahead and try a few things, and it didn't work. It got to the point where I couldn't even throw a baseball because I couldn't hold the baseball in my hand. Yet, they were continually asking me to take batting practice. The press said I just didn't want to play. But what player doesn't want to play?

David Wohlreuter remembered that Roger did want to play. He wrote to the *Sporting News* in 1967 when he was director of sports information at Ithaca (NY) College. He recalled the Roger Maris who played in 1965 in the Hall of Fame game in nearby Cooperstown:

> At the time, Roger was injured. ... With all his problems, he was a gentleman, very cooperative, and a true major leaguer. This is more than I can say for another member of the Yankee outfield, who when he did talk, only complained about having to play at the Hall of Fame on his day off.

Finally, Big Julie acted on Maris' behalf: "The pain in Roger's hand was not to be endured. He could hardly stand up. How could anybody say that he was faking it? I looked into finding the best doctor for Roger's injury and brought Roger there. Nobody knew this, and that included Keane and Houk."

The X rays showed that Roger had broken a bone in his hand and a fragment of that bone had lodged in the upper right side of his hand. While the results of the X rays may have upset Maris and his friends and family, Houk had apparently known about the severity of injury for some time. In 1970 Maris first revealed to Sheldon Ocker of the *Akron Beacon Journal* what happened between him and Houk following that diagnosis.

Finally with about two weeks left in the season, I went up to his office and told him I wanted permission to go home and take care of my hand. I said, if he didn't give me the OK, I'd go anyway. Then he said to me and I'll never forget it. Houk said, "Rog, I might as well level with you, you need an operation on that hand." Now, what do you think?

The media finally exerted enough pressure to convince the Yankees to announce Roger's upcoming scheduled surgery. A writer noticed that rookie Horace Clarke had taken over Roger's locker, and the journalists demanded an explanation. The Yankees quickly scheduled a press conference with the club physician. Dr. Sidney Gaynor gave his statement:

Maris has a bone fracture...Maris goes into the hospital Monday and will be operated on Tuesday. He should be released by Thursday, and the recuperation period will be about six weeks. We expect 100 percent recovery.

The hook of the hamate bone (lower left area of the right hand under the flesh of the palm) was torn loose. It is a small thing, about one-third the size of your pinky. We had hoped that nature would reunite it to the hamate bone, which often happens. In this case, it didn't. We hoped surgery wouldn't be necessary, but when we saw that the hook was not going to rejoin the main bone, we decided to operate.

At first, Roger opposed the surgery, for he saw little hope that the hand could improve. After his visit to New York surgeon Dr. J. William Littler, Roger changed his mind. Maris related to reporter Milton Gross: "He [the surgeon] told me that I might be able to get by without the operation for a while, but eventually I wouldn't be able to do anything with the fingers – a job or anything. I knew that one little slip and I could wind up with no feeling in the fingers, but I knew I had little choice. I said, 'Go ahead and have it out.'"

Before checking in for surgery, Roger said that the entire season had been "a total waste. I feel like a bump on a log. There's no real way to describe it. You can use any word you like: frustrated, disgusted, or anything like that, but it's even worse than that. Do you know how tiresome it gets just sitting around doing nothing?"

On September 28 Dr. Littler performed a three-hour surgical procedure on Roger's hand. The surgeon's records indicate that the reparative surgery on Roger's injury demanded great care to prevent damage to the adjacent motor branch of the ulnar nerve. Littler, internationally acclaimed as the father of hand surgery, maintains a file describing Roger's operation, since it was the first such operation he had performed. His notes read: "Via an incision in the palmar surface of the hand over the hamate bone, the hamate was exposed, carefully retracting the deep branch of the ulnar nerve and the ulnar artery. ... The free-floating fragment was then removed. ... The patient withstood the procedure well and left the operating room in good condition."

Roger recuperated in Roosevelt Hospital, while the dethroned Yanks finished the year in sixth place. In October Roger returned to New York to have the cast removed, the final step in what was termed a successful operation.

Maris' surgery had strained the relationship between Roger and Yankee General Manager Houk. Roger had not consulted with Houk or other Yankee officials before consenting to the operation, an omission that greatly displeased the team management.

Big Julie claims that to overcome Roger's reluctance to undergo surgery, Isaacson solicited Houk's guarantee to maintain Maris' 1965 salary level in 1966 if Roger would have the operation. At first Houk balked, but then he went along with the deal. According to Big Julie, Roger agreed to the operation but left the hospital when the Yanks called a press conference about his condition.

As a member of the Cards in 1967, Roger charitably defended his former boss. "Maybe it's unfair to the individual player not to have it known generally when he's paying under par," Roger said, "but it's potentially beneficial to the opposing team to know the truth. So I don't blame a manager for concealing the extent of injuries from the other side."

Whatever the source of friction between them, Roger refused to attack Houk publicly. In 1978, Maris told Peter Golenbock:

I'm not going to knock Mr. Houk. I'm not going to knock anybody. Everybody's going to draw their own conclusions. There are just a lot of things that I don't understand, and I never will. A lot of things. I just don't want to get into knocking Ralph. I've got my own personal feelings. I feel that a lot of things could have been handled a lot differently than they were.

However in 1985, while terminally ill, Roger could criticize the treatment he had received: "The Yankees didn't take care of me. They didn't send me to the right doctor. They were only interested in getting me back in the lineup. ... Ralph knew how bad I was hurting. He should have told the press. Instead they kept on with that day-to-day crap so that it looked like I was a malingerer."

An example of press dissatisfaction with the Yankee cover-up appeared in the *New York Daily News* on October 18. In a story headlined "Maris Now it Can Be Told," Gene Ward reported that the Yanks had finally revealed the extent of Maris' injury. Ward wrote:

Their candor came very, very late. And when they [the doctors] told him, they told nobody else except the Yankee brass. A lot of fans and some players went right on thinking Maris was goldbricking on a team that was sorely in need of his talents.

I think the Yankee public relations staff goofed in not revealing the seriousness of Maris' injury long before they did.

Tony Kubek, one of Roger's teammates who played under Houk, records in *Sixty-One:* "I asked Ralph about Roger's wrist, and he acted as if nothing was wrong. It wasn't something he cared to discuss. ... Neither man [Roger and Houk] was willing to make the first move to sit down and talk over what had happened. And over the years, the misunderstandings grew and festered until it was impossible to really know the truth."

The 1965 episode soured a professional relationship that had greatly benefited Roger's career. Houk ran interference for Maris when the press pilloried him during the drive for the 61 home-run record. The general manager defended Roger during the trying days of the 1962 training season. In the 1962 off-season Houk supported Roger at Yankee front-office discussions.

But Houk's behavior when Roger injured his hand remains upper-most in the minds of Roger's family, friends, and supporters. In Fargo, Roger's friends censure Houk unequivocally. According to Don Gooselaw, "No one on the Yanks liked Houk, the general manager. ... Houk knew fully what was wrong with Roger and never, until the end, told him the truth. Who's to know what would have happened if Roger had gone to surgery earlier that season?" Said *Fargo Forum* sports editor Ed Kolpack, "Roger never forgave Houk for playing him with a bad hand."

Not only had the injuries taken a physical toll on Roger, but as the 1966 season neared, Roger found that his old excitement about playing baseball had lessened considerably. Roger had been "pushed here, shoved there," said Clete Boyer in *Just for the Record*. Whether it was the Yankee management, the fans, the press, or a combination of all of them, the "desire" to play and win had been "knocked out of him."

In 1965 Roger played in only 46 games, the fewest games-per-season in his major-league career. Roger ended the season with 155 at bats, 8 homers, 27 RBIs, and a .239 average. Despite his statistics and injuries, contract discussions for the 1966 season went smoothly: the Yankees gave Roger the same contract as in 1965. Yankee General Manager Ralph Houk announced, "We didn't feel he should be cut in salary, because he was hurt while playing, and you can't blame a player for that."

Roger genially signed with the Yankees in January. A *New York Daily News* photo shows Maris posing with Houk, smiling and flashing his "once-injured" hand. With great magnanimity Roger Maris explained the Yanks' 1965 diagnosis to the press: "I can see how they would make that mistake. The first X-rays didn't show anything, and later X-rays didn't give them a clear picture, because they were not taken from the proper angle. The pain in my hand prevented me from turning, so they could not get a shot at the proper angle, and from the picture they did take, it appeared that the chip was attaching itself to the bone."

In New York, Roger visited Dr. Littler for a final check-up. The surgeon remembers Roger as "courteous, a gentleman. It was a professional dealing. We talked. He came back for the procedure, and left in good spirits." Dr. Littler examined Roger's hand and pronounced it fit.

Although Dr. Littler had performed a successful surgery, Roger never consistently regained his former power. Worse, he even lost some strength in two fingers.

Dr. Littler offered an explanation of why Roger never again achieved the statistics of 1960-63:

> You must be aware that full recovery does not have to correlate with performance by professional athletes. The difference between successful contact with a ball and failure is ever so slight. I suspect that in Roger's case, where the injury was in the protective pathway, there was an emotional factor that forced him to hold back so that he could not perform at his very best.

During the off-season, Roger had kept himself in shape by golfing near Independence. Since his golf swing seemed accurate and powerful, Maris felt confident that the normal strength in his hand would return. His confidence continued through spring training. Penciled in the starting lineup against the Braves in early March, Maris played his first game as a starter since June 29, 1965. A delighted Roger announced after the game, "I am ready to play every day."

Roger was also delighted with the latest addition-his sixth child, Sandra.

Maris' performance also pleased Joe DiMaggio, a special instructor for the Yankees in spring training. Joltin' Joe observed, "He is in great shape and hitting well." Roger seemed the player to watch in 1966.

Sadly, Roger's body and spirit could not match his early promise. After a slow spring training, Roger hit only .190 in the first 20 games. The skipper benched him against lefties starting at the sixth game of the season. The Yanks, who played as badly as Roger, flirted with the cellar. Desperate, the front office fired Keane on May 7.

Roger's performance improved as soon as Houk returned as skipper. Houk played Roger against all pitchers and Roger responded. In mid-May Maris had a .382 mark, 6 RBIs, and singled-in runs in two consecutive at bats against lefties.

On May 18 the Yankees played against the Tigers, featuring Roger in center field for the first time since the 1964 World Series. In the first inning, Roger attempted to slide home but collided with Tiger catcher Bill Freehan. The catcher's shin guard caught Roger under the knee. The injury that resulted from the freak accident was immediately diagnosed as a "slightly sprained knee."

The damage done to the slugger's knee left it weak and sore for the rest of 1966. He required the proper rest to allow it to heal. However, the Yankees, who had been floundering at the bottom of the league standings, had just taken a 7-2 victory against the Tigers. Having just won four games in six days, the Yanks were unwilling to lose Roger's bat.

The Yanks won their May 25 game against the California Angels, 11-8, but Roger suffered yet another injury. In the second-inning, Roger crashed into the right-field wall after a one-handed grab of a possible homer by Jim Piersall. Maris fell to the ground and was carried off the field on a stretcher. Dr. Gaynor examined the slugger's knees and did not think them seriously injured. Relieved to learn that he had only suffered painful bruises, Roger remarked, "I thought I had broken my kneecaps."

Although Roger was not in top physical condition after those May mishaps, he stayed in the lineup. After the injuries, his batting mark hovered around .230. Maris started September with a .233 mark and 10 homers. At season's end, some of his old spunk seemed to return and he added three more round-trippers.

Roger had orders not to run hard unless his exertions seemed crucial to winning the game in question. He incurred the wrath of both fans and the media when, for the first time in his career, he didn't leg out grounders to the infield. Reporter Paul Zimmerman's story labeled Roger a "$70,000 loaf." A very genial Roger cornered the scribe to correct him: "Quite a story, but I wish you would get it right. I'm a $75,000 loaf."

Roger played his last game as a Yankee on September 30 in Chicago. He ended his pinstripes career with a familiar scenario: Maris answered the fans' boos with a home run.

The best efforts of Roger and all his teammates could not save the 1966 season. The Yanks finished tenth and last in the league, after having set a record for losing ball games by one run. Roger's batting average fell to its major-league low, .233, but he did manage 24 extra base hits, with 13 homers and 43 RBIs.

Big Julie believes that Roger had lost his old spark during the 1966 season. The surgery, the team performance, and the treatment by the front office all contributed to the deterioration of spirit. As an example of Maris' loss of inner fire, Big Julie recalled what was for

Roger an out-of-character incident.

Maris had become good friends with Paul Grossinger, owner of the famous Catskills resort, after Roger had done a Yonkers Police Department benefit there. One Sunday afternoon, Big Julie invited Roger to a birthday party for Grossinger, commenting that Maris might find it difficult to attend because of the Yanks' Sunday doubleheader.

"Roger assured me that would be no problem," Big Julie continued. "Would you believe that Roger got thrown out of the first game midway through, and then Roger sent word to meet him in the club house. 'How about the second game,' I said stunned. 'Let's skip it,' Roger said. 'Nobody will miss me.' That was not typical Roger Maris, but things had hit bottom."

According to a 1978 Golenbock article in *Baseball Quarterly*, Roger told manager Houk in July 1966 of his plans to hang up the spikes. Houk suggested that Roger think it through. If he still felt the same way before spring training in 1967, he could make the announcement. Roger agreed.

Rumors about Roger's possible retirement began to surface in the summer. Roger maintained that much of the speculation stemmed from *New York Post* columnist Milton Gross, who described Roger as "disappointed, disillusioned, and almost in despair." Roger replied to Gross's comments in September, when the Yanks were in Minneapolis: "I know what I want to do, but I haven't told anyone yet."

Eugene Fitzgerald's column in the *Fargo Forum* hinted that Roger would perhaps move back to his hometown. According to Fitzgerald, the Fargo grapevine had reported Roger in the area searching for business opportunities since he had gone to the Yankees. Fitzgerald concluded his article by assessing Roger's 1966 position:

"He said in 1960 he would leave baseball as soon as he felt he could live on his savings.

"He can afford it."

Yankee General Manager Lee MacPhail felt that the team could not afford the leisurely timetable set up by the Maris-Houk agreement on Roger's retirement plans. Soon after the 1966 season ended, MacPhail phoned Roger in Independence, asking whether Roger had had a change of heart. Roger gave the same answer as he did in his summer conversation with Houk. Then, suspecting something afoot, Roger bluntly asked the Yanks GM: "Lee, if you have any intention of trading me, let me know now, and I'll announce my retirement."

MacPhail guaranteed Roger that the Yankees did not plan a trade. Roger reiterated the terms of his agreement with Houk: any announcement of changes in the slugger's status would come in the spring. Macphail agreed to the deal and ended their telephone conversation. A few days later, a photographer waiting on Roger's lawn greeted him with news of his trade to the St. Louis Cardinals.

Pat Maris remembers how she heard of the marketing of the 61-homer king: "On a December day, it was before Christmas, I had just come home from taking some of the children to see Santa Claus. The phone was ringing. The babysitter was in a frenzy. I saw Roger coming in the back door. And there was the photographer. That's how I learned of the trade."

A shocked Big Julie heard the news from Milton Gross. The terms of the swap hit him like a thunderbolt: Roger Maris for Charlie Smith.

The lead of an Arthur Daley column clearly enunciated the degradation of the swap:

> The trade that sent Roger Maris from the Yankees to the Cardinals was an insult to him. He was disdainfully dealt off for the equivalent of a couple of broken bats and a scuffed baseball. That's what gave the transaction such stunning impact, the even-up exchange of a one-time diamond demigod for an undistinguished journeyman, Charlie Smith, a refugee from the Mets.

A few hours before the trade announcement, a column by Milton Richman of United Press International went over the sports wires. Richman wrote: "Roger Maris, the most precious piece of property in all baseball only five years ago, has the same market value as a well-worn 1961 car without any air conditioning. And if you look up those models in the daily ads, you'll find out they bring next to nothing."

After the same wire carried news of the Maris trade, UPI killed the Richman story. Surprisingly, the venerable Red Smith echoed Richman's sentiments when he gave his views of the trade: "More surprising than yesterday's deal and the modest price accepted was the fact that the Yankees found a club willing to accept their damaged goods. There was no secret about the guy's being marked disposable. ...

"Fred Corcoran said it about golf, but it applies in every field: 'In one year he went from *Who's Who* to *Who's He?*'"

Roger had a blunt reaction to columnists' uncharitable opinions: "A bunch of those writers have been trying to get me out of town for years, and they've finally succeeded."

Houk in *Season of Glory* reveals a totally different perspective on the Maris trade:

> After the 1966 season, he told me he wouldn't come back. Just definitely would not come back to New York. When Roger left the Yankees, he was pissed off at the world. Then we made the deal with St. Louis. What we did, we gave him his free agency, really, and he agreed to go to St. Louis because he was from that general area anyway.
>
> That was the best that happened to Roger because, jeez, they really took care of him, gave him that Budweiser dealership in Florida as part of the deal.

Chapter XVII
A Spirit Rekindled in St. Louis

Once Roger lost his initial indignation at the insulting way the Yankees had traded him, he had to decide whether to play in 1967. Big Julie says that Roger's first impulse was to quit baseball. Years later, Maris told Will Grimsley of the Associated Press: "The last six years in the American League were mental hell for me, I was drained of all of my desire to play baseball. They were years of anguish for me, I suddenly lost all my desire to play. I went out and tried. It was no use. I was washed out. The dedication just wasn't there."

Roger would doubtless have complied with his agreement with Houk and retired if the Yankees had not traded him. Retirement became out of the question when the Yanks made Maris a Redbird. As he stated after the trade: "I wouldn't have played in '67 if the Yankees hadn't traded me. But when I was traded I decided to play. I didn't want the press to say I quit because the Yankees traded me."

Soon after the Yankees announced the deal, the Marises and the Musials met for lunch in St. Louis. A few days later Musial sent Roger a letter with a $75,000 contract attached. Roger still felt undecided about his future and put the contract in a drawer for six weeks,

When Stan Musial called again, Roger had decided to sign with the National League's Cardinals. The team called a press conference at Busch Stadium in the second week of February to welcome Roger to St. Louis. Referring to the new addition to the club, Stan the Man said, "We're happy and pleased to have him with us."

Manager Red Schoendienst spoke optimistically at the press conference: "Maris is a real threat. And he'll help in more ways than one. He's a good outfielder and has good judgment on the bases. We were lacking for runs last season, and I think Maris may be just the man we can slip in there to help us. He's always played well when he wasn't injured."

In addition to the generous contract and gracious attitude of the Cardinals, Roger may have had other personal reasons to convince him to forego retirement.

The traveling time between St. Louis and Independence is approximately three and one-half hours by car and fewer than forty-five minutes by plane. The proximity meant Roger could spend more time with his family. "I'll go home now whenever time permits," he said.

Fan sentiment might also have influenced Roger's decision to stay on with the Cards. "Of every ten letters I got, nine are good. Most of the letters say,'play, play, play, and keep on playing.' Maybe they helped me to make up my mind.'"

Kubek's *Sixty-One* cites Big Julie's opinion that a beer distributorship offered by Cardinals' owner Gussie Busch induced Roger to reconsider his retirement plans. Kubek quotes Big Julie saying that St. Louis General Manager Stan Musial "made a deal" with Busch that "Roger could buy one [distributorship] after he retired."

In his early-eighties book, *Where Have You Gone, Vince DiMaggio*, Edward Kiersh also states that the Cardinals promised Roger a beer distributorship for signing with them. Commenting on the book, Roger rejected Kiersh's claim, insisting, "That's not true. I was trying to get a distributorship before I came to St. Louis."

Another version of the story comes from Roger's Fargo friend Bob Wood. "After the Cardinals had won the 1967 World Series, they were whooping it up in the dressing room. A very happy Busch came over to Roger and asked,'What will it take to get you back with us next year?' Roger quickly answered:'a beer distributorship.'"

At Maris Distributing in Gainesville, Florida, Pat Maris dispelled each of those rumors. "Roger was never promised anything when he came to St. Louis. It is true though that Roger's playing in St. Louis made it possible for Mr. Busch to see the type of person that Roger was."

The eager-to-please Cardinals delighted Roger when they announced he would continue to wear his number 9 jersey. Previous St. Louis players to wear number 9 included Bob Uecker, Tim McCarver (in spring training), and most notably Hall of Famer Enos "Country" Slaughter, best remembered for tearing around the bases to beat the Red Sox in the 1946 World Series. A predecessor like Slaughter and the beginning of spring training brought Roger press questions on criticism he had received in New York for his nonchalance in getting from the dugout to the outfield. As usual, Roger replied openly and nonevasively: "I don't believe in false hustle. Why wear yourself out wasting all that energy running to and from your position when you can jog? The games are long enough. I'd rather not be tired when I get up to the plate.

"I've always been ready when my pitcher was. I've never been caught with my back to the pitcher."

All the early press criticism of Roger – before he had even arrived in camp – made many of the Cardinals wary. Mike Shannon, who became one of Roger's close friends, described the Cardinals' attitude in *Just for the Record:* "Everyone was apprehensive because of his New York record." However, Shannon continues, when Roger "put his tail on the line," his teammates "found out in a big hurry what a good person, a good player he was."

Roger found a new spirit in St. Louis. "Maybe it's because there are baseball men running things, Red [Schoendienst] and Stan [Musial], but I've found a relaxed atmosphere." Maris explained his satisfaction with the Cardinals to Red Barber: "Everything is going fine. Red [Schoendienst] was a whale of a pro ballplayer who had his share of injuries and sicknesses. He plays me and keeps me running. I want to get off to a good start and not pull my leg again."

The Cards felt enthusiastic over the prospect of a spirited, healthy Roger Maris helping the St. Louis team better its 1966 sixth-place finish. In an exhibition game against the Mets, Roger teamed with power-hitting first baseman Orlando Cepeda to give the Cards an optimistic preview of the season. Cepeda slammed three hits, among them a homer. Roger banged out four hits and made all the Redbirds smile when he raced home on a short fly to left.

Roger and Cepeda had first met in Arizona in 1958, when Maris was training with Cleveland. Roger recalled, "We talked a little and got along good together then. I like playing on the same club with him. He's a good hitter and I know he's gonna do it. I just hope I can."

Cepeda saw a similarity between his experiences and Roger's. Both Roger and Cepeda had their best years in 1961: the first baseman hit 46 homers, knocked in 142 runs, and showed a .311 batting average. While Roger played alongside Mantle, Cepeda played in the shadow of Willie Mays. Both Maris and Cepeda received criticism for not being team players. Like Roger, Cepeda subsequently suffered injuries and found himself traded like meaningless merchandise.

"What happened to me with the Giants," Cepeda said, "is exactly what happened to Roger with the Yankees I know what it means for him to come to a club like this where everybody looks to help each other. My knee started giving me trouble in 1962 [after a collision with Dodger catcher John Roseboro]. Still I didn't say anything. Then they said I was faking, the same way they said Roger was faking."

Cepeda played hurt for two more years and then was traded in 1966, just as Roger was. "I understand what it means for a fellow like Roger to come here. I understand better maybe than anybody else. "He's good people. Everybody on this club loves him, and if you ask me personally, I don't think they come much better."

Cardinal hitting-coach Dick Sisler told the world what he had discovered about Roger: "I've found that a lot of things written about Roger just don't hold water. I read that he was a loner and wouldn't cooperate. But I often see him with the other players and signing autographs politely, no matter where he is.

"People should know that he really is very friendly and warm. He showed great desire to get into shape and have a good year. I think he'll do it on desire alone."

At the close of spring training, Roger pronounced himself in top condition. He had reduced to his normal 203-pound playing weight. His injured knee even seemed to have improved, and he confidently said, "This is the best and most I've been able to run for some time."

A very impressed Red Schoendienst had noticed that "Roger worked hard in Florida in every way. After playing five or six innings, he'd do a lot of hard running and do his pickups."

Roger had some apprehensions about competing in the National League. Even though the league pitchers would have to learn all about Maris, Roger still felt "It'll be like starting all over. The biggest thing will be learning all the new pitchers."

However, many familiar faces had moved to the National League, including Jim Bunning, Bo Belinsky, and those hurlers who participated in Roger's "61 in '61" season: namely, Jack Fisher, Juan Pizzaro, Bob Shaw, Pedro Ramos, Ray Herbert, Joe Nuxhall, and Milt Pappas.

Roger showed smart batting in the home opener with a double and bunt single against the shift that had three Giants placed between first and second base. The fans cheered when he singled over shortstop in the second but never stopped running, turning a single into a double.

Roger soon knew the rightness of his decision to come to St. Louis.

Neal Russo penned a *Sporting News* story on the Cardinals' opener against the Giants that bore the headline: "Maris Hears Cheers Instead of Jeers." Exhilirated, Maris said: "It was very nice to hear a reaction like that for a change. It's been a long time. I couldn't believe it was for real. I would like to be liked rather than disliked. Just wearing a different uniform this spring seems to have made some difference."

Dr. Surprise believes "the important thing about Roger's outlook for 1967, aside from new fans, new writers, and the like, was that Roger was so close to home. When he was with the Yankees, the entire Maris family would be together for only about ten days a season."

During the brief home stand, Roger belted 8 hits in 17 at bats, for a .471 mark, with two doubles and a triple. He told interviewers, "All I want are base hits. I've got some good hitters like Orlando Cepeda, Tim McCarver, and Mike Shannon behind me."

Roger didn't expect a big home-run year – certainly a most difficult feat with the reduced mobility in his swing. "All I want to do here," he said, "is contribute something to a winning-team effort. If I can do that, I think I've had a good year – a very good year."

A very pleased Schoendienst spoke in superlatives about Roger as the Cardinals came to Shea Stadium early in the season. Beyond Roger's .310 average and 12 RBIs, "He's a real professional," Schoendienst related. "You don't have to tell him anything. He wants to win."

At Shea Roger heard some boos and read some Met bedsheet banners proclaiming "Maris Go Home." When the Cardinals needed a pinch hitter to take advantage of a sinker ball lefthander, they pulled Roger for the first time in the season. Maris' reaction impressed Schoendienst. "He stayed on the bench the rest of the game. He could have gone inside, but he wanted to be out there in the dugout with everybody else."

Fargo's Don Gooselaw remembers that Roger did more than sit in the dugout. "Roger was the dugout cheerleader. He pounded on the garbage can in the dugout to cheer the team on. If you ask Tim McCarver, he'll tell you that it was Roger who was responsible for keying up the Cardinals."

Nothing would keep Roger down. When he chipped a bone in his big toe in a household accident, he was available to pinch hit two days later. Maris started all three contests at Shea.

Maris' major contributions made the Cardinals unstoppable, as they overcame early challenges by the Cubs and Giants. Cardinal shortstop Dal Maxvill soon realized that Roger was "a winning player," whose aggressiveness and determination to win equaled that of the Redbirds' fiercests competitors, Bob Gibson and Mike Shannon. At a mid-May alumni banquet at Washington University in St. Louis, Maxvill referred to Roger Maris as "one of the finest men I have met in baseball."

For the first time in five years, Roger enjoyed playing baseball. The 32-year-old veteran didn't even mind the Cardinals' platoon system that alternated his position in the lineup against righties. "Being in and out of there hasn't bothered me. In fact, at times it has made me stronger. I've been platooned at times before, and I understand it. If you're here to win and the manager thinks that's the way to win, I'm for him."

Sportswriters began to comment on Roger's performance in the clutch. At the end of July, *Post-Dispatch* sports editor Bob Broeg wrote that Roger "has ranked with Orlando Cepeda and Julian Javier for driving in game-tying or winning runs and has rated high, too, in the percentages of runs he has driven in and base-runners advanced."

Unlike the often hostile, abusive New York fans, Cardinal faithful noticed the personality of the man behind the baseball player. Staff Sergeant Anthony DeFazio of Carbondale, Pennsylvania, concluded that "Maris is okay in my book" after reporting a telling incident to *The Sporting News*. As the Redbirds boarded their bus after a game at Connie Mack Stadium, an old man approached a player, begging for a nickel or dime. Roger witnessed the scene from the back of the bus. He took a dollar from his wallet. Then he whispered to John Romano, seated in front of him, and gave the catcher the dollar. Romano handed the old man the dollar through the window, saying, "This is from Roger."

Andy Strasberg, marketing director for the San Diego Padres, has especially fond memories of 1967 and Roger Maris, his boyhood idol. Strasberg recalls that he first met Roger "on a drizzly day in 1963 when I skipped school and went to Yankee Stadium. There weren't many kids around and I had a chance to talk to Roger at length." Young Strasberg asked Roger for a bat and ball. Strasberg got the bat, but Roger told him that he would have to catch the ball himself. Andy fulfilled that dream. In Pittsburgh on May 9, 1967, an older

Strasberg caught a Roger four-bagger in row nine, seat nine, in right field.

Roger called Strasberg his "most faithful fan" and bragged about how much Strasberg liked his company: Andy's 1963 escapade had ended with his apprehension by the truant officer and suspension from school.

Enthusiastic Cardinal fans watched the 1967 Cards take the flag by ten and one-half lengths. Theirs was the first Card squad to win 100 games since the 1942 world champs. En route to that distinction, their 52 road victories set a club mark.

On the surface, Roger's 1967 statistics seem unimpressive: in 410 at bats he compiled a .261 batting average, 9 homers, and 55 RBIs. However, Roger's numbers give no indication of the many power plays that propelled the team to victory. Maris led the club with his 18 "clutch hits" – better described as RBIs – that put the club ahead to stay. Despite his difficulties with southpaws, Roger made some big hits against them. The Cards won 11 of the 12 games he hit safely against left-handed pitching. Of the 15 hits Roger had against lefties, 13 had a part in run-scoring.

Red Schoendienst did not hesitate in selecting Roger over right-thanded outfielder Alex Johnson for the series against the Red Sox. Schoendienst gave the reasons for his choice: "Maris is steady in the field. He rarely makes a mistake out there, and he doesn't make mistakes running the bases. And he has the advantage of being through all that World Series pressure."

Maris' performance in the seven-game clash made Schoendienst's a masterful decision. The obvious Cardinal heroes in their 2-1 opener victory were Bob Gibson, with 10 strikeouts and a six hitter, and Lou Brock, with a series-tying record of four singles. But it was Roger who brought home both runs on groundouts. The gamer came in the seventh with the infield drawn in. Roger hit a sharp shot. Second baseman Jerry Adair grabbed the ball but could not keep Brock from scoring.

After Jim Lonberg tied the series with a shutout, the Cardinals roared back to take the next two games. Gibson shut out the Bosox with a five hitter, but Roger hit an opposite-field double down the left-field line in the first to give the Cards a lead they never relinquished. A few moments later Roger also made the third run possible. He raced to third on a medium-deep fly to right and scooted home as the drawn-in fielders helplessly tried to retrieve McCarver's single. When Gibson was tiring in the eighth with a man on base, Roger closed out the frame by turning in a crowd-pleasing catch after slipping.

The Bosox rallied to take games five and six. Game five was a three-hit Lonberg masterpiece, marred only by Roger Maris' homer – the first run the Cards had managed off the hurler in two games. Game seven became a classic confrontation between the two aces, Gibson and Lonberg. Roger contributed by singling twice, setting up one run, and driving in another with a sacrifice fly. However, Gibson saddened the Fenway Park faithful with his third complete-game victory.

Gibson deserved the *Sport Magazine* outstanding series player award. Brock stole a record-breaking seven bases and hit a lusty .414, so the Cardinals' management awarded him a car. Roger, who earned his third championship ring, also merited recognition. He batted .385 and led both clubs with seven RBIs – the most ever by a Cardinal in the team's 10 years of series play. Years later Ken Smith, Hall of Fame director, would write to Roger: "Funny, instead of the home runs, I remember in the 1967 World Series, how you helped win it by moving runners along, beside hitting."

The public never knew the truth about Roger's physical condition during the series. Throughout, Roger took antibiotics to ward off a "low-grade fever." Maris played with a shoulder so painful that the Cardinal physician, Dr. I. C. Middleman, injected him with novacaine and cortisone after game seven, as he had on six other occasions during the season. Nevertheless, Roger played every inning of the seven-game set.

During the postgame locker-room celebration, pitcher Ray Washburn extended his hand to Roger and said, "Thanks." Then, turning to another teammate, Washburn remarked: "That's got to be the best professional job you've ever seen. He went out and got his hits and made the plays. And he never said a word."

Roger stayed quiet throughout the spirited festivities that began in the clubhouse, continued at the airport, and climaxed at Musial's restaurant, Musial and Biggies. He explained his reticence. "I'm not a champagne guy. Sure, I'm happy. But my thrill is just watching these other guys be happy. That's my thrill. I'm all tied up inside, but I don't show emotion. I've always been that way."

However, Roger could express himself about being with the Cardinals. "I've never been happier in my life. The fans, the writers, the city – they've treated me wonderfully." Pat Maris agreed. "Those years in St. Louis were the fun years. The kids got to see Roger play a lot more. Roger really liked that."

Despite his happiness in St. Louis, Roger would not commit himself to another year in baseball. As the rock-and-roll music blared at Musial and Biggies, and with his wife Pat at his side, Roger said, "I haven't made up my mind what to do. Money won't help me decide. ... I guess you'll have to look in the '68 box scores to find out. I don't know. Honestly."

All the Cardinals, from Stan Musial to Red Schoendienst to the players, hoped that Roger would return. The team remembered outfielder Curt Flood's remark during the season: without Roger the Cards probably would have been a second-division team.

Dal Maxvill, sipping his champagne, spoke for all the Redbirds. "Rog has been just great, and we want him back next year. We don't care how much he got paid this year. ... And if it takes $270,000 to keep him from retiring, then I say, pay him that much."

While the team drank champagne, Roger appeared to be thinking beer. On November 3, 1967, both the *St. Louis Post-Dispatch* and the *Gainesville Sun* reported that Roger had assumed an eight-county Budweiser distributorship in Florida. The *Sun* quoted the comments of an unidentified *Post-Dispatch* reporter that Cardinal owner Gussie Busch had told Roger at a postpennant-winning celebration: "....anybody who hits 33 homers and drives in 100 runs deserves a distributorship."

The papers stated that Roger and Rudy Maris, who had been in business in Youngstown, Ohio, would operate the distributorship. The deal became possible when former distributor Art Pepin took control of the Tampa area.

The stories never openly related a quid pro quo, but the reports did tie the distributorship to Roger's rejoining the Redbirds in 1968. Neal Russo wrote for the *Post-Dispatch:* "Whatever doubts existed about Roger Maris' plans to play for the baseball Cardinals next season were dispelled today when he and his brother had been granted the Anheuser-Busch distributorship in the Gainesville, Florida area."

Roger officially returned to the Cardinals in January when he signed a $75,000 contract for 1968. Dr. Middleman also attended the conference, held in St. Petersburg, Florida, during a sales convention of Anheuser-Busch, Inc.

In the off-season Roger had revealed that for some time, unknown to the Cards' front office, he had suffered from an ailment called Bell's palsy. The affliction causes temporary paralysis of the facial muscles; in Roger's case, the paralysis affected his right cheek. In addition, the facial numbness made him unable to blink his right eye. As a result, vision in his right eye became blurred.

Roger's prognosis seemed very good: Bell's palsy usually lasts only a few weeks and can be treated with massage and medication.

Despite Roger's frequent physical battering, Dr. Middleman reported him in excellent condition at the January press conference. The Redbird management knew of the successful removal of a polyp from Roger's vocal chords. "He's had a 90 percent recovery" from the new ailment, the Cards' surgeon informed the media. Therapy would hasten the remaining 10 percent of recovery, correcting "some drooping of Roger's lower lip." Recurrence of Bell's palsy is virtually unheard of, added the doctor.

Roger realized an on- and off-the-field dream on January 25, 1968. The St. Louis Chapter of the Baseball Writers Association of America presented Maris with the Bob Bauman Physical Comeback Award, named for the one-time trainer of the Cardinals and the University of St. Louis basketball team. At the dinner Roger sat amid an illustrious circle of honorees: Orlando Cepeda, previous Bauman Awardee, St. Louis baseball man of the year (winner of the 1967 National League MVP); Lou Brock, Bob Gibson, Stan Musial, and Red Schoendienst, sharing the J. Roy Stockton award for outstanding achievement in baseball.

Roger devoted his off-season time to his family. "I always wanted a big family," he said. "I guess you'd have to say I've got it....Girls are the greatest. The girls all have time for daddy, but the boys...they don't even realize I'm around most of the time." Nevertheless, the four boys always knew where to find Roger when they needed help. Maris, ever the loving father, delighted in whatever task his children set before him – from fixing bicycles to setting up aquariums.

The Cardinals of 1968 repeated their success of the year before. In June, the Redbirds moved into first place after sweeping a doubleheader from the Mets. Roger scored all the way from first on

Cepeda's pop-fly single in the seventh inning of the nightcap. He made the decisive run in the 3-2 victory.

Roger played in the old Gas House tradition, to the amazement of his teammates. The Maris hustle "surprised us even though we had heard about it when he was in the American League," said Tim McCarver. "He doesn't hit many homers for us, but he wins games in a lot of different ways."

Fargo's Bob Johnson believes that more and more of the media began to learn about the real Roger Maris. Former Cardinal Joe Garagiola asked Roger to appear on his early-morning television program. Even though the scheduled appearance followed a Cardinal night game, Roger responded, "If it'll help you, I'll be happy to come."

Roger found himself playing less and less, and he realized that eventually he would only play on a part-time basis. "The injuries had begun to take their toll," said Pat Maris. "Roger could not be content to sit on the bench. He had to be a good player, to produce. Simply being a pinch hitter would not be enough." Roger knew his happy days in St. Louis would soon end.

In New York, fans greeted him with boos, proving that their feelings toward Roger had not changed. Maris disregarded them. "I couldn't care less what these people think," he said. "I never did and I never will. They can boo me all they want."

A report by *New York Post* columnist Milton Gross spawned much midsummer talk and rumor about Roger's after-the-season retirement. Sarcastically, Roger commented, "It must be right. I read it in the newspaper," adding, "I'm good copy, when there's nothing else to write about."

Maris announced his retirement on August 5, to no one's surprise. He had begun hinting in March that he would retire, and talk of it continued steadily. When he made his announcement, his batting average was .269 in 110 games, with four home runs and 27 RBIs.

At a St. Louis press conference, Roger stated that he made the decision to retire "because I don't have the type of body that can keep going on and on. I have a thickly-set body and heavy legs. I can feel the aches and the pains in the legs and arms when I wake up in the morning. ... I also talked it over with my wife, and we felt I should spend more time with my family." Roger chose to announce his decision before season's end because he "did not really care to be bothered by the press after the season."

Manager Red Schoendienst praised Roger for his numerous key hits during the season and for his excellent fielding and alert base running. "Rog is ready to play whether he's been out a week or a night or two. He' been a great inspiration to the entire ball club. Roger has been a help to some of the young players. He helps without saying much, and he's no popoff."

Roger expressed his thanks to those who appreciated him. "I couldn't have asked for a better place to play than here. The Cardinals have a great organization. Everyone has treated me good. The fans in St. Louis are the greatest."

When someone mentioned Roger's years in New York, he merely replied, "It's like being burned. You never get rid of the scars."

Maris still had his supporters among the sportswriters in the New York media. Dick Young wrote in his August 18 column: "Few men in baseball, in sports, in anything, have been bad rapped so cruelly as Roger Maris. No man was more cooperative, more patient, more understanding than Roger Maris, and under the most nerve wracking of circumstances."

Roger bid his St. Louis fans farewell for the regular season. Before the game on September 29, the Cardinals honored Roger for his achievements in his baseball career, as the Yankees had never done. Roger, Pat, and their six children; Big Julie and Andy Strasberg – two of Roger's biggest boosters – and a crowd of 23,792 enjoyed the ceremonies.

The Cardinals presented the Marises with a Wurlitzer organ, chosen by the family, Pat said, "because I can play it." The master of ceremonies, broadcaster Harry Caray, recited Roger's baseball records. Then, he continued, "such records tell only the story of Maris, the baseball player. In his relatively brief period in St. Louis, we've also come to know and respect him as Maris the man, a gentleman of warmth and humility, an inspiration to youngsters everywhere, a man who has been genuinely a credit to the game."

Roger responded by thanking the Redbirds "for two of my most enjoyable years in baseball and ... the fans here for accepting me the way they did."

The Yanks' meager contribution to the celebration came in the form of a telegram, sent by Vice President Bob Fishel and read by former teammate Tony Kubek, who had become a television broadcaster. The message said:

Manager Ralph Houk, President Mike Burke, Mickey Mantle, and all the present-day Yankees and ex-Yankees join me today in congratulating Roger Maris on his great baseball career, not only the years he spent with the Yankees, but also the two past great years with the St. Louis Cardinals. He is a great asset to the game and will be missed. We all wish him happiness and good health in the many years of retirement from the game, which lie ahead.

Before he would retire, Maris faced the challenge of his final World Series. His regular-season totals reflected the physical wear and tear that had now become obvious. Roger had a .255 batting average, with 310 at bats in 100 games, 45 RBIs, and only five homers.

Neither Roger nor the Cardinals wanted to remember the 1968 World Series. The Redbirds roared to a 3-1 game advantage over the Tigers; then Detroit turned them back. The efforts of Tiger pitcher Mickey Lolich won three games. A frustrated Maris had made only three hits and one RBI for six games of the series. Lolich got Roger to pop out in his last baseball at bat, after striking him out and inducing him to hit into a double play. Roger's baseball career had come to an end, after twelve seasons and 2,253 at bats.

Cardinal Mike Shannon remembers that Roger showed astute baseball sense in his evaluation of Lolich. In July when the Tigers looked like the Cards' opponents, the biggest threat seemed to be Denny McLain, who was headed for a 30-win season. "Forget about McLain," Roger told his teammates. "The guy we have to worry about is Mickey Lolich." Shannon believes this judgment proves that Roger was "especially knowledgeable" about baseball.

The *Post-Dispatch*'s Ed Wilks wrote several stories on Roger Maris, the player and the person. In reviewing Roger's career, Wilks stressed not only Maris' achievements but also his impediments. A weak right hand had robbed Roger of power, and for the past three years he had not been able to grip a bat properly. Still, Wilks wrote, "He was a pro who delivered."

Years later one of Maris' fans, Alan Hays of Washington, Illinois, remembered Roger the Cardinal for the *Sporting News*:

St. Louis fans recognized him for what he was – a first class gentleman and fine professional baseball player.

Personally, I'll never forget his contributions to the pennant-winning Cardinals of 1967 and 1968. I remember him as a team player who could contribute with the bat and in the field. He did everything expected of a professional.

It was very difficult watching the 1977 Cardinals in right field, where balls were juggled, bobbled, and misjudged and where throw-ins missed cutoff men, often went to wrong bases and where outfielders even fell flat on their backsides on several occasions on routine fly balls.

However, when I conjure up thoughts of 1967 and 1968, I recall a right fielder that was tops.

Chapter XVIII
Post-Baseball: As Before, Family Comes First

Roger's sixteen-year professional baseball career sometimes over-shadowed his life outside the ballpark. Once he retired, he could devote the sixteen years remaining to him to his family, his business, his friends and relatives in Fargo, and his associates in the baseball world.

From the day he first put on his uniform in Cleveland to the day he emptied his locker in St. Louis, Roger's family and their welfare were paramount in his mind. Roger cared for them and spent time with them. He also provided for their future as best as he could, through wise investments and conservative – almost frugal – living.

Wayne Blanchard, an assistant vice president at Fargo's First Bank, said of Roger, "Fame didn't change him. He didn't drive new, flashy cars, and he never indulged in spending a lot of money on clothing."

Roger's children remember him as a firm disciplinarian, but primarily as a caring and concerned father. Roger, Jr., his oldest son, remembers that "Dad was always there for us. He was interested in what we were doing and would do it for us whenever he could."

Before Roger died, his son Randy talked about the children's relationship with their father. "We didn't idolize him. He was our dad, first and foremost. We've appreciated the opportunities we've had because of the name, but he was just our father."

Roger Maris centered his life on his six children. Their baseball, basketball, and golf activities meant that sometimes Roger and Pat would attend as many as three sports contests involving the children. Roger frequently golfed with Richard, Randy and Kevin, and proudly boasted, "The two older boys are shooting in the low eighties. I'm a twelve-handicapper myself, so it's getting tougher to beat Randy and Kevin."

Maris had firm beliefs about children and sports. As he told *Forum* sports editor Ed Kolpack: "Children shouldn't be in organized sports until they reach Junior Legion age. Let them play games for fun. There's so much emphasis on winning."

Although Roger took great interest in his sons' sports achievements, he never actively encouraged them to emulate his sports career. Dick Savageau observed that Roger's attitude about possible professional sports careers for his sons was colored by his own experiences. "Roger's wasn't convinced the price a professional athlete had to pay was worth it. I often heard him say, 'I just as soon my children don't go into professional sports.'"

Despite his emotional pounding during the 1961 season, Roger, at an Associated Press awards dinner, clearly articulated that if his sons showed interest in becoming professional baseball players, "I would try to help them if they wanted to play, but I wouldn't force them. What I'm trying to do is fix things up so they won't have to play." Only Kevin and Randy have sports careers, as pro golfers.

Baseball had benefited from Roger's unschooled "keen instincts" and "fine display of common sense," but according to Dr. Surprise, Roger felt that "he lacked a full education." Consequently, the Maris children took advantage of the educational opportunities in Gainesville, Florida. Sandra, Kevin, and Richard enrolled at Santa Fe Community College, where Sandra studied dental technology and the boys participated in extracurricular sports. Their baseball coach Harry Tholen helped the boys develop their skills, and he also observed Roger Maris being a parent. The retired coach said:

> Simply put, Roger Maris was an outstanding family man. Before I came to know him, I sort of had an idea he would be like his press clippings, aloof and unfriendly. But I found him to be a down-to-earth person.
>
> Yes, he was a very private person, and he wanted to protect his family very much. He was an outstanding father. Any man would be proud to have him as a father, not because of his heroics on a baseball field, but because he cared about his children. He was interested in his children's activities. He wanted them to be good in school and very concerned that they be good citizens. He wanted people to be proud of them. You might say that he had the old-fashioned values: hard work, loyalty to family and friends. And, of course, the family was held together by Mrs. Pat Maris, a very strong lady from the word go.

Pat Maris felt that "Roger had good business sense and always knew how to take care of himself." Roger always took great pride in his financial shrewdness and independence. When the Internal Revenue Service challenged some financial planning that Roger had done for his children, Bob Wood recalls that "Roger stood firm and won his case."

Maris' determination had won him the beer distributorship that he had dreamed about for so long. Roger knew that only hard work and discipline would bring him the financial security of a successful business. Still, making the transition from the ballfield to the office had proved difficult even for disciplined athletes. Dr. Steinert cautioned that "Roger was the type of person who needed a routine, a same day-to-day pattern to succeed."

Enter Roger's brother Rudy: family, friend, and key to the success of the beer distributorship. Rudy's business experience had prepared him to perform the important work on the inside, handling the management side of the operation. Roger, Rudy's complement, would work on the outside as the public relations man promoting the product for taverns and supermarkets.

The Maris brothers resolved to succeed. Roger rode the delivery trucks for months, going into taverns and telling owners and patrons alike about the goodness of his beer. To prove his claim, Roger would buy a Budweiser for everyone in the house. The hard work and personal approach paid off: Business tripled in the Marises' eight-county distributorship area.

Ed Kenzler, owner of a building supply company in the Gainesville area and a former University of Florida coach, worked briefly for the Maris distributorship. He said, "I can tell you that the business was run very well and the workers were treated kindly."

The workers decided to test the Maris brothers. The beer handlers went out on strike, making "demands [that] were ridiculous," according to union leader Big Julie. The entire Maris family cooperated to keep the business running. When the workers walked off, Roger and Rudy loaded the trucks themselves, with the help of some of the children. When Maris Distributing made all its deliveries, without missing one, the workers had to settle.

Some of the media persisted in running unfavorable reviews of Roger the businessman. Maris once remarked, "One guy wrote that if it wasn't for the 61 homers I would have been driving a beer truck instead of selling it." These pot shots at the achievements of his former baseball career annoyed Maris less than portraits such as Edward Kiersh's. In *Where Have You Gone, Vince DiMaggio?* Kiersh describes Maris as a goof-off who did not come in to work regularly. To such reports Roger responded, "I'm in the office every day."

Certainly, by the time the business had become a success, Roger had more control over his schedule. He spent more time outside the office, doing public relations for Busch and participating in numerous charity golf tournaments.

From about 1974 until his cancer was diagnosed, Roger played in as many as twenty-five to thirty tournaments a year. "I was gone every other weekend," he said. "It took a lot of time. But I was happy to do it. It was always for a good cause."

The important business of selling beer never kept Roger from acting on his principles. Ryne Duren, a Yankee teammate of Roger's during 1960–1961, had once been a relief pitcher who terrified and overwhelmed the batters. His drinking helped incur his downfall. For years after his retirement, Roger had had no contact with Duren.

After stays in seven hospitals and four treatment centers, Duren finally learned to deal with his alcoholism. He became director of alcoholism rehabilitation at Stoughton Hospital in Wisconsin and currently serves as a consultant on substance abuse rehabilitation. Duren confided:

> Because of my background and present position, I thought Roger assumed we could not get together because he was selling beer. But several years ago, I decided to contact Roger. Let me tell you, Roger is a no-bullshit guy. He said, "Let's see what we can do to correct the lifestyles of the young who might be in trouble." Roger then told me, "Ryne, when you come to Florida, I will arrange for you to speak at the local schools and youth organizations."
>
> Roger kept his word. He was a sound, spiritual type of man willing to present the other guy's point of view.

Larry Guest of the *Orlando Sentinel-Star* wrote an article headlined "Who's the Real Roger Maris?" The story offers some interesting glimpses of the baseball hero-turned-beer distributor who had lived in Gainesville for more than twelve years.

In 1981, the Maris Distributing Company employed a staff of some 50 persons who moved two million cases of Budweiser beer a year.

Guest wrote that the employees thought of Roger as a "a kind, laid-back boss."

A smiling, friendly Roger sometimes rode down the street in his white golf cart. The red-and-black Anheuser eagle emblazoned on the front made him easily recognizable as the Budweiser beer distributor. Guest comments that members at his club considered Maris "generous and unfailingly courteous." University of Florida sports publicist Norm Carlson affirmed the opinion. "I think Roger's a great guy, a funny guy. I've had many good times in his company. He's never been anything but a pleasant person to be around."

Guest found that nothing about the Roger Maris who lived in Gainesville matched the image that had been drawn of him in New York. The "surly" "neighborhood ogre" who isolated himself from the community appeared to have been a media fiction.

Roger himself felt that an unsympathetic press imaginatively created many of the negative things his neighbors supposedly said about him. "I don't think they said some of those things," he remarked. But Maris did concede that his insistence on being a private, faceless citizen might not sit well with some.

> I think some of them thought I was going to be throwing parties all the time when I first came here. And they were probably put out that we don't show up every time somebody throws a cocktail party. I try to be friendly, and if I can help by giving someone a case of beer or something, I'm glad to do that. But parties are not just my thing. I just try to mind my own business.

Maris preferred maintaining his privacy to pursuing material gains. Twenty years after his historic home run, he turned down an enticing offer from a production company interested in a two-hour television movie about the 1961 season. "The offer was pretty good," Roger said, "but I'm not sure I'm ready for that. My life is very peaceful right now."

In 1979, Roger had moved into a new home that augmented the serenity in his life. Located about thirty miles from Gainesville, the house lies adjacent to a golf course and fronts on a lake. When the Maris children began fishing, Roger tried to share their interest and developed a new hobby. Fishing proved to be an ideal leisure activity for a man who shunned the spotlight. On the pier Maris was just another fisherman, talking to fellow fishermen immersed in their craft and not with media looking for a juicy item.

Years had passed since Roger's happy days in Fargo, but he and Pat had a special relationship with their hometown. In Pat's words, "Fargo was always home to both of us. We just never forgot that." A *Fargo Forum* story conveyed the message in its headline: "Roger Maris Still Calls Fargo Home." Whenever an opportunity arose, Roger visited the home where he spent his formative years.

Roger had gained a significant amount of weight after quitting smoking in the mid-'70s. Fargoans saw only a change in Roger Maris' physical appearance, not his personality. Dick Savageau said, "Roger never forgot us up here. The amazing thing about him was for all the notoriety he got, he never forgot a friend. Everyone was his friend."

On those visits home, Roger became a familiar sight at the local Knights of Columbus club. On one occasion some bigwigs from a local country club called and invited Roger to join them. Terry Devine, *Forum* news editor, recalls that incident. "Roger ... said no. It was more important for him to be with his friends."

Often he spent time reminiscing with Don Gooselaw, whose daughter Renee was his godchild. A neighbor of the Gooselaws, Mrs. Jeannette Helgeson, remembers one such visit during the early seventies.

> Roger Maris was having dinner at the Gooselaws'. My son, Jeffrey, then eight, was at the Gooselaws' house, too. Jeffrey went up to Roger Maris and asked him for his autograph. "Give him a chance to finish his meal," Mr. Gooselaw told Jeffrey.
>
> My son came home very disappointed. "Who needs the autograph anyway!" he said unhappily.
>
> It didn't seem long after he'd returned that Susan Maris came to our door with an autographed ball. She said, "My dad would like you to have this, Jeffrey."

Sometimes when he returned home, Roger and his dad would get together to watch American Legion baseball, the developing ground for Roger's training where Roger developed his baseball skills. Barnett Field, where Roger had first attracted the scouts' attention, had made way for an improved Jack Williams Stadium.

Fargo youngsters lionized Maris during his visits. Boyd Christenson, now with WDAY-TV in Fargo, recalled how children's "eyes would pop out when they saw Roger in the flesh. 'You're the guy who hit all those home runs,' they would say in awe."

Roger came to Fargo in late August of 1983 to take part in the 1983 American Legion baseball World Series and attend the banquet at the Holiday Inn. Roger not only renewed friendships at home, but he also rehashed the past with another invitee, Yankee teammate Moose Skowron. The slugger found that on the grounds of Jack Williams Stadium the town had built Roger Maris Park in his honor.

This historic visit for the city of Fargo gave rise to the idea of a Roger Maris Museum. American Legion officials Bob Smith and Jim McLaughlin first broached the subject of the museum at a breakfast meeting at the Legion World Series. Smith said, "We got to talking about it. Roger said it was a great idea. I told him we have the new North Dakota Heritage Center in Bismarck where the museum could be located."

However, Roger insisted that the museum be in Fargo: "I played baseball in Fargo, and that's where I want my things to go." Bill Weaver, who was closely involved in the project, remembers that "Roger was very concerned that the project be first-class, that it be an attractive museum." Maris also insisted on a site ensuring security and maximum visibility. The choice of West Acres, Fargo's busy shopping center, seemed ideal.

According to Bob Smith, he and McLaughlin "made a promise to Roger that if we couldn't do the project right and proper, we wouldn't do it at all. It was going to be great for baseball and great for North Dakota. It was something long overdue."

As plans for the museum took shape, Roger learned that he had cancer. Those involved in the museum project didn't learn about Roger's struggle with the disease until the spring of 1984.

Smith and McLaughlin traveled to Gainesville to inventory Maris' memorabilia for the museum. Maris had made their work easy; according to McLaughlin, "Roger has done a good job of keeping track of his memorabilia."

The original museum collection totaled some 150 items. A taped narration of Roger's last twelve home runs in 1961 announced by Yankee broadcasters Mel Allen and Phil Rizutto draws the most interest. Other objects on view in the three-tier museum include bats, balls, uniforms, awards, photographs, scorecards, rings, cartoons, and other memorabilia of Maris' career.

Maris donated almost everything he had to the museum. However, his Most Valuable Player plaques of 1960 and 1961 remained in Gainesville. The Maris boys could not bear to see the walls of their home Gainesville totally bare. Roger's sons have also kept the four World Series rings.

In the fall of 1984, the *Gainesville Sun* visited Roger's office. The reporter commented on the photo history of his baseball career hanging behind his desk; a second wall had more baseball memorabilia. Roger told Al Hall that the Roger Maris Museum had all the trophies, honors, and other historical highlights. He added, "That makes me feel good because there's not much up that way [Fargo]. If it helps get the place a little attention, then it's good for them. Most of the stuff in this office will go there when I'm through with it. I think that's where it should be." He even promised that the MVP plaques will "go in the museum eventually."

Each museum item, memorable or notable though it may be, has its own fascination. For example, the museum has a badly worn copy of the slugger's autobiography of 1961, *Roger Maris at Bat,* so difficult to obtain that it is not in the Fargo Public Library.

Mementos have continued to arrive even after Roger's death. The Yankees sent Roger's number 9 pinstriped shirt in 1986. Andy Strasberg contributed his Roger Maris baseball cards and a ticket stub from the 162nd game of 1961, when Roger hit number 61.

Nearly 2,000 people came to the opening of Roger Maris Museum on June 23, 1984. Maris' memorabilia, displayed in a 72-foot showcase in the mall, attracted many youngsters on Roger Maris Day in Fargo and in North Dakota. Roger felt it very gratifying "that so many people are interested in what I've done. I know a lot of younger kids are not that aware of it. I'm proud to be from Fargo and North Dakota."

North Dakota officials felt very proud of Roger, too. Governor Allen Olson said Roger "made our buttons pop" when he hit his sixty-first homer. Echoing the sentiments of many that day, U.S. Senator Quentin Burdick stated, "This is a day in history when you recognize the accomplishments of one of our boys."

Following the opening of Roger Maris Museum, the road through Fargo's Lindenwood Park became Roger Maris Drive. A display at the park's entrance carries a picture depicting Maris' sixty-first home run, accompanied by his athletic record. In addition, a summer Park

Board Baseball Program honored Fargo's hero by being named the Roger Maris League. As Sister Bernice of Shanley wrote in the school's *Acorn,* "Who, in Fargo, could not have heard of Roger Maris!"

On June 25, 1984, two days after the Rogear Maris Museum opened, the Oxbow Country Club held the First Annual Roger Maris-Shanley Open in the Fargo suburb of Hickson. Fargo greeted the tournament enthusiastically. The Roger Maris name drew celebrities from baseball and other sports into participation at the dinner and on the golf course. In its second year, the tournament featured nineteen celebrities, six of whom were in the Baseball Hall of Fame.

"The media portrayed Roger as surly, that he was difficult to get along with," said Sid Cichy. "Well, you should see how his former teammates – stars of Yankees and Cardinals – and other players in baseball and other sports have gone all out to get here for the golf tournament, just because Roger was involved. ... Does that sound like someone who couldn't get along with people?"

Roger helped inaugurate an annual event that gave him deserved pride and satisfaction. "Maris Golf Tournament Meaningful," read the headline of a *Forum* editorial at the opening of the Second Annual Tournament. As Roger battled cancer, the tournament was helping defeat the disease: in its second year the tourney added to its beneficiary list the Hospice of the Red River Valley. The editorial concluded:

> When categorizing sports events around here, the word "extravaganza" is not often used. But the Maris golf tournament is an extravaganza. It is big league in every way, just as Maris is big league himself in every way. We hope and pray that he will be able to participate in the event. Maris loves Fargo, and Fargo loves him back.

Roger Maris signs his first contract
with the St. Louis Cardinals.
(Bettman Archive Photo)

Chapter XIX
The Road Back to Yankee Stadium

In an interview after he retired, Roger Maris observed, "Baseball is just like a kid with a train. You got to outgrow it sometime." Roger never outgrew baseball, never lost his love for the game. He bought a satellite dish to follow the teams' contests and rooted heartily for the Yanks. Dr. Surprise believes that while "he was not treated royally in New York ... there was something that Roger liked about the Yankee pinstripes and tradition."

America's sport kept Roger firmly enthralled even though he had retired. Some of his fans would detour through Gainesville from the spring training camps just to try to see or meet Roger. The media continually grilled him about his past or contemporary baseball developments, almost forcing Roger to keep up on the sport. Past friends and contacts – Athletics, Yankees, Cardinals, others – kept Roger in touch with the game. Maris could not forget baseball.

Roger gave few interviews during his first years of retirement, but the tenth anniversary of number 61 did not go by unnoticed. A *New York Times* article by Marty Ralbovsky focused on Frick's ruling and Maris' feelings about the asterisk ten years later. The headline said that Maris "Disdains Use of Asterisk on 61-Homer Mark." The jump headline read, "After 10 Years, Maris Still Resents*."

The article left the reader with the distinct impression that an asterisk in fact appeared in the record books. Ralbovsky thus reinforced a popular myth. Most people did indeed believe that an asterisk not only stood in the book, but also diminished the value of Roger's deserved record.

The lead of the story states that Roger's "memories of 1961 are punctuated with an asterisk." However, Roger said that he tried not to think too much about the home runs. These apparently contradictory statements actually convey Roger's conflicting feelings: he tries not to think about the season and the record, but when he does he sees an asterisk. Maris' unhappiness over the distinction continues. With the 162-game season firmly established, his is the only record overshadowed by and qualified with an asterisk.

Maris feels that the asterisk designation had underlying motives. "A lot of people didn't want me to break Ruth's record at all, especially older people. They tried to make me into the mold of Babe Ruth, and I don't want to fit in anyone's mold. I'm Roger Maris."

Roger Maris the person pays a physical price for his baseball years.

> Every day my body tells me I used to be a baseball player. I can't sleep on my stomach because my rib cage is so tender. It got that way because of how I'd bust up double plays. And my knees hurt if I just brush against them — that's from banging into outside walls. And I still don't have any feel in the ring finger of my right hand, from when I broke my hand in '65. If I had to do it again, I would have been much more careful about my health, not to jeopardize it like I did.

The slugger had not planned to celebrate the tenth anniversary of home run number 61. "I'll just go home and have a beer."

A horde of reporters caught up with Roger in 1973 in Atlanta, where Maris had come to watch the Braves rally and defeat the Mets. The media asked Roger to comment on the pressures facing Hank Aaron as he neared the all-time homer mark of 714. Roger, smiling, said, "I'll be glad when he does it, because it'll take the pressure off me. The girls in the office are taking calls from the press, and it requires a lot of their time."

Roger cited the important differences between 1961 and the Aaron pursuit. One, hammering Hank had no 154-game requirement or 162-game schedule. Two, when Roger broke the record in 1961, the fans expected him to top his performance in 1962. If Aaron were to break the record — as he did on April 8, 1974 — he couldn't repeat his career performance; he could only increase his mark.

Roger wished Aaron well. He had no advice to offer the 39-year-old Aaron, who was only a few months younger than the retired slugger. "What could I tell Hank Aaron that he doesn't already know? He's been around a long time. He knows the ropes. He doesn't need any advice from me."

Aaron himself articulated another important difference between himself and Maris. While both were detested for daring to break the Ruthian records, Hank Aaron became the object of special resentment.

As Aaron observed: "People don't want to accept that a black man is breaking Ruth's record."

Five years later, in 1978, both sluggers met in Orlando at the annual baseball meeting and shared memories, some of them unpleasant, of struggling to overcome Ruth's marks. "For me, it was sheer hell," said Roger. "It was tough. In my case, I felt I had to play every day. One little injury, and I've blown it. They day-to-day pressure was tremendous."

Aaron, now under a five-year, million-dollar contract with Magnavox, conceded, "I thought pressure on Roger was tougher than the pressure on me. He had to get his 61 homers in a set time. Me? I felt it was only a matter of my staying healthy. If I couldn't do it this year, there was always next year."

Aaron and Roger discussed how fans' resentment of their challenges to Ruth spilled into the ballplayers' personal lives. The former Brave revealed, "I never opened my mail for a year. Just lucky someone ran across the letter from Magnavox." On one occasion, a newspaper printed a front-page picture of Hank's wife and implied that she had brought the NAACP and other black activist groups into the "controversy." Aaron answered a particularly sarcastic reporter by hurling a bowl of strawberries in his face. "I couldn't stand it when my family was brought into it," Aaron said. "I don't think I could have gone another month."

Roger disclosed, "I got streams of mail also. A lot of it was of a racist nature. Like Hank, I wasn't allowed to open my own mail. It was a miserable time in my life."

Maris felt bitter not only over the treatment he received in pursuit of Ruth's record, but also over what happened when he achieved it. "Aaron's record was important," remarked Roger, "and mine was trivial. At least that's what's been written. When Ruth held the mark, it was THE one to shoot at. When I broke it, it was a fluke. Now it's the 101st on the list of 100 top achievements."

The Yankee and Brave managements responded differently to their history-making players. When Hank Aaron beat Ruth's 714 lifetime homers by one, Atlanta presented him with 715 silver dollars. "Do you know what I got from the Yankees?" Roger asked sardonically.

The new regime that took over the Yankees in 1973 could not be blamed for Roger's past experiences. George Steinbrenner (the Boss), the principal owner, became interested in the old Yankees — not the least Roger — and organized a Yankee alumni association. Steinbrenner compiled a list of former players' addresses and phone numbers. He had pins and rings made for the alumni. To enable contacts among the former players, Steinbrenner began a newsletter and distributed an alumni address book.

Roger did not cooperate with the Boss' projects. Steinbrenner told the press, "I kept asking our guys, 'Where the hell's Roger Maris? We don't have anything on Roger Maris.'"

Some of Roger's former teammates tried to get him to see the situation from a new perspective. Moose Skowron "told Roger that things were different in New York, that the fans would love to see him and cheer him. I spoke to Roger about returning, more than once. I told him that he also owes it to the other guys on the team who would love to see him. He told me that he'd think about it and perhaps one day he'd come."

Robert Jaynes of the Gannett News Service noticed Roger and former close teammate Elston Howard having drinks in the lounge of the Hilton at the Governor's Baseball Dinner in St. Petersburg, in the spring of 1973. Jaynes relayed their conversation. "You oughta come up," Howard pleaded. "It'll be a great time. Forget all that crap. You'll have a great time." Roger remained adamant. "Nope, Ellie, no."

The Yankees planned to celebrate in 1973 the fiftieth anniversary of Yankee Stadium, the house that Ruth built. Management, players, and fans wanted the home-run champion to participate in the old-timers' game that formed the heart of the festivities. The *Sporting News* of August 18, 1973, reported that the Yanks had initiated a fans' post-card campaign to induce Roger to return to the stadium.

Traditionally, old-timer games brought retired ballplayers together in a nostalgic competition that excited the fans and gave some of them their first chance at seeing the famous in action. Maris had played in several – two in Atlanta and one in St. Louis – with little enthusiasm. "I don't like them," Roger stated. "I can't feel comfortable going out there in uniform any more."

He deliberately avoided the Yankee old-timer game. He not only wanted to stay out of the spotlight, but he also and more specifically wanted to stay out of Yankee Stadium. "The Yankees did him wrong," said Pat Maris, "and he had no interest in going back."

While Steinbrenner was new to the Yankees, Yanks' General

Manager MacPhail was not. MacPhail spoke to Roger at the St. Petersburg dinner, trying to lure him to the stadium. Roger replied sharply, "I'm not an old-timer. I'm only 38. ... I just don't want to go." He concluded with typical candor. "If the Cardinals have an Old-Timers' Day, I go. If you have one, I don't. Is that plain enough?"

MacPhail seethed over Maris' rebuff. His later public reaction only provided Maris with further justification for Roger remaining in Gainesville:

I don't know what you can do. It'll be 12 years this season. That's a long time. But I'm not through yet. I'm going to keep trying.

Actually, we did him a favor by trading him. New York had become a bad situation for him. We gave him new life in St. Louis. He did well there. My gosh, he even got that distributorship from Busch when he retired. I don't think he came out that badly.

Roger found it hard to forget his perception of the Yanks' attitude towards him in '61. "The Yankees always favored Mickey to break the record," he said. "I was never the fair-haired boy over there." Referring to the post-1961 seasons, Maris commented, "When I'd get hurt, they thought I could still play. When Mickey or Tom Tresh or someone got hurt, they'd let 'em rest."

Nor did Roger forget the booing fans, especially during the last years in pinstripes. "If we were playing before 35,000 people," he remembered, "34,000 of them were on my back. It got so baseball was just no fun." The kindness fans showed toward him now "came years too late."

Two publications reported on the conversation between MacPhail and Roger. The articles' headlines caught Roger Maris' mood with their headlines: one, "Maris Still Bitter Over Cards Trade;" the other, "Rog Old-Timer in St. Loo but Not in New York."

While ballplayers and fans alike persisted in their efforts to convince Roger to change his position, the game of baseball went on. In 1974 the media sought Roger's opinions about Yankee hitter Graig Nettles, whose batting performance in April seemed to pose a potential threat to the Maris record. When Nettles' challenge fizzled after April, Roger, referring to the press, said, "I guess they've expected it to happen every year. Their attitude is that if Roger Maris can do it, anyone can do it. It's just one homer every two and one-half games."

Before he died, Roger told a reporter, "Every year a guy gets into the thirties and some newspaperman calls me. We talk a bit and then I always tell them to call back when the guy gets into the fifties. I can relate my experience to his."

By early July, 1976, Dave Kingman of the Mets had connected for 27 homers in a batting performance reminiscent of Maris' in 1961. Kingman's rise prompted Maury Allen to write a *New York Post* column "Remembering Roger."

Conceding that Maris had been wronged, Allen asked Roger to come home to Yankee Stadium:

"Forget it, Roger. These are new people, new times; only the memories are old. Come back, Roger. People won't boo. People will also remember you could run, field, and throw. People remember you took a lot that summer.

"People just want to say thank you for one hell of a summer."

Roger still did not return.

In the spring of 1977, to the surprise of many, Roger again took an active role in baseball. While en route to Marco Island, Florida, to play golf, Maris met the Kansas City Royals' manager. The manager asked Roger to help the team's big, powerful left-handed home-run threat John Mayberry. Roger detoured to Fort Myers, Florida, where he began a stint as hitting instructor to his assigned pupil.

"I did it for Whitey Herzog," Roger explained. "Whitey and I are good friends. I was hesitant at first. You never know how anybody is going to react. ... You can stand there all day long and suggest things, but the hitter still has to go out and execute."

Roger enjoyed his assignment, but he would not guarantee results despite the responsiveness of his student.

The instructions in Fort Myers brought comments from the press. In reply to suggestions that he was "mellowing," Roger retorted, "I'm the same man I was five years ago. It's everyone else who's mellowing towards me." When asked if his temporary return to baseball meant that he would again put on the pinstripes at the stadium, Roger answered, "One day when I get to be an old timer."

The scope of the questions broadened to other topics. Was Roger envious of the hefty salary paid to Reggie Jackson, the Yankees' new, controversial right fielder? "It doesn't bother me at all," replied Roger. "I'm happy I played when I did. The dollar doesn't go anyplace today."

Having encountered the wrath of New York, could Roger advise

Reggie? "I'm not going to give him any advice," insisted Roger. "I could just hear the people saying, 'Who is he to give anybody advice. He couldn't handle his own problems.' I just hope they don't get on him the way they got on me. If they do, it will be miserable for him."

By midsummer, Reggie Jackson began to find incidents in his season that paralleled Roger's tribulations during 1961. "I'm experiencing some of the things Roger Maris went through," said Reggie. "I think I understand him better than I did six months ago.

"I mean, can you imagine what it was like to hit 61 homers in a season? In New York? It would take a new breed of man to do that again. The most amazing thing is that he still has his sanity."

Roger maintained his sanity throughout his Yankee experience; now, as a private person, he persevered in his unshakable insistence on not returning to New York. The Yanks still hoped that he would change his mind, as Rick Ostrow reported on August 14, 1977, in the *Danbury News Times.*

"One source in the Yankee front office reports that Maris' letter of refusal [to] this year's game was warmer than any he's ever sent. Perhaps the day when he does return is not as far away as everyone thinks."

Roger showed no sign of changing his attitude as the 1978 season neared. In his article for the Spring 1978 *Baseball Quarterly,* Peter Golenbock again asked Roger about his refusal to return to the stadium. Roger was not ready to return. The slugger claimed that the Yankees had passed the word that he would not return because he was afraid of being booed. That was not the reason, according to Maris. But aren't Houk and MacPhail gone? the writer asked. Maris replied:

> You've got to understand me. I've never believed in knocking people. Never. It's not my nature. I really don't even care to get into those kinds of things, 'cause all you do is reopen wounds. Right now Roger Maris is in Podunk. Nobody know he's around. You know? Half of us haven't heard of him in the last five years, and it's beautiful. I really hate to reopen old wounds. No news is good news. That is basically what it amounts to.

Roger returned in 1978 for the Yanks' home opener. He said on returning, "I'm here because of George Steinbrenner. He talked me into it." The team had won its first World Series since 1962, and the

Boss wanted to climax the celebration with a flag-raising ceremony with Roger and Mantle. Recognizing Steinbrenner's single-minded determination to bring him to the stadium, and the new, sunnier attitude in the Bronx, Roger relented. But before he agreed, he wanted Steinbrenner to do something in return.

"I'll come back," Roger told Steinbrenner, "and it won't cost you a penny for me."

"Well, what do you want," Steinbrenner asked.

"Sod for the Oak Hill Private School [in Gainesville]."

The Boss granted the request.

"Listen, George, these kids could use some lights, too."

"You got it," said the Boss.

Al Hall in the *Gainesville Sun* relates that Roger also requested and "got Steinbrenner's help" at Oak Hall, where some of the Maris children attended.

Jerry Izenberg wrote a column entitled "The Long Journey Home for Roger Maris" for the *New York Post*. The journalist notes that as the slugger looked at the park and the fans, he said, "Well, it's home."

To avoid potential problems or embarrassments, the Yankees did not publicly public announce Roger's return. The fans in attendance numbered 44,667, nearly double the crowd that had seen him hit number 61. Roger waited in the dugout next to another number 9, third baseman Graig Nettles. "Are you nervous?" Nettles asked. A relaxed Roger answered, "I've got nothing to be nervous about. I don't have to face anybody. I'm not going 0 for 5 today."

Roger still had his crew cut, although for three or four years he had given in to his sons and let it grow longer. As Mel Allen began talking on the field microphone, the video screen in center field showed the confrontation between Stallard and Roger. Roger came out of the dugout slowly. Before he reached home plate the crowd recognized a hero returned. "And then it began," wrote Izenberg "... waves and waves of noise ... different from the jeers and slurs which once were for him a living hell in this ball park. It was a spectacular ovation."

The media wondered, after all these years, what Roger thought of his ovation. Roger responded to his acceptance on April 13, 1978, "It's like obituaries. When you die, they always give you good reviews."

The press persisted. What would have happened if the fans booed? Two versions of Roger's witty retort appeared in the press: "All it would mean is that I wouldn't be back here again;" and "Well, then,

I guess I would have been right in staying away all those years."

Pleased at his stadium reception, Roger stayed in New York long enough to attend a dinner welcoming the 1978 Bombers at the Americana Hotel. Maris received a standing ovation following an introduction by Howard Cosell.

As The Boss was introduced, the band played "Yankee Doodle Dandy." During his invocation, the priest prayed: "Oh, Lord, don't leave it all to George. Even he needs some help." But Steinbrenner did manage to induce Roger back to the stadium in 1978 [not as others, e.g., Kubek and Pluto in *Sixty-One,* have said, in 1984]. Roger told the *Gainesville Sun* in 1984, "I went back again and again, but they sometimes booed Steinbrenner and that bothered me. I haven't really been around George that much, but he's done a lot for baseball in Florida, in South Florida, in Jacksonville. People can say what they want about him, but he's done a lot."

Once Roger had returned to Yankee Stadium, the press seemed to lose interest in him – an ideal situation for Roger. He continued to give occasional interviews, many from the golf links where he played at least once a week.

The year 1981 held historic importance for the sport of baseball. Twenty years after Roger Maris made his 61 homers, baseball parks stood quiet and vacant as a result of the strike-abbreviated season. Sheldon Ocker's article headlined "Maris Scarred by Events of 1961; 20 Years Don't Ease Belittlement of Record, Media Treatment" in the *Akron Beacon Journal* typified most press coverage of the record-breaking anniversary.

Roger hadn't intently followed the strike's developments, but he commented on the economics of the strike and of baseball:

> It seems to me the way the system [in baseball] has gone in the last 20 years is the way the whole country has gone. I certainly don't think players make too much money. ... Baseball players are basically entertainers. No one complains if a movie actor gets a million dollars.
>
> Years ago we were underpaid. People think the Yankees paid their players better than most clubs. But I'd be willing to bet that if it all came out in the wash, other teams had much higher payrolls. I know one thing. They didn't pay me that well.

In 1982, when Edward Kiersh asked him if he would go through that unforgettable season again, Roger said, "Maybe I wouldn't do it all over again if I had the chance. Sometimes I think it wasn't worth the aggravation. Anyway, baseball led to my getting the beer distributorship. Plus, I have the record, and that's the only thing that counts."

Roger stayed active throughout the early eighties. He devoted much time to the Major League Alumni Association, an organization involved with communal and charitable work. Rick Reichardt, a former Angel player and Gainesville neighbor, notes that Roger rarely made public appearances. Consequently, according to Reichardt, "Nobody really knew ... what a caring person he was ... for example, in the appearances he had made at hospitals in Orlando."

Twenty-three years after Roger belted number 61, he made his curtain call at Yankee Stadium. Through the efforts of George Steinbrenner and Howard Cosell, Maris received his due respect as a Yankee during his final, glorious appearance in the "House the Ruth Built." As a feature of the Yankees' annual Old Timers' Day celebration on July 21, 1984, the team would place a plaque honoring Roger alongside those of such Yankee greats as Joe DiMaggio, Mickey Mantle, Casey Stengel, and Thurmon Munson. Fittingly, the site would be close to the memorial to Babe Ruth. As a crowning touch to the ceremonies, the Yankees would retire Roger's number 9.

Howard Cosell informed Roger of the Yankees' plans during an interview for ABC-TV's "Sportsbeat," which was shown on March 31.

Frank Kelly of the *New York Daily News* viewed tapes of the program before broadcast. He wrote, "The look that passes across Maris' normally impassive face ranges from utter disbelief to suspicion to fulfillment."

"You are serious?" an unconvinced Roger asks. Then, believing, Roger says softly: "I think that's very nice. I would say that's the nicest thing that's been done to me. ... It's been 23 years, and it has been hard to get any serious recognition for hitting the 61 through baseball."

Roger's cancer undoubtedly hastened his return to the stadium. However, Steinbrenner had other motives for his prompt actions: "I didn't retire Roger's number and put him on the monument out of sympathy for him because of his illness. I believe in flowers for the living, not just the dead. Twenty-three years was too long to wait. That was a debt that was owed that was never paid."

Steinbrenner waited eleven years to repay the Yankees' debt to

Roger Maris* — A Title to Fame

Roger and retire his number. At the time the Boss bought the team, Nettles wore the number 9. The Boss wanted to retire Roger's number "years ago, but I couldn't very well take the number off Nettles' back." After the 1983 season, when the Yankees traded Nettles to San Diego, Steinbrenner could retire Maris' number 9 without impediment.

Don Gooselaw noticed that "Roger was like an excited youngster who couldn't sit still." Roger had his happiest moments professionally in that brief period before the stadium ceremonies, according to Gooselaw.

On that special, long-awaited day, the Maris family, even the children, could be present at a historic event. Some 250 Fargo citizens made the 1200-mile-plus trip to New York. As a special treat, Roger hosted a reception in his hotel suite for his hometown friends. The honor given Roger Maris also meant glory for Fargo.

"When Roger accepted the honors," said the *Forum*'s Ed Kolpack, "he pointed to his friends from North Dakota who were seated behind home plate. You can bet it was the last – and perhaps the only time – that North Dakota was mentioned on a Yankee Stadium P.A. system."

As Roger stood at home plate, he watched the Yankees also retire the number 32 of teammate and close friend Elston Howard, who had died in 1980. Arlene Howard accepted the honor for her husband. "I'm especially honored," said Roger, "to be sharing this day with Elston Howard. Ellie and I lockered together, and I'm as proud for him today as I am for myself.

The Yankees affixed Roger's bronze plaque on the monument in the memorial park behind the fence in left-center field. The tribute to Roger engraved on the plaque began: "In belated recognition of one of baseball's greatest achievements ever."

The media asked Roger his thoughts on whether the record would be broken soon, if at all. Maris replied, "I think as long as baseball stays with the same dimensions I had throughout the league, it will be pretty tough. Everybody talks about my short porch at Yankee Stadium, but I did hit 31 on the road."

Don Gooselaw felt that the monument and the number being retired "meant more to Roger than his being in the Hall of Fame. He was permanently enshrined in Yankee Stadium, being out there with DiMaggio and Ruth, and, best of all, his family was there to see these honors."

During the ceremonies on his special day, Roger told the stadium crowd: "Every player is always proud to be a Yankee. The Yankees have more tradition, more history." To not only play with the Yankees, but to also merit a plaque and the retirement of one's number is "more than anybody can expect."

The thrill of the day stayed with him. Fewer than six weeks before he died, Roger told the *Gainesville Sun:*

> If nothing else happens to me in baseball, I think the thing that means more to me than anything else is the plaque on the monument in center field. There are a lot of quality baseball players out there, a lot of legends. To be out there is something that I'm very proud of.
>
> I do believe that George wanted to do this for me – not out of sympathy and not for himself but for me.

In Clete Boyer's estimation, Roger Maris loved George Steinbrenner.

The Yankee owner said, "To me, Roger Maris symbolizes the Yankees, just like Ruth, Mantle, DiMaggio, Gehrig. All those guys got their credit. Now Roger has his."

Twenty-three years passed before Roger got his due. The clock might have run out on Roger before he had his hour at Yankee Stadium. As Clete Boyer put it in *Just for the Record,* "If he had died and not returned [to the stadium], it would have been a damned shame."

Chapter XX
'Come Lovely and Soothing Death'

"Come lovely and soothing death."
            Walt Whitman
            When Lilacs Last in the Dooryard Bloomed

In the fall of 1983, Roger Maris consulted a physician about what seemed to be a continuing sinus problem.

Pat Maris remembers that in "the last five years, he got colds and flus. He was able to keep going, but during this period, these colds would really zap him."

During the physical examination, the doctor noticed Roger's swollen lymph glands and ordered further tests. In November, 1983, the doctor diagnosed Maris' condition as malignant lymphoma cancer. Roger had had it for five years.

The doctors told Roger that his type of cancer had an 80 percent cure rate. Pat recalls, "'Cancer' is a scary word. ... We were told that Roger had the 'good' kind of cancer. Roger would joke about this and say, 'If this is the good kind, I'd sure hate to see the bad kind.'

"Roger was diagnosed about five times," said Dr. Surprise, "and ... they said the cancer was due to smoking, but Roger had not been a smoker for many years."

Roger's friends in Fargo soon learned of Roger's cancer. "It was very early in 1984," said Bob Wood. "Roger started explaining to me about the four stages and the remission periods. 'I think we can lick it,' Roger said. I began crying. 'Please don't tell any of our friends,' Roger pleaded."

Bill Weaver didn't know about Maris' condition until the slugger, thinking out loud, inadvertently shared his secret. "It was in 1984," Weaver remembered, "but I can't say exactly when. One day we were driving through Fargo on my way to taking Roger out to lunch. As we passed the cemetery, Roger turned to me and said, 'Bill, I want to be buried in Fargo.' I was stunned. I had no idea that Roger was sick."

By the middle of March, 1984, everyone had learned of Roger's struggle with the disease. A story released by the *Tampa Tribune* revealed that Roger was battling cancer. Roger said, "It looks like it is under control now. I was awfully sick for a while. I mean it's not over, but, well, it's coming. The doctors tell me that if you have to have this thing, this is the best kind to have. It looks like they are right. It looks like we're on our way to victory."

Roger weathered the sickness well, according to Pat Maris. "It was in remission by April," she said, "but when it came back, it was worse. There were chemotherapy treatments. He would look forward to the good days after the chemo because he knew when the good days would be. It was hard for me because I wanted to do something to help him get over this, but I couldn't."

Sister Bertha remarked that Roger had his own inner strength. "Roger was not a stranger to pain and disappointment. He accepted everything God asked him to. The cancer was another thorn in his path that he accepted."

In the spring of 1984 Howard Cosell interviewed Roger Maris. Before a nationwide television audience Roger openly discussed his disease.

> There's what they call lymphoma, which is a lymph-gland cancer. ... I had a couple, three pretty trying months here, starting back in November. Right now I feel very good. The medicine I've taken over the course of the last four or five months seems to have taken care of the problem for now. I think we've got it pretty much controlled. My last check-up, everything looked very good, so I'm encouraged about what's happening. ... Fortunately, in my case I have – if you have to have cancer – the type to have. This is the one they've made the greatest strides to control it and treat it.

In the summer of 1984 Roger still seemed outwardly optimistic. The opening of the Roger Maris Museum, the golf tourney, and his awaited honors at Yankee Stadium all buoyed his spirits. He told Jerome Holtzman of the *Chicago Tribune:* "I consider myself lucky. I could have had a heart attack and died. Now, at least, I have a chance to get well and I feel I am getting well except that I still get tired."

Roger's boyish humor never left him throughout his illness, as

Yankee alumni director Jim Ogle learned. Ogle wanted only the most accurate, up-to-date information on the status of Roger's illness. The *New York Daily News* reports that Ogle heard the latest details on the slugger's condition from Roger, who then said, "By the way, Jim, I died last week, and you are now listening to a recording."

The excitement and appreciation Roger witnessed at the July, 1984, ceremonies at the stadium bolstered his spirits considerably. After the big day in the Bronx, Roger simply said, "I'm assuming I'm in good shape."

Roger again traveled to New York in April, 1985, to attend the Yanks' Welcome Home Dinner where he received the Lou Gehrig Pride of the Yankees award . That spring Roger returned to New York's Mount Sinai Hospital in Manhattan for treatment by cancer specialist Dr. Ezra Greenson. Big Julie was present when Roger suffered a relapse: "It was in the late summer of 1985 that we were in Elmer's Restaurant on Second Avenue. Roger had gotten a good report about his health and we were celebrating the news with champagne. Suddenly, Roger began sweating. He was coming out of remission."

Dr. Surprise claims that Roger's health had been deteriorating since the spring of 1985. "He could only walk a half a block before he tired." On one occasion, Dr. Surprise and Roger spent the day together on Maris' boat. "Roger was in very good spirits," the Independence friend said. "Roger had a Pac-Man and kept on bumping me on to the machine. It was a beautiful day. Roger put the trolling motors on the boat. It was a job that involved physical labor. Roger was trying to get the boat ready so that I could fish. Roger turned gray. 'I don't feel too good,' he said."

No matter how ill he felt, Roger would not refuse an invitation or request from a good cause. He attended the old-timer's baseball game at the University of Florida's Perry Field, wearing a Yankee uniform in the home dugout. Although Maris could not stay long, said the *Gainesville Sun*, "his presence certainly helped boost a program and the young athletes who take part in it."

Ironically, despite his desires, Maris could not attend the 1985 Roger Maris Celebrity Cancer Benefit golf tourney in Fargo. The disappointed tournament chairman Wayne Blanchard had "feared from the very beginning that his health may be a factor in his being here."

Participant Ken Hunt, Roger's former classmate and Yankee roommate, voiced an optimistic assessment of Roger's chances: "I talked to him ten days ago, and he said all the treatment he's received for cancer has left him feeling terrible, like he doesn't have a bone in his body; but if anybody can beat cancer, Roger can because he's always had such a positive attitude about life."

Although Roger had to miss the Fargo tournament, his four sons – Roger, Jr., Kevin, Richard, and Randy – filled in for him. Roger, Jr. spoke for his father at the banquet:

The cause is the main things, because it's going to cancer, and he has cancer. ... He's fighting it. He was in the hospital three weeks ago and he was real weak at the time. But lately he's come on and felt better. He's real susceptible to catching colds and kind of has to confine himself indoors. His white blood cell count is really low, and he just had a transfusion the other day.

The tourney and his son's appearance there meant much to Roger. "To show you what a concerned and involved father Roger was," said Sid Cichy, "Roger phoned the Fargo people after the banquet to find out how Roger, Jr., did."

Although Roger fought lymphoma as best he could, he was resigned to dying if that's how it had to be. Deedee Cosette provides some insight into Maris' attitude: "Roger's thinking was that we all had to die: some earlier and some later. His Catholic training prepared him in this ordeal. And he had the mental ease of knowing that his family had been taken care of financially."

From the moment he learned of his cancer, Roger tried to avoid the outpourings of sympathy that came from the well-meaning. However, the never-ending stream of letters offering prayers and personal messages "was great for my spirit."

Maris found his greatest source of support lay in his friends. Mickey Mantle called every week. Frequent phone contact with other friends – like Mike Shannon, Clete Boyer, and Big Julie – sustained Roger in his last months. "You do find out in a hurry," Roger said, "who your real friends are."

In *Just for the Record*, Mike Shannon describes how well Roger took his illness, never complaining, never speaking about dying. Only once did Shannon hear Roger utter an "I wish." While on the phone with Shannon, Roger saw a couple of golfers going to tee off on the course adjacent to his home. "It's a shame I'm not out there," Roger said.

A satellite dish that the family had bought for him allowed Roger to follow baseball in the summer of 1985. "To show you what a class person Roger was," said Wayne Blanchard, "Roger sent Pete Rose a congratulatory note after he topped Ty Cobb's hit mark. That happened in mid-September when Roger was in a very bad way."

Roger suffered a great deal of pain in the last three months of his life. Shortly before he died he told Dick Savageau, "You can't imagine how much pain I have." Savageau understood: his wife, Mitzie, had died of cancer.

When Roger's condition deteriorated, he decided to try a new, experimental treatment offered under the care of Dr. Robert Oldham of Franklin, Tennessee, near Nashville. Oldham had spent a period of time on staff at Vanderbilt Medical Center and then served as associate director of cancer treatment at the National Cancer Institute in Bethesda, Maryland. In 1985 Dr. Oldham had joined with Dr. William West to organize Biotherapeutics, Inc., a center for cancer research and treatment.

Many prominent people have received treatment at the Franklin Clinic. Doctors there have successfully treated patients who come in at the early stages of the cancer. Some lymphoma sufferers respond well to radiation and drugs. Others who do not, like Roger, receive experimental treatments that involve the body's immune system. Laboratory mice produce antibodies when they are injected with pieces of the tumor removed from the patient. Technicians then extract from the rodents their mouse-produced antibodies and inject them into the patient. According to Dr. Oldham, a successful treatment process takes nine months' to a year's time.

Roger didn't have that much time. His experimental treatments at the Franklin Clinic lasted for about a month. In conjunction with them, Roger underwent the more conventional cancer therapy. The interferon treatment involved the introduction into the body of interferon, a human cell-produced protein, rather than animal antibodies.

Curious, Roger wondered what would happen to the antibodies from his lymphoma if he died before completing the experimental treatment. He learned that the clinic would use the derivative to try to help someone else. Maris never hesitated; "Do it," he said.

In the winter of 1988, Dr. Oldham disclosed that "there had been a measure of progress" in treating Roger's disease. "Roger was a very nice, kind man," Dr. Oldham said. "He appreciated what had been done for him although he was with us only a few days. He was one of several patients undergoing that treatment. Therefore we can't say precisely that what he endured at the clinic definitely helped someone else, but it well might have."

Roger had too little time to utilize the new cancer treatment fully. He checked into the M.D. Anderson Tumor Institute in Houston November 20. "At that time," Gooselaw said, "Roger was not deceived. He knew the end was coming. In fact, in one of our last conversations, Roger told me the next golf tourney in Fargo would be a memorial tournament."

Clete Boyer also visited Roger, as Boyer recalls in *Just for the Record*. Boyer "went through the same" experience with his brother Ken Boyer, an outstanding National League player who fell victim to cancer. That Roger might die seemed hard for Boyer to believe: "We thought he would beat it." In Boyer's estimation, of all his teammates Roger would be the "last to go" because he neither drank nor smoked. Whenever he called Roger, Boyer felt apprehensive: "You don't call because you know the answers you'll get."

Shortly before Maris died, the Major League held its annual meetings in San Diego. A bloodmobile set up at the hotel that hosted the sessions encouraged baseball players to donate their blood. In greatest demand was Roger's own rare A-negative blood; other blood types could be exchanged with hospitals for type A-negative.

Blood donors included Padres' manager Dick Williams, a former teammate of Roger's in Kansas City, and Ken Harrelson, acting general manager of the White Sox. The Associated Press later distributed a picture of Harrelson giving blood. In all, the bloodmobile staff collected twenty-eight pints of blood and sent them to Houston.

Three of the Maris boys tried to donate blood. One son burst into in tears when he learned that his blood was incompatible with his father's.

The Maris family refused to give out any information about Roger's condition or about treatments. Even the *Fargo Forum* lacked information: "It was unknown how long the 51-year-old Maris had been hospitalized."

By Friday, December 13, Roger could hardly talk nor could he receive visitors. When Clete Boyer had wanted to call some days before, Roger told him to his distress, "I don't feel I can see you." The

Maris family turned away the new Houston Astros' coach, who had arrived in Houston and hoped to visit Roger. Yogi Berra remembers: It tore me up not to be able to see him that one last time. I wanted to see him badly. They told me he was too sick."

With the family at his bedside, Roger fell into a coma and died at 1:45 p.m., December 14.

This dark grey granite headstone marks Roger Maris'
grave in Holy Cross Cemetery, Fargo, North Dakota.
(Russ Hanson Photo)

Chapter XXI
In Appreciation of Roger—
After Death

"You end up worth more dead than alive."
Arthur Miller
Death of a Salesman

Pat did not want anyone to know that Roger had lapsed into a coma. Big Julie had wanted to be with Roger when he died, but Pat told him that there was no point in his coming. She suggested to Julie that perhaps the new medication would help and promised to call him the following day.

When she called, Pat delivered a simple message: "Julie, we lost him." Soon Dr. Surprise heard the news. Big Julie and Mike Shannon made calls to other friends and teammates.

After Roger died, Dr. Surprise remarked that "The last five days of Roger's life have been surrounded by much silence. They were exceedingly painful ones. One day Pat will tell about them."

Pat Maris, described by some as "tough as the North Dakota winters," has a strong, commanding family presence that enabled Roger to die a death of grace and grandeur. His passing came as a "relief" to all in the Maris family, she acknowledged. "He suffered so much, but he died the way he lived: strong, private, and doing what he thought was right. He was at peace with himself and his God. Now, he's at rest and happier than we are.

"He is watching me where he is now, and I have someone to pray to and talk to."

Pat expressed bewilderment at why Roger had been so misunderstood during his baseball career, especially in the seven years with the Yankees. She did know that some mistook his openness for surliness. She told the *Fargo Forum*, "I suppose if he had been one of these that buttered up everybody and did what they wanted him to do, he probably would have had a lot of good press. But he kind of just told things the way they were. He really never harmed anybody, that's for sure."

Maris' friends in Fargo praised Roger for his amicable character. Don Gooselaw called Roger "a true friend," and Dick Savageau noted, "The amazing thing about him was for all the notoriety he got, he never forgot a friend."

Sister Bernice, one of Roger's former teachers at Shanley, penned a tribute to Roger for the *Acorn*. In "Saying Good-bye to a Great Guy," the nun wrote:

"Roger was not always a star, but he lived up to his full potential. He was loved and appreciated by his classmates, and this sense of friendship was continued and deepened both with his classmates and teammates in later life. Because of this, I classify him as a star of the highest caliber. ... With JFK, he had a dream and he worked through many adversities to perfect this dream."

A former classmate and teammate Jim Wold spoke of Roger as "the best high school football player I've ever seen ... yet he was quiet and not at all boastful."

North Dakotans throughout the state responded to Roger's death with sadness, remembrance, and reverence appropriate for a fallen hero. The *Grand Forks Herald* announced Maris' burial site with the headline "Fargo, North Dakota, Welcomes Maris Home." Fargoans articulated the pride and gratitude they felt because Roger had shared his life with them. Ed Kolpack's column in the *Forum* carried the headline "Maris Brought Excitement to Fargo." The same theme inspired the *Forum* editorial "Home Runs, Sure, But Home Came First." Roger began his baseball career in Fargo and would return to Fargo for burial. "In between," the editorial concluded, "he gave the nation, but especially his family and his home town folks, a lot of thrills, and an appreciation for the quiet, quality life."

North Dakota Governor George Sinner lauded Roger's honesty: "He said what he believed. You don't get any better credentials than that."

Millions of sports fans had learned of Roger's death during half time of a college basketball telecast. "We have sad news in the world of sports," said Brent Musburger. "Roger Maris has died at age 51."

Shortly after that announcement, Baseball Commissioner Peter Ueberroth issued a prepared statement:

"All baseball is saddened by the loss of one of its true heroes. While he will be remembered for his brilliant assault on the home run record in 1961, we should also remember the courageous battle he fought against this dreaded disease the last two years."

Sports fans across the nation read about Roger's death primarily as interpreted through the reactions of his former teammates, others in the baseball world, and local and national sportswriters.

Managers of the big-league clubs in which Roger played praised his all-around talent and competitiveness. Ralph Houk said Roger "was one of the great ones" who "put winning above his own accomplishments ... a real good family man." Roger's last major-league manager, Red Schoendienst, felt that "Baseball fans should remember Roger as an outstanding ball player. ... He was a complete player." George Steinbrenner, who brought Roger back to claim his deserved recognition from the Yankees, said, "Roger was a most misunderstood young man. The Yankees treated him shabbily."

After Maris' death eulogies replaced the mudslinging that had so plagued him throughout his professional life. Moose Skowron had Maris' detractors in mind when he reacted to Roger's death: "I don't think he got enough recognition as the guy who hit more home runs than anyone in baseball. They'll probably give it to him now that he's gone, but it's too late. You need it while you're alive."

Skowron had an especially memorable day of intense and conflicting emotions on December 14, 1985. "I got a call from my son," Skowron said, "and he told me, 'Dad, you are a grandpa.' Then all of a sudden I got a call from Pat, telling me about Roger. God brings one in and takes one away. And it happened on the 14th, the same number as my uniform. Everything hit me at once. I had to give the phone to my wife. I began to cry."

News of Roger's death reached Mickey Mantle in Miami. In an interview with *WPLG* the Mick tried to put to rest those stories alleging bitter relations between him and Roger: "There was a lot written about the animosity between me and him. But that was the furthest thing from the truth. We roomed together in New York that year [1961] and I don't think we had a single argument. Roger was a great man."

Clete Boyer said that Roger was as close to him as his own brother, whom he had already lost to cancer. Boyer had tried to contact Mrs. Rudy Maris about Roger's condition a few days before he died. When she didn't answer the phone, Boyer realized that his close friend was near death. Finally the phone rang, and Boyer "got a cold feeling when they called me. I went through the same thing with my brother.

You may as well look in the mirror."

According to Boyer, Roger had felt that his achievements had received scant recognition throughout the years. "I know that asterisk really hurt him and took away from him what he had accomplished."

Mike Shannon also thought of Roger Maris as family: "Would you want him as a brother? He was my brother." The former Cardinal "will remember him as a friend and a very compassionate person," one who rarely said no when asked by friends to attend fundraisers for charities.

Cardinal teammate Tim McCarver cited his reasons for respecting Roger. "He was warm, he was giving, and he was one hell of a ballplayer. He was a complete ballplayer. He could run, he could throw, and he gave so much to those championship teams of 1967 and 1968."

Roger's teammates knew the value of Roger as player and person. Fellow North Dakotan, former teammate, and friend Ken Hunt observes: "I don't think he got anywhere near the respect he should have for the achievement he accomplished, but I think that it is all going to come. He is going to get a lot more posthumously than he ever did when he was alive."

Hunt's prediction proved true. The overwhelming majority of sports-column items were very sympathetic and kind to Roger's memory. However, some stories, such as that of Joseph Durso in the *New York Times,* continued to report the harshest aspects of Roger's personality: "'I was born surly,' Maris acknowledged in 1961, when the home run race had ended, 'and I'm going to stay that way. Everything in life is tough.'"

The media again emphasized the asterisk of 1961 as if, in fact, an asterisk stood in the record books. The editorial page of the *New York Times* carried an article entitled "Roger Maris*" that began: "There was nothing personal about that asterisk. It was just one generation's way of preserving a youthful hero undiminished."

The *Kansas City Star* noted in its editorial that Roger's mark of 61 homers "has resisted the onslaught of sluggers for 24 years." However, in 1961 the asterisk overshadowed Maris: "For weeks he was chased by the media, booed by fans, and ridiculed by then-baseball Commissioner Ford Frick, who decided to put an asterisk by the mark if he set it."

The *Gainesville Sun* editorial remarked that "Maris' feat has been noted in the record books with an asterisk." The asterisk had become such an identifying label for Roger that the *Sun* editorial ended: "Gainesville is a better place today because Maris lived here, and his loss is a great one.*" Underneath that final sentence was the note "*No doubt about it."

The asterisk seemed the common element in all Roger Maris stories. George Vecsey writing in the *New York Times* sought to dispel two "misconceptions:" that Roger was a mediocre player and that he was "some kind of asocial being." Those misconceptions have followed Roger "ever since Ford Frick, the presiding keeper of baseball tradition, affixed the infamous asterisk to Maris in the home run season of 1961."

"World Remembers the Courage of Maris" headlines a *New York Times* article by Robert McG. Thomas, Jr. Aside from remembering Maris' record home-run year, the article "recalled [Roger] as a loyal and unassuming friend who had dealt with the cancer that would claim his life in the same way he had handled the pressures of chasing Babe Ruth's home run record—with quiet courage."

In his column Art Spander keenly observed that media coverage of sports and sports personalities changed with Roger Maris. Spander wrote that Roger "couldn't handle the repetitive interviews and questions. ... Maris was perhaps the first athlete to be scrutinized so intensely."

Spander saw more in the death of Roger Maris than the death of a great athlete. Recounting, Spander noted that former Yankee Johnny Lindell had died a few weeks before and Cleveland's Mike Garcia lay in ill health. The columnist observed, "Disease plays no favorites. Life gives no compensation for skill, productivity, or courage. There's one game we always lose. ... Once more, we're reminded of our own mortality."

Bob Verdi produced an eloquent article on Roger's death for the *Chicago Tribune*. The columnist sets forth his theme in the first paragraph: "There are lessons to be learned from the mistreatment of Roger Maris but none more important than these: Treat an athlete for the person he is, not the person we think he ought to be, and judge what he accomplishes according to his era, not another irrelevant time-frame of reference."

Verdi explains that "because Maris didn't kiss the right people in the right places he was kicked for it, and nobody hit him harder than Ford Frick, a clerk of a commissioner. ... So Frick unfurled his asterisk. Not only was the commissioner's brainstorm unwarranted; it was pretty much accepted by the public."

The article concludes with a plea:

> Superior athletes, just as superior salesmen or superior airline pilots, encounter enough pressures each morning. They needn't be artificially compared with other people in other decades. If we so honor records that are made to be broken, we should respect whoever breaks them, whenever, however. Achievers are achievers, and that is the only equitable barometer. If only life had been so fair while it lasted for Roger Maris. They should bury the asterisk and hatchet, too.

Athletes rarely receive the media coverage Roger did when he came home to Fargo for his funeral and burial. In death Roger would receive the praise he could not during his lifetime.

Hector Airport bustled with people the week of the funeral. Don Gooselaw, who had volunteered time away from his business to help with the arrangements, chauffeured many of the VIPs from the airport and around Fargo by van.

North Dakota Governor George Sinner ordered all state flags to fly at half-staff on December 19, the day of Roger's funeral. Ironically, the December 19 date coincided with Ford Frick's birthday.

Pat Maris planned all the details of the funeral. She scheduled December 18 for open-casket public visitations at both the Boulger Funeral Home and at St. Mary's Cathedral.

Fargoans streamed in to the funeral home, signed the visitation book, and looked upon a national hero and a fellow Fargoan for the final time . An early visitor, former mayor Herschel Lashkowitz, remarked: "I've known Roger for years. These are sad days. We were good friends." Chip Litten, a former Fargo Central High and Minnesota Gopher football hero, felt that even though Fargo appreciated him, "Roger never got the recognition he deserved," .

Some visitors never identified themselves when they came to pay their respects. One former American Legion ballplayer said: "I'm like Roger. I like to be in the background."

Approximately five hundred people braved two feet of snow and six-below weather to attend that evening's fifty-minute prayer service in St. Mary's. The service brought Roger's friends from Fargo and from baseball together in a celebration of Roger's life. Clete Boyer summarized the thoughts of all those who had known Maris and had played with him: "Roger was a great family man and a great athlete. I'm proud to be here." Jim McLaughlin, an active personality in Fargo Legion baseball, grew emotional as he voiced the sentiments of all Fargoans, "We're very proud that Roger chose to come back here to be buried."

At noon on December 19, snow fell softly to the ground in the two-degree temperature. About eight hundred mourners filled the pews of the state's largest Catholic church. One hundred more grievers stood along the walls of the century-old, alabaster-columned church. An additional one hundred participants sat on folded chairs in the basement and watched the services on closed-circuit television.

The oak casket had twelve pallbearers: six former teammates and six other personal friends. The Yankees' Mantle, Boyer, Skowron, and Ford; the Cardinals' Shannon; and the Athletics' Herzog represented Maris' ties with the sports world. The remaining six bearers were Bob Allison, a Minnesota Twins player and Roger's friend since their Raytown days; Dr. George Surprise from Independence; New York's Big Julie Isaacson; Don Gooselaw, Dick Savageau, and Bob Wood.

The members of the immediate family — Pat Maris and her six children, ages 20 to 28; Roger's mother, Connie; his father, Rudy, Jr.; and his brother, Rudy — stood near the coffin, united in tragedy.

North Dakota Governor Sinner, former Governors William Guy, Art Link, and Al Olson took their places in the sanctuary. American League Vice President Bob Fishel represented Commissioner Ueberroth, and Maris' former teammate Roy White, the newly named Yankee coach, represented George Steinbrenner. In addition to the Yankee pallbearers, Yankees Bobby Richardson, John Blanchard, Bob Cerv, and Ryne Duren sat in the pews.

The Reverend John Moore of the Blessed Sacrament Catholic Church of West Fargo, who reportedly persuaded Roger to attend Shanley, celebrated the funeral Mass. Cocelebrants in the first part of the Mass included Bishop James S. Sullivan, the Reverend Al Bitz, and Brother Bob Dufford. The Northern Plains Brass Quartet provided the instrumental music; Edwin Hawkins soloed, and the Shanley Boys Chorus sang vocal choruses and solos.

Moore peppered his eulogy with baseball language. God is "the great umpire of our lives, which is the way it should be," he said, because man often muffs the calls.

Moore continued:

> Some might say Roger struck out in his final at bat. However, Roger got a base on balls, a free pass to heaven. ...
>
> It is one thing to come here for a golf tournament in the summer time when everything is lush and green. It is another to come at this time of year and brave the elements. It shows how much you cared for Roger.
>
> We are here to pay tribute to a great athlete, a great man. Death was especially difficult because he was in the prime of life.

The priest quoted Wisdom 4:7-15 as appropriate to Roger's life:

> "But the just man, though he die early, shall be at rest. For the age that is honorable comes not with the passing of time, nor can it be measured in terms of years."
>
> Roger was a just man, a good man. His family always came first. I suppose that was one of his troubles in New York, his problem with the press. He did his job and he did it to the best of his ability, and then he wanted to go home to his wife and family.

For these reasons, he said, Roger's burial in Fargo is fitting because "it is truly his home, and the people here dearly love him."

After a reading from Wisdom by Roger Maris, Jr., James Carvell, Roger's brother-in-law, read from 2 Corinthians. Tim Kasper sang a responsorial Psalm, "On Eagles' Wings" written by Michael Joncas.

Serving as gift bearers, Tasha Carvell, Roger's grandniece, and Steven Maris, one of his two grandchildren, carried the eucharistic elements to the priest. Roger's brother-in-law and niece, Walt Seeba and Ann Schneider, were the special ministers of Communion. Brother John Foley also participated in the Communion rite.

Bobby Richardson fervently eulogized his former teammate's athletic skills and the personal qualities the press never acknowledged. According to Richardson, Roger—perhaps the Yanks' best rightfielder ever—had a "cannon arm" and was "one of the most feared power hitters in the American League."

Roger was "misunderstood," continued Richardson. "He was a

private man who wanted to go home after the game, be with his family. He didn't take too much to the acclaim and adulation of the hero. ... [He was] a wonderful father and husband ... being dedicated to his family and to his inner circle of friends."

The eastern media didn't appreciate Roger's humor as Richardson did. Giving an example, Richardson recalled one day when he and Roger watched an American Legion game in Richardson's South Carolina hometown. As they sat in the stands, Roger saw a ball sail over the head of Richardson's son in the outfield. Roger poked Richardson and chuckled, "He's been watching me too much."

Roger Maris, Jr., spoke for the family in discussing his father's values: "His number one priority was to live and see that he could give as much love as possible. ... [He was a] "great humanitarian. ... [Roger Maris] "treated every person as if they were standing on a pedestal and looking eyeball to eyeball. He said if you could treat everybody as you would like to be treated, it could make you a better person."

Following the Communion reflection by Bill Lane and Roger Nichols, a recessional ended the hour-long Mass.

The poignant service left Mantle wiping away the tears from his eyes. Chuck Haga of the *Grand Forks Herald* devoted his column to "Honoring the Heroics and the Hurt." Haga had idolized Mantle who now "grieved for his friend Roger. Maris was heroic, too, and I felt his loss. I felt compassion for his family and friends, and I felt pride and gratitude that Maris had asked to be buried here. ... "

If Haga could have spoken to Mantle, he would have told him: "Thanks for being, for trying, for failing sometimes, for playing hurt, for growing and maturing these last few years, for coming to Fargo, for crying for Roger, for saying on television that you loved him."

All who came to the funeral felt a sense of fulfillment, especially the youth. Todd Colliton, a member of the Shanley Chorus, considered it "an honor to be here. We were chosen by Mrs. Maris." Todd's father had quarterbacked for Shanley in Roger and Rudy Maris' era. Another Shanley Chorus member, Tom Hall, "wanted to be here." His father had been bat boy for the Fargo-Moorhead Twins when Roger played for them. Young Hall said: "I've heard all the Roger Maris stories. I heard about the sportswriters—they didn't like him. But they didn't understand him. Dad said he was shy."

Eric Nelson, 10, attended the funeral with his father. The boy announced to reporters, "I just checked out a book on Roger Maris from our school library." When asked "Why?" Eric readily answered, "Because Roger Maris was one of the greatest baseball players in the world."

A surprised reporter commented, "But you never saw him."

Innocently, Eric said, "I saw him last night."

The media deployed in full force. Television stations pooled their resources to cover the funeral. Roger's Fargo friend Boyd Christenson, then public affairs director of Prairie Public Television, coordinated the media efforts. The sight of the shivering press trying to take notes or snap pictures made Christenson smile. "I have to think Roger got the last laugh," he said. "After his running gun-battle with the press, he got them to come to North Dakota and stand around with freezing fingers taking notes. Knowing Roger, I think he's smiling."

After the service, mourners in cortege drove three miles through a gentle snowfall to the Holy Cross cemetery in North Fargo. Family and friends huddled together against the cold, sheltered by an undertaker's tent, as the Reverend Al Bitz prayed for Roger's soul. Following a short prayer service in the frigid prairie air, Roger Maris was laid to rest in the same cemetery where Pat Maris' family is interred.

Pat Maris exhibited a stoic strength throughout the Mass and burial that gave courage to her family and friends. Andy Strasberg, who flew in from San Diego, found the services an overpowering emotional ordeal. The prayer service on the eve of the funeral left him overcome with grief. Pat Maris came to his aid. "Can you believe, I had to console him," she said.

Accounts of the funeral had an emotional impact on countless baseball fans throughout America. Fargoans saw the death of Roger Maris as more than just the passing of a great athlete. Despite his death, Roger could never be separated from Fargo, and not only because he was interred there. *Forum* editor Joe Dill wrote of this indissoluble relationship in an article aptly titled "Maris and Fargo: Never the Twain Shall Part." In his tribute, Dill speaks not only of the bonds between the two but also of the regional qualities that helped shape Roger's personality:

Fargo shed tears last week when adopted son Roger Maris was returned to the town that always was home for him. But they were quiet tears, not convulsive sobs. That's the way it is here.

In a twist of irony, the man who loved privacy was never more public than in death. This says more for the man, and more for his understanding family, than any mere words.

The family shared Roger with the Fargo-Moorhead area for two days last week, ...

Maybe what the eastern media considered surliness was nothing more than the demand by a man of the prairie for his space, his right to privacy. In this part of the country, a person says what's on his or her mind candidly, works hard, and values the family. ...

Broadcaster Boyd Christenson ... had keen insight: "To us in this part of the country, he was more than a guy with a bat, wearing pinstripes and a number 9 on his back."

As his priest friend put it, "What a beautiful person Roger was. He was one of us."

Happily, they talked about Roger Maris the person rather than Roger Maris the legendary baseball player.

The tears Fargo quietly shed last week would have sent a living Maris running from the room, but it's okay, Roger. The tears were of pride as well as grief. You gotta expect that when you're back home.

So, the man who ascended to the absolute heights of major league baseball fame is back where he started, back home. Fargo always was a big part of Roger and, thank God, the man who thrilled the country when he hit 61 will always be a part of Fargo.

The passing of Roger Maris revivified days gone by for Jim Naughton. In an article for the *New York Daily News* sports wire, Naughton recalls his "earliest memory," sitting in a barber chair listening to Mel Allen present the 1961 confrontation between Roger and Hoyt Wilhelm. Naughton's whole life might have been different if his first recollection had not had Roger as its "focal point":

Certainly there were other compelling bits of raw material available in 1961. Perhaps I would have gone to law school if my earliest memory involved the Bay of Pigs. Or maybe I would have had a better social life if it involved

Elvis Presley.

But there is Roger Maris, with the shoulders of a comic-book hero. He is smiling at me from an old box of Post Alpha-Bits. And here I am, 23 years later, wondering what to make of him.

In 1979 Naughton covered an oldtimers' game where he saw Roger. The sportswriter wanted to tell the old Yankee what an impact he had made on Naughton's life and how its memories still lingered. Naughton could not do it: "You just cannot walk up to a person and tell him that two decades earlier, he helped you discover your imagination. You have to find another way to say 'thank you.'"

Chapter XXII
Preserving a Legacy

Countless other "Naughtons" wanted to say "thank you" and to preserve the legacy of Roger Maris. George Steinbrenner gave New Yorkers that opportunity two days before Christmas, on December 23. "The Boss" arranged for a Mass to be said for Roger at St. Patrick's Cathedral in New York, the city where Maris achieved his greatest success.

When Babe Ruth died of cancer in 1948, fans thronged to St. Patrick's for his funeral. Only two other figures in the sports world, football's legendary coach Vince Lombardi and now Roger, had the honor of requiem services in this world-famous cathedral.

Nearly three thousand persons came to the cathedral, not to grieve Roger's death, but to celebrate his life. The front cover of the church program depicted a young, smiling Roger in spring training, with the number 9 and Yankee logo set off by New York pinstripes. The back cover showed the plaque hanging at Yankee Stadium and the date of its installation, July 21, 1984.

The program text included two familiar biblical quotations: "For everything there is a season, and a time for every matter under heaven; a time to be born, and a time to die; ... a time to weep, and a time to laugh; a time to mourn and a time to dance." (Ecclesiastes 3: 1-8); and "Whatever is born of God overcomes the world; and this is the victory that overcomes the world, Our Faith" (I John 5:4).

Steinbrenner had not only proposed the tribute, but once he received permission for it, he also invited the dignitaries by telephone or mailgram. Personalities from the baseball world, past and present — including former Yankee teammates — and a number of public figures attended the service.

The notables from public life included former President Richard M. Nixon; former New York Governor Hugh L. Carey; New York City Mayor Edward I. Koch; former New York City Mayor Abe Beame; U.S. Attorney Rudolph Giuliani; New York State Attorney General Robert Abrams; and New York City Police Commissioner Benjamin Ward.

Among the baseball delegation were Commissioner Peter Ueberroth, former Commissioner Bowie Kuhn, American League President Bobby Brown, and Houston Astros owner John McMullen. Former Yankees Yogi Berra, Jim Bouton, Joe Collins, Phil Linz, Ed Lopat, Sparky Lyle, and Phil Rizzuto attended. Coaches Gene Michael, Jeff Torborg and Roy White, and Roy Cohn, the team's attorney, represented the present-day Yankees. Former Brooklyn Dodger Ralph Branca and former Madison Square Garden president Sonny Werblin also came to pay their respects.

The crowded cathedral accommodated countless Yankee fans and curious passers-by who had interrupted their Christmas shopping to attend the Mass. Those who arrived late found only standing room available.

Pat Maris, her six children, and grandson Steven occupied the front pews, while Steinbrenner sat across the aisle from the Marises.

His Eminence John Cardinal O'Connor, the celebrant and homilist, said to the congregation, "It is only fitting that we honor the great Yankee in this place and in this way." Looking at the Maris family, O'Connor continued: "This is where her husband and their father sprang to his great fame. This is a fitting cathedral in the heart of the city to honor him."

The cardinal reminisced about growing up with his father, a diehard Yankee fan in Philadelphia who still idolized Babe Ruth. "When Ruth died in 1948," Cardinal O'Connor said, "the Yankees played their scheduled game that day, and my father was very upset. He would not go to another Yankee game. He said there would be no Yankees without the Babe."

Roger's advance on the Ruthian mark "crushed" O'Connor's father, who reacted as many Yankee fans did in 1961: "My father talked of the length of the season and the lively ball, and I could not convince him otherwise. My father was my father. I finally got him to go to a Yankee game and he saw the young Maris and he said, 'I must admit he sure does look like a fine, young fellow.' That was canonization by my father. Of all the accolades, none will surpass those of my father's."

Five Maris children — Susan, Kevin, Randy, Richard, and Sandra — took part in the Offertory Procession, while Roger Maris, Jr., spoke for the family. To accentuate his dad's vigorous family attachment, He read the last verse from the prophet Malachi: "And he shall return the heart of the fathers to the children, and the heart of the children to their fathers."

The broadcast announcer of the historic sixty-first homer, Phil Rizzuto, read the Prayer of the Faithful. "For Roger Maris," he said, "that he find peace in God's merciful judgment, we pray." The congregation responded, "Lord, hear our prayer."

Opera star Robert Merrill sang "The Lord's Prayer." A long-time admirer of Roger, Merrill often performs the national anthem before Yankee games.

Howard Cosell presented the Words of Tribute, which expounded further on the theme of the day: Roger Maris as father, husband, and athlete.

"We celebrate him in death as we should have long ago," Cosell began. "Roger Maris was the equation for guts. Courage, integrity, character, and principle. It was the way he lived his life."

Roger was not only a feared home-run hitter, continued Cosell, "but a complete ballplayer's player," who cared more about the team's winning than about his own statistics. "He would make key plays that were an integral part in victory."

Cosell detailed Roger's "heartache" after surpassing Ruth's seemingly untouchable record. Not only did Roger smash the mark of the much-worshipped immortal, but he also beat out "the adopted successor to the legend, Mickey Mantle."

Following the tribute, organist John Grady played and cantor Harry Danner sang.

The cardinal then came forward to offer some closing words. Alluding perhaps to Roger's misrepresentation by the press or. his negative reception by the fans or his career's domination by the purported asterisk, the cardinal said: "We believe if there were any faults remaining that have not been covered, so to speak, that we do so today."

In commemoration of the cheers for Roger Maris that rocked Yankee Stadium too infrequently, the cardinal asked the congregation "for one last burst of applause to honor this man."

The hushed assembly, including some dozen priests at the altar, rose as one. The enthusiastic applause began softly in the front rows. It grew in intensity into an ovation that lasted nearly a minute and resounded throughout the cavernous cathedral.

Cardinal O'Connor looked down at Roger's grandson Steven, in a gray suit and red tie. "You were not around to hear your grandfather applauded in the stadium. This [applause] is for you. You will remember this always, O.K.?"

Steven nodded, serious in demeanor.

A photograph of this moment later featured in the nation's press showed a determined-looking Pat Maris with her arms around the cherub.

Richard Nixon remained after the service to talk about Roger with the press. An avid baseball fan, Nixon saw parallels between himself and Roger – difficulties with the press and possessing "inscrutable" personalities. Nixon recalled the emotional hardships Roger endured after the record-breaking season. The former President used a quote from the Greek dramatist Sophocles, "One must wait until the evening to see how splendid the day has been," to emphasize that years later Maris – and others – began to appreciate his achievement.

With the memorial service now ended and the funeral in Fargo behind them, the Maris family looked ahead to a painful holiday. As Cardinal O'Connor had told them before the service, "It may be a white Christmas here or in North Dakota, but it will be a blue Christmas in your heart."

The Maris family almost welcomed Roger's death, coming as it did after he had suffered so much. As Pat Maris later confessed, "He was sick, so sick for so long. You knew it was coming, but it was a shock and not a shock at the same time. You just go on, like anything else."

Although she had courageously faced the ordeal of Roger's cancer, Pat had difficult adjustments to make after he died. "It was hard at first for Pat to go back to things as they were," said Dr. Surprise. "After all, she had known Roger for some 35 years as friend and husband, and they were so close. That would leave a void in anyone's life. For a while she had some thoughts about resettling in Fargo."

Instead Pat chose to stay near her family in Gainesville, content to be a mother and grandmother. "While there are still many pleasant memories and close friends in Fargo," Pat Maris said, "I could not return because the winters there are simply too long, and we had already gotten used to Gainesville."

Pat Maris adjusted to her life without Roger. Although she has had some back problems, she seems cheerful, happy to reflect on her good days with Roger, and grateful for them.

On the other hand, when Rudy Maris lost his son, he lost his entire reason for being. He could not face life without Roger. At the time of Roger's death, Rudy was "spaced out" and withdrawn from the family. The *Fargo Forum* never interviewed him, and none of his thoughts appeared elsewhere in the press. However, when interviewed by Maury Allen for his biography of Roger Maris, Rudy's responses carried an unmistakable note of alienation and rejection: "I wasn't even invited to the St. Patrick's event. I don't know who was responsible for that. I wanted to be there. I should have been there. I don't know why I wasn't asked."

In September, 1985, one Fargoan said, "Rudy is just too depressed" to speak about his son. None of the immediate members of the Roger Maris family, especially Pat, has cared to comment about Rudy Maris since Roger's death. Other Fargoans say that Rudy has "bad-mouthed" Pat to friends and neighbors in Florida, suggesting, for example, that she was not strict enough with the children.

Rudy Maris attended the banquet preceding the 1987 Roger Maris tourney without being introduced to the large audience. Unable to cope with the tragedies in his life, Rudy Maris "hears" but is unaware of the world around him. He walks in silence, locked in depression, and strikes out against those dearest and truest to him.

Life in Fargo went on without Roger Maris after his death. Few presumably noticed the headstone that appeared on his grave in Holy Cross Cemetery in time for Memorial Day 1986. Pat Maris had designed the stark, gray-black marker in a diamond shape that extends three and one-half feet from home plate to second base. The stone bears an engraving of Roger swinging a bat, with number 61 above and below it in recognition of his 61 homers in 1961. The marker rests on a four-foot-long, eight-inch-high base, its rugged exterior partially rock-pitched. The Dakota Monument Company had engraved the eight-inch thick, African granite headstone and sand-etched its inscription, "Against All Odds."

Befitting the privacy Roger sought in his lifetime, the headstone placing occurred without ceremony. Dorothy and Gus Duchschere attended the placing by chance. Classmates of the Marises at Shanley, they had come to the cemetery that day to place a wreath at her father's grave. The *Fargo Forum* reported Dorothy's observation, "It looks nice."

The Maris grave attracts visitors, some from great distances. The community frequently hears proposals for adding to the many public memorials to Roger in Fargo. With the approach of the baseball season, a *Forum* editorial called for building a park named for Roger on the site of the old Barnett Field. The site of Roger's pre-major-league heroics, Barnett Field fell to the demolition crews in the sixties. The *Forum* said:

> We think visitors as well as local folks will want to offer some silent thoughts on Roger's grave. It would also be fitting if they could capture something of what happened on the field where he and others performed in their years of spring. We call on the Fargo Park District to undertake this project in conjunction with the Fargo schools.

That summer a Fargo panel announced a contest for best billboard design declaring the city the home of Roger Maris. The city of Fargo and the American Legion would pay for the billboard that would direct visitors to the Roger Maris Museum at West Acres. City Commissioner Jeff Frankhauser noted that the proposal originated with Fargo residents who wanted to "More visibly identify [themselves] with Roger Maris on some type of permanent basis." In addition, the billboard "would help people traveling to remember Fargo as a city that is proud of Roger Maris and his accomplishments."

The winning billboard design, by Fargo artist Robert Washnieski, showed Roger swinging a bat and read, "Home of the Roger Maris Museum."

Roger had also made Fargo the home of the annual Roger Maris golf tourney. The city of Fargo – and the Maris family – determined to make the sports event an annual high point in Fargo life and a continuing memorial to its founder. A *Forum* editorial announced the tourney:

> Long live the Maris event. It's important to his memory that the celebrity golf tournament continue. The tournament was important to Maris because the proceeds went to charity. ... We want it to continue for many, many years — for just as long as sports stars are willing to come to Fargo to help those who need help, and because of a man who quietly cared.

Some 1,500 spectators came to see the 23 celebrities among the 260 golfers. Notable participants included baseball Hall of Famers

Enos Slaughter and Warren Spahn; former Yankees John Blanchard, Clete Boyer, Ryne Duren, Ken Hunt, Tony Kubek, Don Larsen, Hector Lopez, and Moose Skowron; ex-Twins' Bob Allison, former New York Met Jerry Koosman, and Frank Quilici; football star Dave Casper; and actor Dale Robertson.

The tourney drew baseball fans such as Dennis Vadnais, who drove to the competition with his sons, Matt and Josh, from Crookston, Minnesota, 80 miles away. His reasons for attending seemed similar to those of others in the audience. He told the *Grand Forks Herald,* "We came down here to get autographs and to watch the ballplayers. For me, it's like reliving your childhood, a chance to see your childhood heroes. I don't play much golf; it's just being here and being a part of it."

The Maris family were integral to the tournament, and memories of Roger pervaded the occasion. At this, the first tourney since Roger's death, Pat Maris said, "I do really feel he's here. I feel he's out there watching somewhere."

Randy played in the tourney, as did the other sons, Roger, Jr., Kevin, and Richard. The oldest son, Roger, Jr., spoke of life without his father, verbalizing feelings shared by the other children. "There have been some hard times," Roger, Jr., said, "but I remember so many good things about him. It's almost like he's off somewhere playing ball. You think he's going to return, but you know he's not. ... I talk to him when I pray at night. He always seems like he's there, so I say hello and stay in contact with him."

Roger, Jr., remembered that his father "wanted to be sure that everyone had fun" at the event. This tourney brought enjoyment to participant and spectator alike. Its record-setting proceeds benefited the Hospice of the Red River Valley and Shanley High School. A profitable sports equipment auction helped boost the fun and the funds. This Roger Maris Golf Tourney scored a success on all counts.

Before the 1987 tourney, two events relating to Roger Maris brought his name before the public in a non-sports context and reinforced his image as a caring and courageous human being.

On November 9, 1986, David A. "Sonny" Weblin, president of Madison Square Garden, received the first Roger Maris Memorial Award at the twentieth annual banquet of the Brooklyn School for Special Children. The interracial, nondenominational school provides a place of learning for the brain-damaged and mentally and emotionally handicapped.

Big Julie, a member of the dinner committee, explains the honor's designation as a Roger Maris Award: "Simply put, most of those who are being helped at the school are kids. And with kids, there was nobody better than Roger."

A galaxy of celebrities from the sports and other entertainment fields attended the black-tie dinner at the Waldorf-Astoria. Roger Maris, Jr., represented the Maris family and continued the Roger Maris tradition of caring. "That might be the only Roger award presented by the school," said Rabbi Morris J. Block. "But just think of the children whose lives may have added meaning because Roger Maris' name was lent to us for that evening."

The city of Fargo also intends to name a medical unit for its favorite son. A press conference called for May 1987 and attended by Pat Maris and son Kevin announced that the Fargo Clinic and St. Luke's Hospital/MeritCare would call its soon-to-be-built outpatient facility the Roger Maris Cancer Center.

The 30,000-square-foot center — only a few blocks from St. Mary's Church — would emphasize cancer prevention, as well as education, early detection, and research.

"We are really excited," said Pat Maris, "that St. Luke's Hospital and the Fargo Clinic elected to name this after Roger. Fargo has always been special to us."

Kevin Maris succinctly stated the family's feelings on the facility. "After what my father went through," he said, "it means a lot to have his name associated with this."

As the time for the 1987 golf event approached, Fargo tourney officials grew worried. Don Gooselaw said, "We were concerned that more than a year after Roger's death that the tournament might not be able to attract as many celebrities as before. But we were gratified that the stars came." On hand in 1987 were Hall of Famer Enos Slaughter, Tracy Stallard, former umpire Ed Runge, in addition to former Yankees Hank Bauer, John Blanchard, Ryne Duren, Ken Hunt, Don Larsen, and Moose Skowron. Other participants were former Major Leaguers Bob Allison, Roy Sievers, and Frank Quilici. Nonbaseball sports heroes also competed: Johnny "Red" Kerr, basketball; John Henry Johnson and Lou Cordileone, football; John "Gino" Gasparini, hockey; Larry Ziegler, golf.

The 1987 tourney auction – a notable success – brought in $9,000.

The profits stemmed from the sale of sports memorabilia, such as a collection of Roger Maris baseball cards; a Yankee Stadium seat; a 1977 ticket for the game in which Lou Brock broke Ty Cobb's base-stealing record; a Wayne Gretsky hockey stick; a Michael Jordan basketball; round-trip airline tickets from Fargo to San Diego, with hotel accommodations and tickets to two Padres games; and a Gerry Ford presidential golf wedge imprinted with the presidential seal.

With baseball fans around like Marv Kereluke of Regina, Saskatchewan, the tournament can never fail. The Canadian police officer left the auction with a Roger Maris Louisville Slugger bat — at $80, a "steal." Although Kereluke neither saw Roger in action nor met him in person, he like countless others feels, "Roger was an inspiration to me at age 14 when he hit 61 homers. He was the underdog."

Hank Aaron and Roger Maris in 1977,
two all-time home-run champions.
(Bettman Archive Photo)

Chapter XXIII
Of Heroes and Cooperstown

To many, Roger Maris seemed the perennial underdog because of the obstacles that he encountered — and overcame — during his baseball career. His talents as a rookie drew comparisons to Mickey Mantle's, but injuries dulled the promise of his early years. Nevertheless, a host of teams recognized the quality of his sports performance. Finally in 1960 he donned the Yankee pinstripes and began to earn recognition as one of the game's best all-around players.

In 1961 "against all odds," Maris won out over Mickey Mantle in a media-inspired competition to become the home-run king. Roger bested Babe Ruth's record by one, yet the ensuing asterisk furor pitted Roger Maris against Babe Ruth, 1961 against 1927, and the modern sport against the old-timers' game. The Fargo slugger sought evaluation for only his own accomplishments and his own merits, not in comparison with his predecessors.

Roger Maris, the underdog, stood alone amid the media free-for-alls and the manic adulations and execrations of the baseball faithful. Unprotected by his team; untutored by agents, lawyers, and publicists; and armed with only his innate openness and honesty, Maris braved the rigors of being in the public eye.

Maris deserves enshrinement at the Hall of Fame in Cooperstown, New York. His title to fame arises out of his achievements during his twelve-year Major League career and his accomplishments during 1961, and the proper interpretation of Rule 5 for Hall of Fame election.

The Hall of Fame in Cooperstown, New York, has just celebrated its fiftieth anniversary as America's foremost baseball shrine. William Guilfoile, associate director at Cooperstown and responsible for its promotion, stated that "people have a comfortable feeling when they visit Cooperstown. Baseball is a family sport and visitors come as families. And the association between the invention of baseball and Cooperstown certainly makes the Hall that much more attractive to those who flock here."

Legend goes that Abner Doubleday, an instructor at a nearby military school, invented the game of baseball. Doubleday, later a major general and combatant in the Mexican and Civil Wars, never himself claimed to be the father of baseball. Baseball historians attribute that distinction to Alexander Cartwright.

However, Cooperstown native Abner Graves, a mining engineer, remained fully convinced that Doubleday invented baseball. Graves maintained that in 1839 he had witnessed the 19-year-old Doubleday "carve out" the first baseball diamond from a local pasture. Graves's assertion became more plausible with the 1934 discovery of a well-worn and beaten crude hardball among his possessions in Fly Creek, three miles west of Cooperstown.

Cooperstown's Stephen C. Clark, the Singer Sewing Machine Company magnate, purchased Graves's homemade hard ball for five dollars. Around that memento rose the National Baseball Museum, inaugurated on June 12, 1939. The museum displays the Doubleday Baseball – as it is now called – in the Cooperstown Room. The text on the wall that accompanies the artifact tells of Abner Doubleday, "who started baseball in Farmer Phinney's Cooperstown Pasture [and is] remembered as the lad in the pasture where the game was invented."

When the National Baseball Museum opened its doors to the public, it had already installed twenty-five American heroes, including Babe Ruth, Ty Cobb, Honus Wagner, Cy Young, Walter Johnson, Grover Cleveland Alexander, Tris Speaker, Napoleon Lajoie, and Connie Mack. To affirm Babe Ruth's position in the history of baseball, the builders of Cooperstown appended to his image the caption: "Greatest drawing card in history of baseball." No American hero in sportsdom has loomed larger than Babe Ruth.

Although the residents of Cooperstown number fewer than 2,500, the exhibit at Cooperstown attracts some 250,000 visitors a year. The sightseers come not only to pay homage to their American baseball heroes, but also to enjoy the displays of more than 20,000 baseball artifacts — bats, balls, gloves, uniforms — and newsreels of great moments of baseball history.

In *American Heroes: Myth and Reality* Professor Marshall W. Fishwick stresses the importance of heroes to American culture.

Without the symbols, heraldry, inherited titles, and traditions which Europeans exalt and revere, Americans have concentrated their attention on a few men. ... Because it answers an urgent need, hero worship is an integral part of American life.

We identify ourselves with greatness by means of a signature in an album, a lock of hair, a photograph, or a baseball that has scored a home run! We haunt stage doors and locker rooms; we pursue our favorites with candid cameras and sound recorders.

America's obsession with sports heroes has led to the establishment of several centers for the glorification of a sport and its top players: Professional Football Hall of Fame in Canton, Ohio; College Hall of Fame in Kings Island, Ohio; Soccer Hall of Fame in Oneonta, New York; Basketball Hall of Fame in Springfield, Massachusetts; Hockey Hall of Fame in Eveleth, Minnesota; Bowling Hall of Fame in St. Louis, Missouri; Horse Racing Hall of Fame in Saratoga Springs, New York; Tennis Hall of Fame in Newport, Rhode Island; PGA-World Golf Hall of Fame in Pinehurst, North Carolina; Track and Field Hall of Fame in Indianapolis, Indiana.

These halls, however, all lack the mystique of the shrine at Cooperstown. Professor Fishwick tells us: "There is nothing like Cooperstown. It was the first sports shrine to be established, and, therefore, is the granddaddy of all the others that are simply spin-offs."

Guilfoile attributes the majesty of the hall to a "sense of continuity in baseball that is not found in other sports." He explains: "We had our heroes when we were youngsters, and now that we are older and our heroes are even older, we follow them. That might explain why there is so much interest in their election to the Hall and resentment when our heroes are rejected."

Baseball is America's pastime. The excitement and controversy surrounding the selection process for investiture at Cooperstown are unique to the sports world. Baseball heroes such as the Babe and others enshrined in the hall fulfill a crucial need for many Americans. In Fishwick's words: "They give us blessed relief from our daily lives, which are frequently one petty thing after another. Hemmed in by our little horizons, we hear the hero's voice, clear and confident. ... He gives meaning to all we do and why. He helps us to transcend our drab back yards, apartment terraces, and tenements, and to regain a sense of the world's bigness."

By 1990, the exclusive membership of the Cooperstown Hall of Fame had grown to 206 baseball veterans: Negro League players; managers; umpires; pioneers; executives; and nearly 150 former players from the Major Leagues.

Very specific rules govern an individual's election to the Hall of Fame. Members of either the Baseball Writers' Association of America (BBWAA) or the Baseball Hall of Fame Committee on Baseball Veterans can designate a baseball notable as an American hero.

Only active and honorary BBWAA members who currently practice the craft of baseball writing can vote to introduce a player into the Hall of Fame. More than 400 such writers usually qualify for eligibility any given year. The writers can vote for a maximum of ten candidates. Each eligible candidate must have played for at least ten years and have been retired for five years.

Rule 5 offers the baseball writer precise guidelines for his choice of candidate: "Voting shall be based on the player's record, playing ability, integrity, sportsmanship, character, and contribution to the team(s) on which the player played and not what he may have done otherwise in baseball."

Sportswriter Dick Young said, "There is no tougher electorate, no more stringent rules than govern entry to baseball's shrine at Cooperstown. To be chosen, a man must obtain 75 percent of the popular votes cast. If our nation were run by the same high standard, we'd never elect a president."

Former players who have not achieved election can remain on the ballot for 15 years. After a three-year waiting period, they become eligible for election by a 20-member (recently expanded from 18) Committee on Baseball Veterans. On this committee sit former players now in the Hall of Fame, individuals associated, past or present, with baseball in an official way, or members of the BBWAA.

Former hall director Ken Smith discusses the turmoil over the selection process, especially during the hall's early years, in his book *Baseball's Hall of Fame.* "Editorials demanded Hall of Fame justice," writes Smith, "in outrage against the exclusion of old favorites. ... Scribe was arrayed against scribe in the who's who wrangle. One magnate thought one way, another disagreed, and fans wrote all sorts of suggestions about who should be in the Hall and how he should be elected. Everybody took the controversy very seriously."

Smith points out that two divergent philosophies ruled the hall in its first years. Tom Swope of the *Cincinnati Post* opposed limiting the hall to the "super-great": not everybody had to be a Ruth, Cobb, Mathewson, or Young. "Baseball has plenty of great stars and figures of whom it is proud," said Swope. "To have the Hall of Fame only half filled gives the impression the game is short of talent."

On the other hand, Bill Brandt, baseball writer, National League service bureau head, and radio announcer, championed Cooperstown's Hall of Fame as an "ultra exclusive" gallery of baseball players. According to Smith, Brandt had a long-lasting influence on elections to the hall because he "advocated rigid barriers."

Commissioner Ford Frick followed the philosophy of Brandt. Frick insisted on a "very exclusive" Hall of Fame and conveyed these thoughts in an August 16, 1944, memo to Cooperstown President Stephen Clark.

Smith questioned an election system that excluded many worthy candidates from their rightful places in the hall. "Was the trouble merely too many equally good men from whom to single out the one or two best by such an overwhelming majority as 75 percent?"

As the years passed, others voiced their concern that less-than-heroes were being inducted into the hall. A shocked Shirley Povich, BBWAA president and *Washington Post* columnist, in 1955 expressed fear that there would be "a gradual cheapening of the honor of being in the Hall of Fame." In 1968, C.C. Johnson Spink, editor and publisher of *Sporting News*, wrote, "Who belongs in the shrine? ... We feel that the Hall of Fame is intended only for the 'great ones.' The near great don't belong although some of them have been selected."

Today's electors seem to share Spink's belief. In 1988 only Willie Stargell, in his first year of eligibility, gained admission to Cooperstown. For the twelfth time, the electors denied induction to Jim Bunning, who played a perfect game and won 100 games in each league. However, the big story of 1988 centered on the blank ballots returned by nine writers who had found no worthy candidate. The blank ballots expressed the sentiment that if no candidate meets the voter's standards, no candidate should receive a vote. Hall of Fame President Ed Stack ruled that election required "a pure" 75 percent — not 74.9 percent — of all ballots cast, both signed and blank. "Once again," wrote Dave Anderson of the *New York Times,* "the Hall of Fame emerges as a philosophy as much as a museum."

The nine scribes who sent in blank ballots all felt that standards for admission to the Hall of Fame had been declining. Therefore, those players enshrined must be more than excellent; they must be great. By returning a "no" vote, Bill Madden of the *New York Daily News* gave "a statement of my Hall of Fame philosophy" that the hall is reserved "for only the truly greats, not the almost greats or less. Madden believes that nominees of greatness "were all players who dominated the game at their positions for significant periods of time which is the one criteria I have always adhered to in voting for the Hall of Fame."

In a column next to Madden's, Phil Pepe said that the great are "the creme de la creme, the Ruths, Cobbs, Youngs, Mantles, Mayses, DiMaggios, Aarons." For the first time, in 1988, Pepe cast his ballot with no selections to make a clear statement: "I think we slowly have eroded the standards of the men we put in the Hall of Fame, and I did not want to contribute to that erosion."

Another first-time voter, Fred Lief of United Press International, also searched for greatness among the candidates. "For somebody to be in the Hall of Fame, he really should have illuminated baseball in his time," he said. While excellent candidates appeared among the 1988 would-be heroes, "did they illuminate the game? I don't think so."

Many members of the BBWAA feel that the Veterans Committee — the final adjudicator of Roger Maris' title to fame — does not adhere to the standards necessary for "regular" admissions to the hall. Baseball writers have now assumed responsibility for maintaining the standards of greatness that govern investiture in the hall.

In his 1944 memorandum, Frick insisted that the Veterans Committee not diverge from the standards followed by the baseball writers. Bob Broeg, a columnist for the *St. Louis Post-Dispatch*, lamented in the 1969 *Stadium Van Magazine*, "A chummy 12-man veterans committee has jeopardized the selectivity of Baseball's Hall of Fame." In 1976 Dick Young called the Veterans Committee the "back door to Cooperstown": "a bunch of nice old codgers, baseball people, who sit around a room once a year, have a few hot toddies, and decide to put one or two of their contemporaries into Cooperstown."

John Leo, a contributing writer for *Time* magazine, directed his wrath at the committee while offering his own plan for maintaining greatness at Cooperstown. In 1987 Leo used the *New York Times* to publicize his "Housecleaning Plan for the Hall of Fame," a proposal analogous to Metropolitan Museum of Art Director Thomas Hoving's method of revitalizing the museum's collection. "While deliberately cleaning house," Leo noted, Hoving insisted that "he wasn't getting rid of masterpieces, merely 'deaccessioning' a few works the museum no longer needed."

Leo continued his analogy. Cooperstown must be exclusively for the great. The hall should deaccession those who do not belong in Cooperstown, discarding many of its "embarrassing" would-be heroes. Leo mentions more than 20 "truly demented selections" of the "perennially woeful Committee on Veterans."

Critics say that the Veterans Committee has outlived its usefulness. It had been established to accord recognition to older heroes who might have been overlooked by the younger generation of writers. Enough time has passed that the committee's rationale for existence no longer applies. Now, according to Leo, "all the committee does is second-guess the real voters and recycle rejects."

In 1988 the Veterans Committee met in Tampa, Florida, to consider the names of 29 potential Hall of Famers — Rizzuto, Ashburn, Hodges, and ex-umpire Al Barlick among them. The committee received further censure when it selected none of the nominees. A member of the veterans group, Hall of Famer Monte Irvin, said the committee was "wasting time to meet and not elect anyone. With all those deserving people, someone should have been elected." Committee member Buzzy Bavasi has a different opinion. "The Hall of Fame is an exclusive club. Let's keep it that way."

Cooperstown opened it's doors in 1989 to Veterans Commettee selections Al Barlick and Red Schoendienst, who joined BBWAA choices Johny Bench and Carl Yastrzemski. In 1990 there were no selections from the Veterans Committee, but Jim Palmer and Joe Morgan became the newest honorees, selected by the baseball writers.

Do the criticisms of the Veterans Committee imply lesser honor for enshrinements at Cooperstown won through committee vote? Enos Slaughter retired in 1959 but waited for 26 years before the veterans said yes to him. Twenty-eight years after Johnny Mize played his last game, the veterans finally said he belonged. Do these unwarranted delays degrade the honorees and the hall?

"When a man is in, he's in, and we should be happy for him," says Seymour Swioff of Elias Sports Bureau, as quoted by Roger Angell in the *New Yorker*. While this may be true, the methods by which a player gains entry to the hall may mitigate the happiness. The Board of Directors of the Hall of Fame elects only 20 members to the Veterans Committee, and each serves for six years. With such a small number of committee members empaneled for a comparatively lengthy time, a concerted, directed action in favor of a candidate may facilitate his installment. Although baseball writers – not the veterans – named Cleveland hurler Bob Lemon to the Hall of Fame, Lemon benefitted from an orchestrated letter campaign in the last years of his eligibility. Steinbrenner and others in the Big Apple launched a campaign for Rizzuto that has not convinced the Veterans Committee. However, Maury Allen believes that the Veterans Committee must feel that a would-be honoree has the loyal support of his admirers. The *New York Post* scribe says the fans "must organize a campaign of support, write the committee members letters, prepare slick brochures for submission at the meeting, badger the committee members wherever and whenever they can be found. That's how this system works."

Pete Carvella of Ellwood City, Pennsylvania, worked the system in his successful ten-year effort to get fellow townsman Hack Wilson into Cooperstown. The Lawrence County chapter of the Pennsylvania Hall of Fame arose specifically to further this mission. As Carvella told the *New Castle News*, each member of the Veterans Committee received letters "so they wouldn't forget about Hack Wilson. We never gave up."

Like Carvella, Bill Guilfoile knows the workings of the Veterans Committee as few people do. An experienced baseball administrator whose tenure at Cooperstown began in 1979, Guilfoile previously served as director of public relations and assistant to the general manager of the Pittsburgh Pirates. As part of his Cooperstown duties, he takes the minutes of the Veterans Committee election proceedings.

Guilfoile notes the deliberateness that marks committee composition. "We seek a balance: six former players, Hall of Famers, three from each league; six writers; six baseball executives; and two broadcasters. Members are carefully selected by the Hall of Fame administration. There have been cases, such as that of Ted Williams, where a veteran has asked to serve on the committee." The recent deaths of baseball executive Bob Fishel and writer Joe Reichler have reduced the committee to 18.

Hall of Fame President Ed Stack's voting procedure includes an early February mailing to Veterans Committee members. The material sent includes a letter that lists the new candidates recommended for consideration, and a booklet of statistical information on the candidates. The "preliminary ballot" has room for 30 candidates "deserving of further consideration."

The members' evaluations extend beyond raw statistics. "This is one area where we need the Veterans Committee," Guilfoile said. "It looks at the total player. The Committee is in a better position to evaluate players who were in the Majors 25, 30, or 40 years ago than those writers who have been following baseball for only a comparatively short time."

If the assessments of the Veterans Committee are so necessary, what justifies the secrecy of their proceedings, particularly the precise voting? "People have asked to bring the deliberations of the committee out into the open, going as far as to request taping the meetings," said Guilfoile. "But what has made the committee effective has been the discussion process, the interchange between members, and this would not work out if put out into public view."

Replying to attacks on the specific rejections of the Veterans Committee, Guilfoile asked: "Where were those writers when the candidates were eligible to be elected by BBWAA? Writers complain, for example, that the committee is ineffective because it hasn't selected Rizzuto. But did Bill Madden and others vote for him before his name came to the Veterans?"

Guilfoile rebuffed charges of cronyism on the committee, insisting that it had little effect in an election decided by 3/4 of the members. "If one member has a 'crony,'" he said, "how many votes does that mean: one, two, but certainly not enough to elect."

The late Joe Reichler, a member of the Veterans Committee, agreed that cronyism is restricted, but cited another unavoidable factor that influences voting. "The people who do the voting," he said, "are always inclined to vote for the players they saw most often. And they are doing it in all honesty. Other players may have been just as great, but anyone who plays in New York is always bigger than a player who does the same thing somewhere else."

Over the years, sportswriters have decried the Hall-of-Fame votes given to players with qualifications focused on or limited to one particular achievement, no matter how magnificent that accomplishment might be. This category includes Bill Wambsganss of Cleveland, who turned in an unassisted triple play in the World Series; Hub Pruett, the St. Louis pitcher who regularly struck out Babe Ruth but won only 29 games in his Major League career, and Dick Kerr, the Chisox pitcher who remained free of the Black Sox taint but won only 53 victories in his big-league career.

To avoid the enshrinement of such mediocre players or one-day wonders, the Hall of Fame adopted Rule 5 — Automatic Elections: "No automatic elections based on performances such as batting average of .400 for one (1) year, pitching a perfect game, or similar outstanding achievement shall be permitted."

The Veterans Committee will first consider Roger Maris for the Hall of Fame in 1992.

Is there much more to Roger Maris than the "similar outstanding achievement" of 61 in '61?

Does Roger Maris have a title to fame?

Chapter XXIV
A Title to Fame

Over the years, the media have carefully examined Roger Maris' athletic prowess in regard to his enshrinement at Cooperstown. Journalists of the press and airwaves have scrutinized the voting patterns for and against Roger's installment, as well as the responses and reactions to his failure to gain entrance to the hall. When Roger again becomes eligible for election in 1992, his admission rests on the vote of the heavily attacked Veterans Committee. It will decide the most important question: Is Roger worthy of enshrinement with the other baseball immortals?

Maris retired in 1968 and first became eligible for election five years later, in 1974. In 1988 he failed to achieve election for the fifteenth year, thus exhausting his chances of election by the writers. His vote totals ranged from 69 votes in both 1982 and 1983 to a high of 177 in 1986. While the rules of enshrinement require a vote from 75 percent of the voters, Roger's highest ballot count in 1986 brought him only as close as 42 percent.

Roger played down his first rejection. However, his comments over the years revealed his realistic view of his prospects. While he yearned to be among the chosen, he determined to mask to the rest of the world his disappointment in being passed over.

In a 1975 interview with the Associated Press, he commented on his acknowledged lack of support from the writers.

> I'm not paying much attention to it, but if I were ever voted in, I would consider it a great honor. The Hall of Fame is something you think about from childhood if you play ball.
>
> Maybe I'm not worthy of it. I don't know. But if I am worthy, I've my doubts I'll make it. I'll just leave it to the geniuses who vote on it.

Roger's reaction to being turned down in 1977 resulted in a UPI headline that read "Maris Isn't Interested." According to the story, Roger's intense involvement with his beer distributorship allowed him little time to follow baseball. In fact, UPI noted that "unless a newsman called to tell him" about the Cooperstown balloting, "he wouldn't know it." Besides, the story quoted Maris, "Baseball is just like a kid with a train. You got to outgrow it sometime."

Afflicted with cancer in the last years of his life, Roger seemed outwardly unperturbed at the many years' snub by the writers. The retirement of his Number 9 and the plaque in the Memorial Park section at Yankee Stadium in 1984 meant more to him than election to Cooperstown. "The Hall of Fame could not compare with this honor," he said proudly. "I've always been proud to be a Yankee. I may have played other places, but I was always a Yankee. The Yankees have had so many great ballplayers, but not too many of them had their numbers retired or had a plaque in their honor put on that wall out there."

Ever aware that baseball writers' votes decided the election, Roger made an honest assessment of his chances in 1984. "You have to look at where I'm coming from, knowing who votes, that the Hall of Fame is not a realistic hope."

Nevertheless, Roger added, he had his place in the hall. "It [election to the hall] doesn't matter now anyway. It's not something that's gonna change my life any. The way I look at it, I'm there in every way but name. My bat, my uniform – all of it is there."

Roger reiterated this theme again in 1985, following the last election before his death. After garnering 128 votes to finish seventh in the balloting, he remarked in Gainesville, "I think at one time it would have been an honor. Today it's so immaterial it's ridiculous. If you ask the average fan is Roger Maris is in the Hall of Fame, he'll say yes. The bat I used to hit the sixty-first home run and the ball are there. That's one thing they cannot take away – the display is already in Cooperstown."

Despite his stoic attitude and public stance, Roger certainly must have wanted formal acknowledgement as an American hero. Enshrinement in Cooperstown would have granted him appropriate recognition of his title to fame. However, Roger had no intention of pandering for votes or groveling for a groundswell of support generated through a public relations campaign. Shortly after the writers again rejected his candidacy in 1978, Roger remarked to Will Grimsley of the Associated Press: "The Hall of Fame is charity – it's something they give you – not something you necessarily earn. I'm not one to ask for charity."

Although Roger spoke bitterly about his hellish relations with the press during the Yankee years, he still asserted: "I'm going to be in there [the Hall of Fame] some day. If the writers keep me out, there are other ways." His "other ways" of attaining membership probably referred to his last chance – the Veterans Committee, with its membership of Hall of Famers, former players, executives, and broadcasters – in addition to writers.

Through the years, Pat Maris has had almost nothing to say about Roger's continued rejection from the Hall of Fame. When asked if she would attend the Cooperstown ceremonies if Roger were elected, she tactfully replied, "That's a situation that I will not have to deal with right away."

Roger's sons, on the other hand, have given much thought to their father's omission from the hall.

Only five months before Roger's death, his sons came to Fargo for the Celebrity Benefit Golf Tournament. In a *Forum* article by Brian Wicker, the boys stated that the press had portrayed Roger so unfairly. Wicker wrote, "It is part of that lingering resentment the family believes that has kept Maris out of baseball's Hall of Fame.

Randy Maris spoke of the significance of enshrinement: "He's had so many achievements but not the Hall of Fame. If he had been out [of baseball] for a couple of years and then got in [to the Hall of Fame], it would have meant more to him instead of the press holding a grudge against him all these years."

In his book, Maury Allen relates that when the family gathered in Fargo for Roger's funeral, Kevin Maris seemed concerned with thoughts of Cooperstown. On that somber occasion the boy asked the journalist, "Will my father get in the Hall of Fame?"

Roger's longtime friends differed on Roger's continued rejections. Don Gooselaw did not believe that Roger had felt "deprived" because he was not in Cooperstown. As proof, Gooselaw cited Maris' comment made in reference to his bat and ball, "I'm in the Hall of Fame anyway."

However, another lifelong Fargo friend, Dick Savageau, said, "Roger never made any public statements about his actual feelings on the hall. But there is no doubt that he would have liked to have been elected to the Hall of Fame."

Even though Roger would not make public statements, Fargoans and other North Dakotans pulled no punches. "Tell the writers [in New York] in no uncertain terms that they have been terribly unfair to Roger Maris," said Joe Paper, president of the Fargo Hebrew Congregation.

North Dakotans anxiously sought the recognition due to its favorite son. Roger's abbreviated life had little time left for enshrinement in the hall through the "regular" election process. State Senator Herschel Lashkowitz, formerly mayor of Fargo, sponsored a resolution urging Roger's election to the Hall of Fame. The resolution cited Roger's involvement in charitable causes for the deprived and handicapped and highlighted his athletic achievements. When North Dakota adopted the resolution, it sent the message to the sports world "with a resounding and enthusiastic and unified voice."

The North Dakota campaign for Roger's election to the Hall of Fame began in the spring of 1984, with the announcement of the prospective ceremonies at Yankee Stadium. "The honors are beginning for New York Yankee home run champion Roger Maris," said the April 24 *Fargo Forum* editorial "Maris Due Fame Honors." The meaningful and merited Yankee Stadium ceremonies are not enough, concluded the editorial. Without Roger, "The baseball Hall of Fame still is not complete."

North Dakotans could only feel bitter disappointment that the Hall of Fame still eluded Roger as he heroically succumbed to cancer. The reportage on his death inevitably involved the theme of immortality at Cooperstown. What Roger could not achieve in life, he would achieve in death, according to the Dakota press.

North Dakota "now waits impatiently for his election to the Baseball Hall of Fame," wrote Chuck Haga in the *Grand Forks Herald.*

"We believe that Maris deserves Hall of Fame recognition for his pure baseball skills," proclaimed a *Forum* editorial. "If he is not elected to the Hall of Fame, it will be a travesty."

North Dakotans believed that the obstacles to Roger's instatement stemmed from the long-standing feud between Roger and the press. The editorial reasoned:

> Sports writers, especially those in the big city press, had problems with Maris' restraint. He turned away questions that tried to invade his privacy. There is a prevailing suspicion that he has never been elected to the Baseball

Hall of Fame ... because the selections are made by baseball writers who are not willing to forget a timidity which they mistook for surliness.

Forum sports editor Ed Kolpack picked up on the theme and wrote, "Some say Maris' attitude toward the writers was the reason he was not voted into baseball's Hall of Fame. Hall of Fame inductees are chosen by writers. I wonder what one man has to do to be recognized." Rationalizing that the Hall of Fame is only a shrine for mortals, Kolpack continued, "Who needs a Hall of Fame governed by men? He is ready to enter another Hall of Fame, which already includes Lou and Ty and Roberto and Case. And the Babe."

The eulogies at Roger's funeral alluded to Roger's absence from the Cooperstown shrine. Former teammate Bobby Richardson noted directly that Roger's battles with the media might deprive him of his title to fame. Still, remarked Father Moore, Roger was among the true immortals in "God's Hall of Fame. In life, the honors are soon forgotten. God's Hall of Fame is for eternity."

The controversy over Roger's induction into Cooperstown has stimulated spirited media debate ever since Maris became eligible for the Hall of Fame. Those favoring Roger's election into Cooperstown cite his career that went far beyond 61 in '61. Those who feel Roger unworthy of a place in the hall point to his relatively short career both in years and in achievement, with the notable exception of his home-run record.

Sports columnist Greg Hansen found it amazing that Roger could only muster 72 votes in the 1977 balloting, finishing fifteenth in the field. His all-around skills went unappreciated. Hansen reflected, "While Maris was matched in an unholy war against the sporting Gods of Ruth and Mantle, he never got the recognition he deserved for his abilities away from the plate." Hansen described Roger's skills by quoting Golenbock's *Dynasty:* "Maris played right field with unmatched skill; he displayed speed and disregard for his personal safety. On base he was a daring and aggressive base runner whose steamrolling blocks were famous throughout the league."

The sports columnist drew the bottom line on Roger's poor showing in the balloting at the writers who clung to the media perception of an "unfriendly" Yankee. The writers were at fault. "Someone once wrote," Hansen said, "that Roger Maris suffered so much character assassination that if he had discovered a cure for cancer he still would have been thought of as an arrogant and aloof scientist."

According to Roger's long-time booster Jerry Izenberg, Roger deserves to be in Cooperstown not only for his 61 homers, but also for his motivation, for being a team player, and for such heroic feats as the throw in game six of the 1962 World Series. Izenberg's argument still centers on the overwhelming achievement of 1961. "The case here is simple," Izenberg wrote. "It took a monumental span ... concentration and ability to accomplish a feat nobody ever thought possible ... to chase the Ghost of Babe Ruth and contend with all that went with such a contest."

Twenty years after the historic 1961 season, Jack Herman interviewed Roger for the *St. Louis Globe-Democrat* when Roger trailed in that year's balloting. The "chances are Maris will never be elected," Herman complained, even though "He knew how to play the game, defensively and offensively. And he was a winner, even under intense pressure."

Roger's death prompted the expected media comments and analyses about his electability to the hall. Bob Broeg, *St. Louis Post-Dispatch* sports editor and a member of Cooperstown's Veterans Committee, noted that Roger always lagged behind in the voting. His batting mark was an "undistinguished .260," and he offended some reporters and stonewalled others, especially in New York. Notwithstanding, Broeg considered Roger to be Hall of Fame material. Roger "was one of the most underrated baseball players ever. He was a great fielder with a strong arm, and he possessed base running wisdom, if not speed. In addition to an obvious ability to hit home runs, including a record 61 in one season (1961), he also had the ability to hit in the clutch."

Broeg had the statistics to back up his statements. In four of Roger's five pennant-winning seasons with the Yankees, he batted "remarkably well" with men on base: .411, .375, .440, and .426.

The headline for a story by West Coast columnist Roger Murray read "Hall of Fame Struck Out With Maris." Murray fulminated, "I am angry" that Roger Maris "has never been considered seriously for the Hall of Fame." Although Murray wrote of Roger's base running, defensive play, and career highlighted with two MVP awards, the columnist rested his case on Maris' 1961 achievement.

"Roger Eugene Maris, 51, died Saturday of cancer," Murray mourned. "We owe him. Baseball owes him. It would be far too little, far too late, but I hope the Hall of Fame is listening."

The Cooperstown balloters heard none of the pleas from Murray and the others. In his last year of "regular" eligibility, Roger again fell short. Harvey Araton took up the cudgels for Roger Maris in the *New York Daily News*. When Maris missed once more in 1988, an amazed Araton reflected that Roger's bat and ball of that homer heard around the world is in Cooperstown, but not Roger himself. "The enormity of the record and the pressure of the chase" gave enough reason for enshrinement, but Roger Maris' career had more than one season:

"Wasn't Maris a dominant player for a solid half-decade (back-to-back MVP's, 275 career home runs), and the essence of a complete player for all of his 12 years? Was he not a certified winner, with seven pennant winners and three championships for teams in both leagues?"

Araton also knew the reasons behind Roger's perennial rejection. For years, Araton wrote, the Hall-of-Fame voters have been saying that they "found Maris abrasive, aloof, a pain to work with. Not enough impact years going by the numbers."

The sportswriter concluded that such reasoning is shortsighted because "The name Maris transcends the game because of 1961."

Roger's fifteen-year rejection by the BBWAA members proves that the previous baseball logic impressed too few writers. Fellow *New York Daily News* writer Phil Pepe covered the funeral in Fargo, then wrote a story headlined "Maris Doesn't Merit Hall." Perhaps some copy editor misrepresented Pepe's words with the headline, because the journalist found much to like about Roger. Pepe thought Maris "grossly misunderstood, greatly unappreciated, unfairly scorned. He was a remarkably talented baseball player, possessed of wonderful instincts for the game, good speed, defensive skills, and, of course, that beautiful, sweet batting stroke."

In quickly reviewing the cold statistics, Pepe all but asked, "Are those Hall of Fame numbers?" Alluding to Rule 5 of Hall of Fame elections, Pepe stressed that one season's "outstanding achievement" did not entitle a player to enshrinement at Cooperstown. Similarly, Don Larsen's perfect World Series game did not merit him the Hall of Fame when evaluated in conjunction with his lifetime mark of 81–91.

Pepe said that he had never voted for Roger and would not now.

"His credentials didn't get better, just because he died," Pepe continued. Knowing Roger, as Pepe thought he did, the writer decided that the slugger would not have "wanted a sympathy vote."

Roger got neither the vote nor the sympathy of Associated Press writer Hal Bock. A few days after Roger's funeral, Bock's article headlined "In Long Run, Roger Did Not Earn a Place in Hall" tacitly asked the baseball world, "Are those Hall of Fame numbers?"

Bock thought it "a nice sentiment" that Roger's death might generate support for his instatement at Cooperstown, but "It is also a bad idea." Bock conceded that Roger was a "fine player" whose career showcased the 1961 season and two MVP awards, but that was not enough. Although hitting 61 homers "was a singularly spectacular achievement accomplished under the most trying of circumstances," Bock still insisted that Roger did not compare favorably with the 26 non-pitchers eligible in the 1986 elections: only two had career averages lower than Roger's; seven candidates had more career home runs; and 12 had more career RBIs.

Nearly a year after Roger's death, the baseball world observed the twenty-fifth anniversary of Roger's sixty-first home run. The event sparked a discussion of Maris' Hall-of-Fame credentials on the NBC-TV show "Today." Host Bryant Gumbel briefly recited the cold statistics and then challenged his guests. He asked Tracy Stallard and Maury Allen: "Are those Hall of Fame numbers?" Allen responded with a recital of Roger's achievements, but Gumbel continually interrupted with the refrain, "But, are those Hall of Fame numbers?"

If Roger has no title to fame, as opinions such as Gumbel's dictate, what can be done about him? Bock suggests that the solution for Roger and others like him is to "establish a separate wing in Cooperstown, a place for short-term achievements." Roger's 61-home-run feat would share the new category with Larsen's perfect game, Bill Wambsganss's unassisted triple play, Bobby Thomson's pennant-winning homer, Dennis McLain's 31-victory season, and the like.

Bob Costas, the NBC announcer, also believed that Roger Maris' accomplishments should not remain unappreciated; however, he did not feel that Roger belonged in the circle of Cooperstown winners. "As much as I admire Roger Maris," Costas told the *Forum*, "I think it is fair to say that his entire career doesn't place him at the same level as Hall of Famers Babe Ruth, Ty Cobb, Willie Mays, and Mickey Mantle."

During the spring of 1987, the announcer suggested a way of resolving the problem of granting Roger proper recognition for his achievements and remaining within the limitations of Rule 5. On his "Coast to Coast" show Costas proposed a "second-level" at Cooperstown for those who, like Roger, were first-rate, outstanding players, but do not – according to some criteria – belong in the category of the great.

Who can best judge whether a player is outstanding, great, or entitled to fame? Former players or others who have seen an athlete perform can judge stardom as well as anyone else – perhaps better.

During his lifetime Roger received his most striking endorsement from Hank Aaron in 1978, when they met at the annual baseball meetings in Orlando. Aaron thought Roger's exclusion from Cooperstown was an injustice. "What irritates me," Aaron said, "is the suggestion that Roger was just a fluke who had one good hitting year. ... I played against him. He was one of the best all-around outfielders I have ever seen."

Many have supported Roger's enshrinement more vocally since his death. Their advocacy of Roger's induction into the hall increases his chances in future consideration by the Committee on Baseball Veterans.

Hall of Fame pitcher Warren Spahn "voted" for Roger at the Fargo banquet preceding the Celebrity Golf Tournament. "The 61 home runs by Maris," said Spahn, "is the greatest record in baseball. It is the greatest because it is the only record that has a time frame. I want to see Roger inducted [into the Hall of Fame]."

Umpire Ed Runge, in Fargo for the 1987 tournament, also cited the 61 record as his reason for wanting Roger in the hall. "He broke the most impressive record in baseball books," Runge said, "and that enough merits a place in the Hall of Fame."

Discussions of worthiness for the Hall of Fame often involve somewhat illogical comparisons between Roger and his 61 homers and Don Larsen and his one-time shot at fame, his perfect game. Larsen thought the comparison "dumb." At the 1987 Fargo golf tourney, he said, "I am proud of my achievement, but how can you put that on the same level, what I did in one afternoon, with what Roger accomplished in one season, with all that pressure on his back. Without qualifications, Roger belongs in the Hall of Fame."

As expected, the Yankees and Cardinals – those who played with him – have been Roger's biggest boosters. The 1961 Yankees produced three Hall of Famers: Berra, Ford, and Mantle. Roger's former roommate unequivocally supports Roger for the fourth 1961 Yankee in Cooperstown. After Maris finally returned to the stadium in 1978, Mantle stated his position: "Roger's 61 home runs is one of the greatest feats in sports. He definitely deserves to be in the Hall of Fame." He was even more emphatic on the Bob Costas show of February 26, 1989, calling Roger, "one of the best all-around players I ever saw in my life. He never made a mistake, just like Willie Mays."

Yankee infielders Clete Boyer and Tony Kubek also endorse Roger's title to fame. "He belongs in the Hall of Fame," said Boyer. "Roger could do everything. We had 25 great players on our teams [in the early 1960s]. But it was Mickey Mantle and Roger Maris who were the stars."

On the twenty-fifth anniversary of Number 61, in 1986, Kubek spoke of the "misconception" that Roger was only a home-run hitter, "a one-dimensional player. He was a solid outfielder with the best arm of anyone I ever played with, and he ran the bases hard. And he had six or seven years when he was as good an all-around player as anyone in the game."

Kubek comments reflected his disappointment that the baseball writers had rejected Roger for the fifteenth time in 1988. Many of them had felt that Roger did not have the "numbers." Kubek responded: "Numbers? People who look at numbers all the time never really see what's going on on the field. But if you asked all the great players of his era – they'd tell you Maris was deserving."

George Steinbrenner, who honored Roger and celebrated his return to Yankee Stadium before his death, hasn't made much of an issue of Roger's exclusion from Cooperstown. In contrast, the Boss has actively promoted Rizzuto's election, even going so far as to threaten a boycott of the annual Cooperstown game if the Scooter were not enshrined. However, while commenting on Roger's death, Steinbrenner stressed that the slugger had never received proper recognition in the baseball world. "In my opinion," the Boss said, "Roger is one of the greatest Yankees of all time. There is no reason why he is not in the Baseball Hall of Fame.

"His record of 61 home runs in 1961 and Joe DiMaggio's consecutive hitting streak are the two greatest records in the game today. The magnitude of Roger's record is so great when you consider he hit

61 home runs, and now with the lively ball, the leaders are always around 35-40; Roger had 33 percent more."

Surprisingly, one member of the Yankee family dissented from the team consensus on Maris and the Hall of Fame. The late Bob Fishel, then executive vice president of the American League and member of the Hall's Committee on Baseball Veterans, formerly acted as public relations director for the Yankees during part of Roger's quest for the home-run title. Ex-PR man Fishel felt somewhat responsible for his failure to "protect" Roger from the media onslaught. However, when he attended Roger's funeral in Fargo, Fishel told the *Forum*'s Ed Kolpack that "one requirement" for election to the hall "is that a player have 10 outstanding seasons." Both Roger and Don Larsen of the perfect World Series lacked this requirement; according to Fishel, neither slugger nor hurler would get into Cooperstown.

The 10-season "requirement" that Fishel cites has no official source. A close look at the hall's "Rules for Election" reveals no such provision. The rules simply require a candidate to have "been active" as a Major League player for 10 years. In fact, another of Roger's teammates, Cardinal Tim McCarver, demolished the 10-season fantasy without referring to Fishel when Roger was again rejected in 1988.

McCarver, now the Mets' announcer, offered the career of Dodger superstar Sandy Koufax as a counter-example. The hurler had only six outstanding years; in the next 6 he posted a sub-par, below .500 won-loss mark. Yet, the Koufax plaque appeared in Cooperstown in his first year of eligibility.

The announcer argued, "Maris' career is comparable to Koufax. When you consider the 61 home runs, the MVPs. ... the world championship and all, is Sandy's 6-year period that much better than Roger's, so much so that one guy is automatic, and the other doesn't get in?"

Fans, who have no vote in the Cooperstown enshrinement process, agree that McCarver's argument makes sense. "After the elections," said Bill Bean, a Hall-of-Fame librarian, "we often get an outpouring of mail from fans who blame us, the Hall of Fame administration, for denying a place to their heroes. In recent years, Rizzuto and Maris have been two of the leading players that the fans have written us about."

Neither the Hall-of-Fame administration nor the Baseball Writers Association can usher Roger Maris into the Hall of Fame now. From 1992 on, the Veterans Committee — the court of 18, barring resignation or death — will vote on Roger's title to fame.

Charles Segar, former baseball executive, chairs the Veterans Committee. Some committee members had taken a particular interest in Roger's career. Broadcaster Red Barber was a member of the Yankee family when Roger played for New York. Al Lopez served as skipper when Roger was on the Cleveland team. As general manager of Pittsburgh, Joe L. Brown tried to obtain Roger from the Athletics. Stan Musial was an executive with the St. Louis Cardinals when Roger joined with them. Bob Broeg, sports editor of the *St. Louis Post-Dispatch,* and Joe Reichler, former baseball editor of the Associated Press, had both written extensively about Roger. Throughout his professional career, Roger had idolized Ted Williams.

The committee is also comprised of former players Roy Campanella, Charlie Gehringer (also an executive), and Monte Irvin (also an executive) — past and present baseball executives — Buzzy Bavasi and Gabe Paul; scouts Buck O'Neil (formerly a Negro League player and manager) and Birdie Tebbets (formerly player, manager and executive); past and present baseball writers — Allen Lewis, *Philadelphia Inquirer;* Edgar Munzel, *Chicago Sun-Times;* Shirley Povich, *Washington Post;* and Detroit Tiger broadcaster Ernie Harwell.

Some of Roger's supporters argue that Roger compares favorably with other right fielders, e.g., Harry Hooper and Tommy McCarthy, and center fielder Hack Wilson, who had a National League season high of 56 homers. "If the standard is, 'Is Roger as good as some players who are already in the Hall,'" said Bob Costas, "then the answer is 'yes.' He does belong."

In 1986 Ralph Houk advocated that Roger enter the hall because he "set a record which may never be broken." Citing the comparable merit issue, Houk continued: "There's a lot of players in there [Hall of Fame] now that aren't as deserving as Roger. I won't name names, but Roger is much more deserving." However, in *Season of Glory* (1988), Houk's bitterness over his past dealings with the rightfielder surfaces, as he implicitly rejects Maris' candidacy: "Few people would put Maris on a level with Al Kaline ... the Tigers' fine rightfielder, now deservedly in the Hall of Fame."

Roger would never have wanted a place in Cooperstown if it were based on how he compared with others. Nor can Maris' performance be measured by the feats of Babe Ruth, Ty Cobb, Mickey Mantle, or any standard other than what he solely accomplished himself.

Roger's career stats — .260 batting average, 1325 hits, 275 homers,

851 runs batted in — may not be Hall-of-Fame numbers, but Roger Maris' career, like so many sports careers, cannot be honestly evaluated by the raw, cold data.

Those seemingly uninspiring numbers placed Roger at the time of his death high on the list of heroic pinstripe sluggers: sixth on the all-time slugging list (515) and seventh in homers (203).

In each of four Yankee pennant-winning seasons, Maris had a sparkling on-base batting average: .411, .375, .440, and .426. By winning the American League's Most Valuable Player awards in 1960 and 1961, Maris became one of only five league players to have received the MVP honor in consecutive years. Roger's hitting 100 home runs in 1960 and 1961 allowed him to join Ruth, Foxx, and Kiner – all Hall of Famers – in the select group that has accomplished that feat. By hitting 61 homers, he counts among only ten individuals who have hit 50 home runs or more. Still, despite all of his achievements, Roger is the only 50-plus slugger not in the hall, except for George Foster who has not yet attained eligibility.

The cold statistics do not reveal that Maris played key roles in leading his teams to seven World Series. His career summary does not show his outstanding fielding record, baserunning, competitiveness, and influence on the younger players. The "Hall of Fame numbers" cannot describe the magnificent throw that saved the 1962 World Series. The dry statistics hold no memories like that of former Cooperstown director Ken Smith: "I remember in the 1967 World Series, how you helped win it by moving runners along."

Roger should not be judged against his forerunners like Ruth and Cobb; nor should he be compared to his contemporaries like Mantle and Mays. For those who insist that Roger – and others – must be the predominant player at the position assigned him by his team, the response is simple: among American-League right-fielders, only Al Kaline surpassed Roger in accomplishments, all-around ability, and value to the team.

His detractors will say that all this rhetoric for Roger rests on his one phenomenal season in 1961. Who would Roger Maris be, critics will continue, without that 1961 season? Doesn't Rule 5 "warn" against elections for a .400 batting average, a perfect game, or "similar outstanding" accomplishments?

Without 61 in '61 Roger Maris would be an outstanding, competitive player. However, can all Roger's detractors who hide behind Rule

5 honestly compare what a perfect game pitcher does in one glorious outing or what one batter does in a magnificent .400 season to what Roger Maris achieved in a period of unprecedented pressure in sports history?

"Unbreakable sports records are few and far between," wrote the *Kansas City Star* in 1985. "The Maris mark of 61 home runs in 1961 may be one." Babe Ruth's mark of 60 fell 34 years later; Roger's record has not been seriously challenged and still stands 28 years later. "More home runs are being hit by more people today than ever before," celebrated baseball statistician Allen Roth said. "The fact remains Maris is the only one to ever hit 61. It's a great achievement." Mantle and countless others feel it's the greatest feat in sports.

Roger, however, did more than just smash a sacred, seemingly untouchable record, and more than endure the unendurable in the process. Most important, Roger Maris did something for baseball and for its myriad fans.

Phil Pepe has never entered Roger's name on a Hall-of-Fame ballot. But, inspired by Graig Nettles's fast home-run start in 1977, Pepe said many kind things about Maris in a column titled "The Greatest Record of Them All."

"Baseball owes a great deal to Roger Maris. It owes its survival to him. Maris came along when the game was at its lowest ebb. Public apathy was at a high pitch. ... Along came Roger Maris as its saviour. He renewed public confidence with a barrage of home runs that stimulated the people and brought 'em back to the ball park."

Ted Smits of the Associated Press referred to the unprecedented interest in baseball Maris ignited in 1961. "It's the biggest story I've handled since I became sports editor 16 years ago. I've never known anything to match it for interest and suspense."

Harold Rosenthal in *More Sport, Sport, Sport* wrote that not Babe Ruth, Jack Dempsey, Red Grange, or Joe Louis – none of them – "did conquer the imagination of the American sports-loving public" as Roger Maris did. The writer notes that Roger "enjoyed" media coverage – especially radio and television – as those earlier stars could not. Untold numbers of fans followed Roger's "excruciating efforts in the late stages of the campaign as he struggled with the dwindling calendar." The fans "lived vicariously" during his ordeal. "Identities of housewives, office workers, truck drivers, school boys, and musicians all merged to become a single crew-cut, heavy-shouldered young man out of the Midwest."

Yes, Roger dazzled for only one summer, one season, but what he did has no parallel in a perfect game in October or a season-ending feat of a .400 batting mark. Does Don Larsen's masterpiece have a long-lasting effect on a teenager grown older? What enduring quality remained after Bill Terry made his .401. In contrast, nearly 30 years later, fans still remember 61 in '61, Ken Clarke, a staff writer for the *Gainesville Sun,* had never met his fellow Floridian but went public on the twentieth anniversary of number 61 to say, "Hey, Roger: Thanks for '61 Memories."

> You have no idea of the thrills you provided a 12-year-old baseball fan during the summer of '61. It is the stuff of private pleasure, tucked away in my memory and always brought forth with a smile.
>
> Actually, there were millions of us out there sharing the emotional ups and downs of your chase. The fact may have been lost to you because of the glare of the media and some of the unpleasantness you had to endure. ...
>
> The biggest fans in the world are 12-year-old boys, you know. Having not yet discovered girls, they devote all of their emotional energy (and much of their physical energy) to the game, memorizing statistics, daydreaming of heroics and keeping up with the heroes.
>
> So there I was, hanging on your every swing and driving my parents — who never understood such things — crazy with my newspaper clippings, my baseball cards and charts. ...
>
> It is a credit to my parents' patience and understanding that they not only tolerated my gyrations and shouts, but they also — finally — seemed to appreciate your feat. ...
>
> Thanks to you, it was great to be a kid during the summer of '61.

Jim Naughton, only four that summer, still retains impressions of Roger's success.

> I'm sure there are scientists and accountants and bartenders and mechanics who carry some mental snapshot with them, too.
>
> Maris was one of those people whose accomplishment was woven into the fabric of the moment. It has become a

way of telling time, a common point to start, a conversation among strangers. Not so much "where were you when ..." because 61 homers require a well-sustained excellence. But "what were you doing the summer of ... ?"

If Roger Maris' career statistics, his accomplishments that do not show in the numbers, and the year 1961 do not prove his title to fame, critics and electors must examine carefully the words of Rule 5:

> Voting shall be based upon the player's record, playing ability, integrity, sportsmanship, character, contributions to the team(s) on which the player played, and not what he may have done otherwise in baseball.

The "cold" record, the statistics, presents itself for judgment: the batting averages, the runs batted in, fielding percentage, career wins, and the like. Evaluating a player's *ability* requires more subtlety: assessing the fielding (beyond the percentages), running, special batting and pitching skills. The player's contribution to his team has a non-numerical quality. Could the team have won without him? How did he influence rookies and other inexperienced players?

Guilfoile states that the last provision in Rule 5 ("what he may have done otherwise ...") is intended to separate what the player achieved on the field from what he accomplished in other roles, such as in the front office.

But how does the voter analyze *integrity, sportsmanship, character?* Are these qualities visible on a television screen or obtainable from a computer fed data and asked, "Are those Hall-of-Fame numbers?"

Guilfoile says that these qualities are "pretty much left up to the interpretation of the voter ... are intended to be applied both on and off the field." Guilfoile claims that the electors have much leeway. "There is nothing in that rule that defines what is meant by character, integrity, or sportsmanship," he said. Nor is it made clear what aspects of a candidate's off-the-field or post-baseball career a voter should consider. "In recent years," Guilfoile observed, "we have had renewed interest in the case of Joe Jackson, who was involved in the Black Sox scandal. We are certain that when Ferguson Jenkins comes up for consideration, the drug episode will be a factor to be weighed."

In January of 1991 Ferguson Jenkins was elected to the Hall of Fame, along with Rod Carew and Gaylord Perry.

Guilfoile's words antedated allegations of Pete Rose's gambling activities, but undoubtedly Rule 5 will receive much attention when Charlie Hustle becomes eligible for Hall of Fame election in 1992, the same year the Veterans Committee votes on Roger Maris.

On Feburary 4, 1991 a decision will be made as to whether or not Pete Rose will be on the 1992 ballot.

Fortunately, some use Rule 5 fully as a basis for voting. Stan Hochman of the *Philadelphia Daily News* referred to it to justify his 1988 vote for Jim Bunning and to attack the nine no-voters:

> You were supposed to vote on the basis of distinguished playing career, character, integrity, sportsmanship. Bunning belongs on every count.
>
> The nine clods who botched the electoral process with their empty ballots that matched their empty heads should be ashamed of themselves.

The dictionary definition of *integrity* reads: "The quality or state of being of sound moral principles, uprightness, and sincerity."

Did any player ever have more integrity, i.e., honesty, than Roger Maris? He put integrity before the deceit, hypocrisy, and dishonesty that would have enhanced his image before the media and advanced his career. Most noticeably in 1961, Roger adhered to the Shakespearean maxim, "To thine own self be true." Roger always acted on his innate honesty; he could not assume a role that did not fit him.

"I wish I had been able to spread a little bull around," Roger once said, not out of regret but rather as a reflection on the price he had paid for his integrity. As a man of integrity, he never romanticized his profession, nor did he idealize or glamorize his accomplishments. At his core, Roger wanted the best for his family. The better he played, the better he could provide for his wife and children.

To Roger, integrity meant being open and direct, and answering all questions honestly. Years after he retired from baseball, Roger remarked, "I've always said that Howard Cosell got his idea of 'telling it like it is' from me. It made Howard a big success, but it never worked for me."

It is easy to act with integrity when things run smoothly. In 1961, when Roger achieved his record, *Kansas City Star* sports editor Joe McGuff commented on the difficult challenge Roger faced in maintaining his integrity "despite unrelenting harassment and hostility.

... I can think of no other athlete who experienced such great success under such difficult circumstances."

Roger displayed the same integrity on the field as he did off the field and after his professional career. In the early seventies, Ken Smith wrote of Roger, "One comes away from a visit ... realizing that here is a gentleman who doesn't truck with anything phoney."

Roger Maris exemplified integrity, and made an ideal role model for "character," as stipulated under Rule 5. Roger's behavior on and off the diamond cannot be more important than the roles he performed as husband, father, friend, and citizen. "What Roger achieved in life," said Ryne Duren, "is greatness, and that is what the Hall of Fame should represent. He was a great husband, a great father, a great citizen, and, most of all, a great human being."

More than 250,000 people come to the baseball shrine annually, many as families or as members of a younger generation in search of more than statistics from their American heroes.

Many Americans demand heroes with greater distinctions than "Hall of Fame numbers," heroes distinguished by character and integrity. Roger Maris personified both character and integrity and entered the realm of the hero. Despite the ravages of his own terminal illness, he strove to augment his hometown's civic pride. As his legacy to Fargo, he established a permanent baseball museum to attract tourists and an ongoing golf tournament to benefit educational programs and cancer victims.

In one of his columns reflecting back on Roger and 1961, Phil Pepe observed, "Baseball owed him a great deal. ... How could it ever repay him?"

Baseball can "repay" Roger Maris by bestowing upon him his title to fame – not out of guilt, not out of pity, but simply because he deserves it.

Appendix

Memorabilia from Roger Maris' career is on permanent
display in the Roger Maris Museum, located at
West Acres Shopping Center, Fargo, North Dakota.
(Russ Hanson Photo)

Outstanding Dates
of the Year 1961

Jan. 20 – John F. Kennedy inaugurated as 35th president of the United States.

Apr. 3 – U.S. State Department demands that Cuba divorce itself from international communism.

Apr. 11 – Adolf Eichmann brought to trial in Jerusalem, Israel, for crimes against Jews and others during World War II.

Apr. 12 – Soviet cosmonaut Yuri Gagarin becomes first man to successfully orbit the earth.

Apr. 17 – Cuban rebels, backed by the U.S. government, invade southern Cuba, establishing a beachhead at the Bay of Pigs.

Apr. 18 – Soviet Premier Khrushchev demands that the U.S. withdraw support from the rebels and promises USSR support for the Cuban government. President Kennedy tells the Soviets that the U.S. will not permit outside military intervention.

Apr. 20 – Cuba claims to have quelled the Cuban rebel invasion.

Apr. 21-22 – French Army troops in Algeria revolt and take control of Algiers.

May 5 – U.S. Commander Alan B. Shepard, Jr., becomes the first American in space.

May 13 – Film star Gary Cooper, who portrayed Lou Gehrig, dies.

May 14 – White mobs in Alabama attack white and black integrationists protesting segregated bus facilities throughout the South.

May 20-21 – Continued racial violence in Montgomery, Alabama, leads to the imposition of martial law.

May 30 – Generalissimo Trujillo, military dictator of the Dominican Republic, falls victim to an assassin in Ciudad Trujillo.

May 31 – South Africa becomes a republic and cuts its ties with the Commonwealth of Nations.

June 3-4 – President Kennedy and Premier Khrushchev meet in Vienna, Austria, to reaffirm their support of Laotian neutrality and to discuss the nuclear test ban, disarmament, and the German situation.

June 15 – Premier Khrushchev in Moscow states that the USSR will conclude the German peace treaty by year's end and that the Soviets will "rebuff" any Western attempts to enforce access rights to West Berlin.

July 2 – Noted American novelist and Nobel Prize winner Ernest Hemingway commits suicide in Ketchum, Idaho.

July 8 – Premier Khrushchev suspends announced Soviet cutbacks in the armed force and increases defense spending as a result of the Berlin crisis.

July 14 – Pope John XXIII issues an encyclical condemning birth control and materialism, supporting private property rights, approving aspects of socialism, and requesting aid for the Third World.

July 15 – U.S. sends note to Moscow, charging the Soviets with undermining the nuclear test ban talks at Geneva.

July 17 – U.S., Britain, and France reject the Soviet proposals on resolving the Berlin crisis.

July 17 – Legendary diamond hero Ty Cobb dies.

July 19 – French and Tunisian soldiers join in battle at a naval base in Bizerte.

July 20-21 – Capt. Virgil (Gus) Grissom becomes the second American in space.

July 25 – President Kennedy addresses the nation on the Berlin crisis and proposes increases in the armed forces and defense spending to counter the "worldwide" Soviet threat.

Aug. 12-13 – East Germany closes the border between East and West Germany to stop the flow of refugees.

Aug. 20 – Fifteen hundred U.S. military personnel enter West Berlin to bolster Western garrisons.

Aug. 23 – East Germany issues new restrictions on East Berlin travel; Allies position tanks along the East-West border.

Aug. 24 – U.S. warns Soviets that its interference with free access to West

Berlin would be an "aggressive act."

Aug. 31 – U.S.S.R. announces its resumption of nuclear testing.

Sept. 5 – President Kennedy orders nuclear weapons testing to be resumed without radioactive fallout.

Sept. 9 – General de Gaulle unhurt following an assassination attempt.

Sept. 9-13 – Hurricane Carla strikes the Gulf Coast, killing 40 and causing an estimated twenty million dollars in damages in the nearby gulf states.

Sept. 12 – Philosopher Bertrand Russell and spouse jailed in Britain for protesting against nuclear arms.

Sept. 14 – Big Four Western ministers meet in Washington to discuss the Berlin crisis.

Sept. 15 – U.S. explodes a low-yield nuclear device underground in Nevada.

Sept. 18 – U.N. Secretary Dag Hammerskjold dies in airplane crash in Northern Rhodesia.

Oct. 10 – Britain's minister Macmillan cautions Gromyko against Soviet unilateral action on Berlin, calling it a "grave danger."

Oct. 13 – Soviets claim they will accept the U.N. Acting Secretary-General with full executive powers.

The Roger Maris Cancer Center was opened in 1990 as
part of St. Luke's Hospitals/MeritCare in Fargo, N.D.
(Russ Hanson Photo)

Babe Ruth's 60 Home Runs – 1927

Home Run #	Team Game #	Date	Opposing Pitcher, Club, City	Pitcher's Record, '27 W-L	ERA	Inning	On Base
1	4	Apr. 15	Ehmke (r.), Phila., home	12-10	4.21	1	0
2	11	Apr. 23	Walberg (l.), Phila., away	17-12	3.98	1	0
3	12	Apr. 24	Thurston (r.), Wash., away	13-13	4.48	6	0
4	14	Apr. 29	Harriss (r.), Boston, away	14-21	4.17	5	0
5	16	May 1	Quinn** (r.), Phila., home	15-10	3.17	1	1
6	16	May 1	Walberg (l.), Phila. home	17-12	3.98	8	0
7	24	May 10	Gaston (r.), St. Louis, away	13-17	5.00	1	2
8	25	May 11	Nevers (r.), St. Louis, away	3-8	4.92	1	1
9	29	May 17	Collins (r.), Detroit away	13-7	4.68	8	0
10	33	May 22	Kerr (r.), Cleve. away	3-3	5.02	6	1
11	34	May 23}	Thurston (r.), Wash., away	13-13	4.48	1	0
12	37	May 28#	Thurston (r.), Wash., home	13-13	4.48	7	2
13	39	May 29	MacFayden (r.), Boston, home	5-8	4.27	8	0
14	41	May 30##	Walberg (l.), Phila., away	17-12	3.98	11	0
15	42	May 31	Quinn (r.), Phila. away	15-10	3.17	1	1
16	43	May 31+	Ehmke (r.), Phila., away	12-10	4.21	5	1
17	47	June 5	Whitehill** (l.), Detroit, away	16-14	3.36	6	0
18	48	June 7	Thomas (r.), Chicago, home	19-16	2.97	4	0
19	52	June 11	Buckeye (l.), Cleve. home	10-17	3.95	3	1
20	52	June 11	Buckeye (l.), Cleve. home	10-17	3.95	5	0
21	53	June 12	Uhle*** (r.), Cleve. home	8-9	4.36	7	0
22	55	June 16	Zachary (r.), St. Louis, home	4-6	4.38	1	1

Home Run #	Team Game #	Date	Opposing Pitcher, Club, City	Pitcher's W-L Record, '27	ERA	Inning	On Base
23	60	June 22#	Wiltse (l.), Boston, away	10-18	5.09	5	0
24	60	June 22#	Wiltse (l.), Boston, away	10-18	5.09	7	1
25	70	June 30	Harriss (r.), Boston, home	14-24	4.17	4	1
26	73	July 3	Lisenbee (r.), Wash., away	18-9	3.57	1	0
27	78	July 8+	Hankins (r.), Detroit, away	2-1	6.43	2	2
28	79	July 9#	Holloway (r.), Detroit, away	11-12	4.09	1	1
29	79	July 9#	Holloway (r.), Detroit, away	11-12	4.09	4	2
30	83	July 12	Shaute (l.), Cleve., away	9-16	4.23	9	1
31	94	July 24	Thomas (r.), Chicago, home	19-16	2.97	3	0
32	95	July 26#	Gaston (r.), St. Louis, home	13-17	5.00	1	1
33	95	July 26#	Gaston (r.), St. Louis, home	13-17	5.00	6	0
34	98	July 28	Stewart (l.), St. Louis, home	8-11	4.27	8	1
35	106	Aug. 5	Smith (r.), Detroit, home	4-1	3.93	8	0
36	110	Aug. 10	Zachary (r.), Wash., away	4-7	3.68	3	2
37	114	Aug. 16	Thomas (r.), Chicago, away	19-16	2.97	5	0
38	115	Aug. 17	Connally (r.), Chicago, away	10-15	4.09	11	0
39	118	Aug. 20	Miller (l.), Cleve., away	10-18	3.21	1	1
40	120	Aug. 22	Shaute (l.), Cleve., away	9-16	4.23	6	0
41	124	Aug. 27	Nevers (r.), St. Louis, away	3-8	4.92	8	1
42	125	Aug. 28	Wingard (l.), St. Louis, away	2-13	6.58	1	1
43	127	Aug. 31	Welzer (r.), Boston, home	6-11	4.45	6	2
44	128	Sept. 2	Walberg (l.), Phila., away	17-12	3.98	1	0
45	132	Sept. 6#	Welzer (r.), Boston, away	6-11	4.45	6	2
46	132	Sept. 6#	Welzer (r.), Boston, away	6-11	4.45	7	1

Home Run #	Team Game #	Date	Opposing Pitcher, Club, City	Pitcher's W-L Record, '27	ERA	Inning	On Base
47	133	Sept. 6+	Russell (r.), Boston, away	4-9	4.10	9	0
48	134	Sept. 7	MacFayden (r.), Boston, away	5-8	4.27	1	0
49	134	Sept. 7	Harriss (r.), Boston, away	14-24	4.17	4	1
50	138	Sept. 11	Gaston (r.), St. Louis, home	13-17	5.00	4	0
51	139	Sept. 13#	Hudlin (r.), Cleve., home	18-12	4.01	7	1
52	140	Sept. 13+	Shaute (l.), Cleve., home	9-16	4.23	4	0
53	143	Sept. 16	Blankenship (r.), Chicago, home	12-17	5.05	3	0
54	147	Sept. 18##	Lyons**** (r.), Chicago, home	22-14	2.84	5	1
55	148	Sept. 21	Gibson (r.), Detroit, home	11-12	3.70	9	0
56	149	Sept. 22	Holloway (r.), Detroit, home	11-12	4.09	9	1
57	152	Sept. 27	Grove**** (l.), Phila., home	20-13	3.20	1	0
58	153	Sept. 29	Lisenbee (r.), Wash., home	18-9	3.57	1	0
59	154	Sept. 29	Hopkins (r.), Wash., home	1-0	5.00	5	3
60	155	Sept. 30	Zachary (r.), Wash., home	4-7	3.68	8	1

New York played 155 games in 1927, with one tie game on April 14. Babe Ruth participated in 151 games.

#	First game of a doubleheader	*	248 career wins
+	Second game of a doubleheader	**	218 career wins
##	Afternoon game of a split doubleheader	***	200 career wins
		****	260 career wins, member, Hall of Fame
		*****	300 career wins, member, Hall of Fame

Roger Maris's 61 Home Runs – 1961

Home Run #	Team Game #	Date	Opposing Pitcher, Club, City	Pitcher's W-L Record, '61	ERA	Inning	On Base
1	11	Apr. 26	Foyack (r.), Detroit, away	11-10	3.92	5	0
2	17	May 3	Ramos (r.), Minn., away	11-20	3.95	7	2
3	20	May 6n	Grba (r.), Los Angeles, away	11-13	4.25	5	0
4	29	May 17	Burnside (l.), Wash., home	4-9	4.54	8	1
5	30	May 19n	Perry* (r.), Cleve., away	10-17	4.70	1	1
6	30	May 20	Bell (r.), Cleve., away	12-16	4.11	3	0
7	32	May 21	Estrada (r.), Balt., home	15-9	3.69	1	0
8	35	May 24	Conley (r.), Boston, home	11-14	4.91	4	0
9	38	May 28	McLish (r.), Chicago, home	10-13	4.39	2	1
10	40	May 30	Conley (r.), Boston, away	11-14	4.91	6	2
11	40	May 30	Fornieles (r.), Boston, away	9-8	4.69	8	2
12	41	May 31n	Muffett (r.), Boston, away	3-11	5.85	3	0
13	43	June 2n	McLish (r.), Chicago, away	10-13	4.39	3	2
14	44	June 3	Shaw (r.), Chicago, away	3-4	3.80	8	2
15	45	June 4	Kemmerer (r.), Chicago, away	3-3	4.36	3	0
16	48	June 6n	Palmquist (r.), Minn., home	1-1	9.43	6	2
17	49	June 7	Ramos (r.), Minn., home	11-20	3.95	3	2
18	52	June 9n	Herbert (r.), Kansas City, home	3-6	5.36	7	1
19	55	June 11+	Grba (r.), Los Angeles, home	11-13	4.25	3	0
20	55	June 11+	James (r.), Los Angeles, home	0-2	5.32	7	0
21	57	June 13n	Perry* (r.), Cleve., away	10-17	4.70	6	0
22	58	June 14n	Bell (r.), Cleve., away	12-16	4.11	4	1

Home Run #	Team Game #	Date	Opposing Pitcher, Club, City	Pitcher's W-L Record, '27	ERA	Inning	On Base
23	61	June 17n	Mossi (l.), Detroit, away	15-7	2.96	4	0
24	62	June 18	Casale (r.), Detroit, away	0-6	5.25	8	1
25	63	June 19n	Archer (l.), Kansas City, away	9-15	3.20	9	0
26	64	June 20n	Nuxhall (l.), Kansas City, away	5-8	5.34	1	0
27	66	June 22n	Bass (r.), Kansas City, away	11-11	4.68	2	1
28	74	July 1	Sisler (r.), Wash., home	2-8	4.20	9	1
29	75	July 2	Burnside (l.), Wash., home	4-9	4.54	3	2
30	75	July 2	Klippstein (r.), Wash., home	2-2	6.75	7	1
31	77	July 4+	Lary (r.), Detroit, home	23-9	3.24	8	1
32	78	July 5	Funk (r.), Cleve., home	11-11	3.33	7	0
33	82	July 9+	Monbouquette (r.), Boston, home	14-14	3.39	7	0
34	84	July 13n	Wynn** (r.), Chicago, away	8-2	3.52	1	1
35	86	July 15	Herbert (r.), Chicago, away	9-6	4.04	3	0
36	92	July 21n	Monbouquette (r.), Boston, away	14-14	3.39	1	0
37	95	July 25	Baumann (l.), Chicago, home	10-13	5.60	4	1
38	95	July 25#	Larsen (r.), Chicago, home	7-2	4.14	8	0
39	96	July 25+	Kemmerer (r.), Chicago, home	3-3	4.36	4	0
40	97	July 25+n	Hacker (r.), Chicago, home	3-3	3.70	6	2
41	106	Aug. 4n	Pascual*** (r.), Minn., home	15-16	3.46	1	2
42	114	Aug. 11n	Burnside (l.), Wash., away	4-9	4.54	5	0
43	115	Aug. 12	Donovan**** (r.), Wash., away	10-10	2.40	4	0
44	116	Aug. 13+	Daniels (r.), Wash., away	12-11	3.44	4	0
45	117	Aug. 13#	Kutyna (r.), Wash., away	6-8	3.92	1	1
46	118	Aug. 15n	Pizarro (l.), Chicago, home	14-7	3.05	4	0

Home Run #	Team Game #	Date	Opposing Pitcher; Club, City	Pitcher's W-L Record, '27	ERA	Inning	On Base
47	119	Aug. 16	Pierce***** (l.), Chicago, home	10-9	3.80	1	1
48	119	Aug. 16	Pierce (l.), Chicago, home	10-9	3.80	3	1
49	124	Aug. 20	Perry (r.), Cleve., away	10-17	4.70	3	1
40	125	Aug. 22n	McBride (r.), Los Angeles, away	12-15	3.64	6	1
51	129	Aug. 26	Walker (r.), Kansas City, away	8-14	4.82	6	0
52	135	Sept. 2	Lary (r.), Detroit, home	23-9	3.24	6	0
53	135	Sept. 2	Aguirre (l.), Detroit, home	4-4	3.27	8	1
54	140	Sept. 6	Cheney (r.), Wash., home	1-3	8.70	4	0
55	141	Sept. 7n	Stigman (l.), Cleve., home	2-5	4.64	3	0
56	143	Sept. 9	Grant (r.), Cleve., home	15-9	3.86	7	0
57	151	Sept. 16	Lary (r.), Detroit, away	23-9	3.24	3	1
58	152	Sept. 17	Fox (r.), Detroit, away	5-2	1.42	12	1
59	155	Sept. 20n	Pappas****** (r.), Balt., away	13-9	3.03	3	0
60	159	Sept. 26n	Fisher (r.), Balt., home	10-13	3.90	3	0
61	163	Oct. 1	Stallard (r.), Boston, home	2-7	4.87	4	0

New York played 163 games in 1961, with 1 tie game on April 22. Roger Maris participated in 161 games.

n   Night game
First game of a doubleheader
+   Second game of a doubleheader

*   215 career wins
**   300 career wins, member, Hall of Fame
***   A.L. leader in strikeouts, 1961-63
****   Leader in earned run average, 1961
*****   211 career wins
******   209 career wins

Further Reading

Alanen, Arnold R.. "The 'Location': Company Communities on Minnesota's Iron Range." *Minnesota History*, Fall, 1982. 94-107.

Allen, Maury. *Roger Maris: A Man For All Seasons.* New York: Donald I. Fine, 1986.

Angell, Roger. "Up at the Hall." *New Yorker*, Vol 63, August 31, 1987, 35-38.

Broeg, Bob. "Maris Memories of '61 Still Stir Pain, Pleasure." St.Louis *Post Dispatch*, Sec. B. March 28, 1972.

Clarke, Ken. "Personal Thanks to Boyhood Idol. Gainesville Sun, Sec. D. October 1, 1981.

Creamer, Roger W. "Gift for Making a Bad Situation Much Worse." *Sports Illustrated*, Vol. 18, May 27, 1963, 48-49.

Daley, Arthur. *Man Out of a Shadow.* Columbia, Vol. 42, February, 1962, 17-19.

Duffy, Bob. "Roger Maris: A Beleagured Champion Finally Finds Peace." Boston *Globe*, Sec. B. December 15, 1985.

Fishwick, Marshall W.. *American Heroes: Myth and Reality.* Washington Public Affairs Press, 1954.

Ford, Whitey with Phil Pepe. *Slick — My Life in and Around Baseball.* New York: Morrow, 1987.

Golenbock, Peter. "1961: A Year to Remember For Everyone Except Roger Maris." *Baseball Quarterly*, Spring 1978, 43-49.

Gray, Sid. "A Man Named Maris." New York *Post*, July 31, 1961: 40; August 1, 1961: 58; August 2, 1961: 64; August 3, 1961: 51; August 4, 1961: 52.

Gross, Milton. "Last Chance for Roger Maris." *Sport*, April 20, 1966, 27-29.

Gunther, John. *Inside U.S.A.* New York: Harper, 1951.

Houk, Ralph and Robert W. Creamer. *Season of Glory: The Amazing Saga of the 1961 New York Yankees.* New York: Putnam, 1988.

Kahn, Robert. "Pursuit of No. 60: The Ordeal of Roger Maris." *Sports Illustrated*, Vol. 15, October 2, 1961, 22-25.

Kolpack, Ed. "Maris Brought Excitement to Fargo." Fargo *Forum*, 1985.

Koppett, Leonard. "Mighty Mr. Maris." *Saturday Evening Post*, Vol. 234, September 2, 1961, 24.

Kubek, Tony and Terry Pluto. *Sixty-One: The Team, The Record, The Men*. New York: Macmillan, 1987.

Lebovitz, Hal. "Maris Always Knew He Couldn't Miss." *Sporting News*, May 1, 1957, 7-8.

Mantle, Mickey with Herb Gluck. *The Mick*. New York: Doubleday, 1985.

"Maris". *New Yorker*, Vol. 36. August 13, 1960.

"Maris Image Incorrectly Portrayed." Gainesville *Sun*, Sec. E., December 15, 1985.

Maris, Pat. "'My Husband,' as Told to Deirdre Budge." *Look*, Vol. 26, April 10, 1962, 38-40.

Maris, Roger and Jim Ogle. *Roger Maris At Bat*. New York: Sloan and Pearce, 1962.

Meany, Tom. "Roger Maris: The Man Who Shook Up the Yankees." *Sport*, November, 1960, 61-68.

McGuff, Joe. "Maris Does Not Want to Be Traded." Kansas City *Star*, May 24, 1959, 28.

Naughton, Jim. "Rog a Cut Above All: HR Chase in '61 Stir Memorials." New York *Daily News*, Sec. C. December 1985, 35.

New York Yankees. *Pinstripe Power: The Story of the 1961 New York Yankees*. New York, 1986.

Ogle, Jim. "Fact and Legend of Roger Maris." *Sporting News*, January 14, 1967, 25-26.

Ralbovsky, Marty. "After Decade, Maris Resents Asterisk." New York *Times*, October 1, 1971, 49.

Reston, James. "The Asterisk That Shook the Baseball World." New York *Times*, SEc. 4, October 1, 1961, 8.

Rice, Jack. "Quiet Home Base of Roger Maris." St.Louis *Post-Dispatch*, Sec. F, October 8, 1961, 2.

Rosenthal, Harold. *More Sport, Sport, Sport*. New York: Watts, 1962, 179-94.

Sherman, William C. and Playford V. Thorson, Editors. *Plains Folk: North Dakota Heritage*. Fargo ND: North Dakota Institute for Regional Studies, 1987.

Smith, Ken. *Baseball's Hall of Fame*, 4th. Ed. New York: Bantam, 1981.

Stewart, Bob: Jack Orr, Editor. *Baseball's Players Today*. New York: Watts, 1963, 19-25.

Trimble, Joe. "Maris Hits Hard in Life, Too." New York *Daily News*, September 29, 1961, 72.

Wilks, Ed. "The Spirit of St. Louis Kept Slugger Roger Maris in Baseball." St. Louis *Post-Dispatch*, Sec D. September 25, 1967, 1.

DATE DUE

MR 23 '92			
JAN. 1 1 1993			
MR 22 '93			
JUL 2 1993			
MR 2 3 '95			
MAY 1 6 1996			
NOV 1 9 1996			
MAY 2 0 1997			
MAY 2 4 1998			
JUN 0 1 1999			

DEMCO 38-297